Contemporary Work and the Future of Employment in Developed Countries

Whilst only in the second decade of the 21st century, we have seen significant and fundamental change in the way we work, where we work, how we work and the conditions of work. The continued advancements of (smart) technology and artificial intelligence, globalisation and deregulation can provide a 'sleek' view of the world of work. This paradigm can deliver the opportunity to both control work and provide new challenges in this emerging virtual and global workplace with 24/7 connectivity, as the boundaries of the traditional organisation 'melt' away.

Throughout the developed world the notions of work and employment are becoming increasingly separated and for some this will provide new opportunities in entrepreneurial and self-managed work. However, the alternate or 'bleak' perspectives is a world of work where globalisation and technology work together to eliminate or minimise employment, underpinning standardised employment with less and less stable or secure work, typified by the rise of the 'gig' economy and creating more extreme work, in terms of working hours, conditions and rewards. These aspects of work are likely to have a significant negative impact on the workforce in these environments.

These transformations are creating renewed interest in how work and the workforce is organised and managed and its relationship to employment in a period when all predictions are that the pace of change will only accelerate.

Peter Holland is a Professor of Human Resource Management and Director of the Executive MBA at Swinburne University of Technology, Melbourne.

Chris Brewster is now a part-time Professor of International Human Resource Management at Vaasa University in Finland; Henley Business School, University of Reading in the UK; and Radboud University in the Netherlands, specializing in international and comparative HRM.

Routledge Research in Employment Relations

Series editors: Rick Delbridge and Edmund Heery,
Cardiff Business School, UK

Aspects of the employment relationship are central to numerous courses at both undergraduate and postgraduate level.

Drawing from insights from industrial relations, human resource management and industrial sociology, this series provides an alternative source of research-based materials and texts, reviewing key developments in employment research.

Books published in this series are works of high academic merit, drawn from a wide range of academic studies in the social sciences.

For more information about this series, please visit: https://www.routledge.com

Contemporary Work and the Future of Employment in Developed Countries

Edited by
Peter Holland and
Chris Brewster

Routledge
Taylor & Francis Group

LONDON AND NEW YORK

First published 2020 by Routledge

2 Park Square, Milton Park, Abingdon, Oxon OX14 4RN
605 Third Avenue, New York, NY 10017

Routledge is an imprint of the Taylor & Francis Group, an informa business

First issued in paperback 2021

Publisher's Note

The publisher has gone to great lengths to ensure the quality of this reprint
but points out that some imperfections in the original copies may be apparent.

Library of Congress Cataloging-in-Publication Data
A catalog record for this title has been requested

ISBN: 978-1-138-49063-5 (hbk)
ISBN: 978-1-03-217713-3 (pbk)
DOI: 10.4324/9781351034906

Typeset in Sabon
by codeMantra

Contents

1 The Changing Nature of Work

*Jeffrey Saunders, Chris Brewster
and Peter Holland*

There is a tremendous upside to technological change. It has the potential to improve lives and wellbeing, save time and effort… But agreeing that technological change can improve living standards does not mean dismissing the real fears that people have about where, or whether, they fit in the workforce increasingly dominated by machines

(Chalmers & Quigley, 2017:1)

Introduction

The above quote reflects an ongoing fear people have had regarding technology and change. But, is the world of work really changing that much? For many generations people have bemoaned the way things 'ain't what they used to be' and there have certainly been lots of messages recently about the 'constant white water' of change (Shea & Gunter, 2016). But perhaps things were ever thus, and each generation feels that it is under more pressure than the one before. It is certainly possible to find quotes from Marx and Engels from not far short of two centuries ago arguing that things had never moved so fast and the threat to work was increasing exponentially. As the French would say – *plus ca change, plus c'est la meme chose.* We address the changing nature of work in more detail in our final chapter, but here we just note that the changes we are seeing that are leading us into the Fourth Industrial Revolution (following the mechanisation of production, the massing of production and the IT of production) build, like each of its predecessors, on what has gone before – but add a fusion of the physical, biological and, crucially, digital spheres. We are talking about the impacts of smart technologies, robotisation and artificial intelligence (AI) combined with the mass collection, storage and analysis of data in near real-time, the continued integration of humans with technology, leading to debates over human augmentation and performance enhancement, and deregulation, on the way we work (Cho & Kim, 2018; Friedman, 2016; Harari, 2016).

Commentators, observing these phenomena, are divided among the techno-optimists and the techno-pessimists. Techno-optimists tend to be the 'digital geeks' and often represent or are connected to major tech companies. These individuals share visions of a world undergoing a new technological renaissance (Economist, 2016), where the end result will be a world with more wealth, more leisure time and better work (a point alluded to by Toffler nearly 40 years ago at a similar time of change). They opine that all previous industrial revolutions have ended up creating more of these things and that, despite the developments in robotisation and AI, high-income countries have almost unprecedentedly low levels of unemployment and, indeed, are 'sucking in' migrants in ever-increasing numbers. Even in medium- and low-income countries in Asia, automation and the implementation of information and communication technology (ICT) systems have led to an employment boom, where the number of jobs created by technology have outstripped those destroyed through automation by more than 20 million (Asian Development Bank, 2018).

There are, however, others who argue that the destruction of jobs that results from these new technological developments, and the reinforcing of the neo-liberal approach to economics that will occur, will lead to increased poverty and imbalances of power (Chalmers & Quigley, 2017; Rayner, 2018). These commentators note that previous technological shifts caused 'skills' dislocation that negatively impacted segments of the labour market whose skills became irrelevant. These commentators are concerned about the ability of affected populations to adapt and learn new skill sets sufficient to maintain or even improve their quality of life. They often use a variation of the postulate that "two-thirds of today's five-year olds, will in about 15 years find themselves in jobs that do not exist. And the jobs that do exist will not necessarily be located where job seekers live" (Dell and IFTF, 2017; Schwartz et al., 2019).

So how is work and employment changing in the 21st century? The key drivers appear to be technology, globalisation, increased life expectancies, individualisation, commercialisation and deregulation. On their own these have all had a major impact on work, but, in combination, they will fundamentally reshape the nature of how we work, where we work, when we work and how work is managed.

As with many discussions, definitions and nuance are important. Many of the commentators – optimistic and pessimistic – are often arguing about different issues and time scales when they discuss robotisation and AI, and there is little discussion as to how technology diffusion and adoption will proceed within markets around the world. It appears as if the prevailing assumptions are that diffusion and adoption will happen across all sectors in all countries simultaneously. This will not likely be the case. This nuance is critical for understanding the implications of robotisation (automation of a task or process through software automation, industrial automation and robotics) and AI on work now and in the future.

AI, in particular, has become a catch-all phrase that some use to describe the "special sauce" in a company's product or service offering and that others use to describe the "ticking time bomb" that could not only automate work, but also ultimately lead to end of human dominance or even humanity itself as we are superseded by the machines we created (Bostrom, 2014).

As with many phenomena, there are several definitions and ways to categorise the development and future of AI (Partnership on AI, 2019). In this book, we will use the definition and categories developed by the US Defense Advanced Research Projects Agency (DAPRA). This agency was one of the key initiators and funders behind the autonomous vehicle revolution and many other AI initiatives (Launchbury, 2017). DARPA defines AI as a "machine's *programmed* ability to process information". AI systems have varying abilities and can be categorised according to their capacities to perceive (rich, complex and subtle information), learn (within an environment), abstract (to create new meanings) and reason (to plan and to decide). DARPA views AI as an evolution of technology coming in three supplementing waves or ages (Launchbury, 2017; Vorhies, 2017). These are the:

- *Age of handcrafted knowledge* – this age is characterised by systems that have been developed to augment human intelligence by distilling sizeable bodies of knowledge into intricate decision trees built by subject matter experts (Vorhies, 2017). The structure is defined by humans and the specifics are explored by the machine. Examples include TurboTax, chess and chess-like games, logistics programs and scheduling programs. These systems are good at reasoning through predefined problems but have no learning capability and little handling of uncertainty (Launchbury, 2017).
- *Age of statistical learning* – this age represents the current stage of development and is based on probabilistic approaches to handling information based on statistical learning. In this stage, engineers create statistical models for specific domain problems and train the models on large and dynamic data sets. These machines have nuanced classification and predictive capabilities but do not yet possess the ability to understand the contexts in which the data is taking place and abstract information from one domain to another. These flaws can be exploited. Examples include voice recognition, face recognition and autonomous vehicles (Launchbury, 2017).
- *Age of contextual adaptation* – this is the emerging future age of AI, which would create systems that are able to explain their reasoning, which would enable the validation of the process and outcome. Examples of this include programming generative models from which systems would learn the underlying context. For example, teaching how each letter of the alphabet is written to discern bad handwriting automatically with much less training data. The hope among researchers is that these contextual models will be able to perceive, learn, reason and abstract (Launchbury, 2017; Vorheis, 2017) – see Figure 1.1. This version of AI has raised the concerns of such philosophers like Nick Bostrom and serial entrepreneur Elon Musk, who are

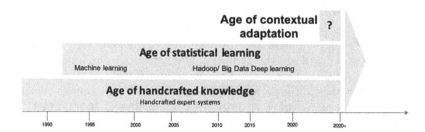

Figure 1.1 Three Ages of AI. Adapted from Launchbury (2017) and Vorhies (2017).

concerned that this age of AI could eventually lead to the emergence of a Super-intelligent AI that can emerge in future. Estimates as to when this type of AI could emerge range from decades to centuries (Bostrom, 2014).

While the first two are currently having significant impact on business and the labour market, they require significant interventions by specialist labour to define the algorithms, label training data, etc. For example, Google Assistant, which interprets 26 languages, relies on the efforts of a large team of linguists who label training data for Google Assistant to work. Facebook's content moderating AI system requires thousands of human content moderators. Amazon's Alexa has global teams of transcribers. These systems require labour until the AI systems have automated the tasks away (Hao, 2019). It is the final stage of AI development that alarms the likes of Stephen Hawking, Nick Bostrom and Elon Musk.

The impacts of these changes, however, will vary according to markets, skill sets of labour, economic sector and geopolitics. Over the last few years, technology development, diffusion and adoption are becoming geopolitical flashpoints among the USA, China, European Union, Russia and India. The current trade and access to market disputes occurring between China and the USA over 5G infrastructure and the Chinese firm Huawei are a good example of this trend. Concerns over national security combined with regional differences in laws covering use of personal data (e.g. the recent introduction of General Protection Data Regulation or GDPR in Europe) could limit organisations' and individual's ability to acquire and apply technologies globally (Bey, 2016; Milner & Solstad, 2018).

The impact on workers will depend upon the pace and degree by which the underlying technologies within the robotisation and AI defuse and other smart technologies are adopted. Although one may argue that technologies are defusing globally more rapidly, McKinsey Global Institute (2017) did an historical analysis of adoption rates (using relative over absolute amounts) and found that even when we account for highly popular social media applications, adoption rates for technologies have not increased over the last 60 years.

In a review of case studies from organisations who have applied AI technologies in their workplaces, uptake depended upon buy-in from management and workforce and return on investment, which can be difficult to attribute solely to AI. The impact on labour varied, and while none of the companies under study reported layoffs to date, effects were difficult to measure and cascaded beyond firms under review to third-parties and broader ecosystem (Partnership for AI, 2019).

These fundamental changes that are taking place in the Advanced Market Economies (AMEs) are also impacting on the quality of work, the underlying theme of this book. One subtle consequence of these changes is the impact or dislocation these factors are having on the employment relationship, where a fundamental break in (guaranteed) work and (secure) employment and regulation is gaining momentum. The consequences of these changes on the labour force will likely be mixed. For some, it will create opportunities for them as individuals or small teams to offer their services globally, as efficiently as, and with greater agility than, large organisations. For others, it will create a class of precarious workers who will lack opportunities for long-term employment and financial security.

The transformative technologies involved in the fourth industrial revolution are already leading to the reorganisation of working processes, automating routine knowledge work, production and services. We are seeing the continuing emergence of new digital platforms and productive ecosystems of companies large and small, and of individual freelance working. Seven of the 12 largest companies in terms of market capitalisation and over 70% of unicorn companies (start-ups valued more than one billion USD) operate a digital platform-based business model (Hirt, 2018). This could be seen as allowing for the liberation of labour for work involving innovation, creativity, research, development, in short, the kind of work that cannot easily be summarised in formulas or be automated (Fridman, 2016). The successful harnessing of such capacities, it can be argued, will create greater economic growth and progress as we move to a global virtual labour market (Ross, Ressia, & Sander, 2017).

Technological development is giving workers access to a range of cheap, powerful tools that would have been unimaginable a few decades ago. Knowledge workers have access to ever more powerful devices, personal computers, smart phones and tablets. These are increasingly being supplemented with ever more affordable 3D printers; virtual, augmented and mixed reality devices; wearables; and programmable robots. Due to the emergence of increasingly powerful connectivity, workers gain access to inexpensive or even free software, tools and services, including AI platforms and free online education, professional networks, cloud storage and tools, collaboration platforms, global product, job markets and more. This, in addition to ongoing improvements in real-time translation, could remove language barriers and create a truly global market for labour – especially in knowledge work (Saunders & Mogensen, 2017).

None of this is new of course. In the 'Book of the Machines' section of his Dystopian novel *Erewhon*, first published in 1872, Samuel Butler has the narrator of the book predicting a future where machines will take over from humans:

> There is no security ... against the ultimate development of mechanical consciousness ... reflect upon the extraordinary advances which machines have made in the last few hundred years, and note how slowly the animal and vegetable kingdoms are advancing. The more highly organised machines are creatures not so much of yesterday as of the last five minutes, so to speak, in comparison with past time... what will they not in the end become?
>
> (Butler, 1996: 142)

It is too late for us to adopt the Erewhonian solution and smash all machines, including even the narrator's watch; we will have to live with the consequences.

Karl Marx too in the famous 'fragment on machines' in *Grundisse* predicted that the rise of new machinery would create radical change in the role of workers, leading to the loss of jobs. Norbert Weiner, who established the science of cybernetics in the interwar years, predicted the same effects; and at around the same time, on the other side of the Atlantic in France, Georges Freidmann made similar points. In the UK, John Maynard Keynes, as far back as 1933, raised concerns about the potential for widespread technological unemployment due to the rapid advances of technology (Frey & Osbourne, 2017). In the USA, in the 1960s, then President Lyndon Johnson established a Presidential Commission to investigate concerns that automation would permanently reduce the amount of work available (Borland, 2017). The contemporary pace of changes underpinned by ICTs and AI has seen these questions re-emerge in terms of the capacity of the economy to replace jobs (Ross et al., 2017). Research by Frey and Osbourne (2017) suggests that up to half of all jobs are susceptible to automation in the next two decades. And yet, in most advanced economies, unemployment rates have rarely been lower, and employers are complaining about major shortages of labour (Fleming, 2018).

One question is whether technological change over the coming decades will be 'skills-biased', more negatively affecting one skills group over another? For example, the ICT revolution of the last few decades has complemented the work of highly skilled workers, whilst substituting the easily programmable work of low-skilled workers. Currently, there is no clear indication as to the direction of impact. One could point towards AI-based assistants enabling nurses to perform tasks that have until now been the sole purview of physicians, while elite surgeons would be able to serve a global market-place through robot assistants and ICTs (McKinsey Global Institute, 2017). This issue of the effects of technology on work is a recurring theme throughout this book, as we look at its impact on work.

Robotisation and the development of AI is another in a long list of technological developments that have continued through the centuries. In all previous cases new jobs have been developed to replace those that have become redundant. Blacksmiths may have lost the chance to shoe horse, but they could become motor mechanics. When Gutenberg invented the printing press, it displaced the work that many monks had, hand copying books. However, since the price for production fell dramatically, the market for printed materials expanded greatly in scale and created opportunities for new products, including flyers, posters, newspapers, magazines and books. It likewise led to the introduction of new associated jobs like journalists, editors, illustrators, booksellers and newspaper delivery logistics. Similar jobs have grown in the digital age, including app developers, web designers, vloggers and bloggers, and cybersecurity specialists (Saunders & Mogensen, 2017).

In each case, the Jeremiah's we cited above are both right and wrong. Technological advances did create massive changes in jobs, but still most people managed to find employment. Now, however, we argue, with Stephen Hawking, that things may have reached a tipping point. Hawking argued, in *The Guardian* newspaper in 2016, that the automation of factories has already decimated jobs in what would be described as traditional manufacturing and the rise of AI is likely to extend this job destruction deep into the middle-class or white-collar work, with only the most caring, creative or supervisory roles remaining – a point reinforced by Susskind and Susskind (2015), who argue that even the supervisory roles may be replaced by AI. Hawking also agreed with the point made by others that new technology will widen the inequalities in society so that it makes it possible for increasingly small groups of individuals to make enormous profits while employing less and less people, which he said is both inevitable and socially destructive.

It is easy to find many other examples of people through the years claiming that technological developments would lead to the destruction of various kinds of employment, and easy too to find examples of people who point out that although there may be fewer workers in various traditional occupations, in fact other kinds of work have arisen. In many of the developed countries today, unemployment remains at historical lows. As MIT economist David Autor commented, if you told an American farmer in 1900 the coming century would bring a 95% reduction in farm employment, it's a safe bet the farmer would not have predicted we would be developing apps instead (cited in Engelbert, 2017). But there is a difference between the past and the present: in the current case the new kinds of work could also be performed by robots and AI. In other words, the new jobs that are being created as replacements for the jobs destroyed by robots will themselves be done by robots.

We have known since Meehl (2013), in the 1950s, that statistical prediction invariably outperforms subjective judgement, and this approach has been applied to the world of work too. We, of course, follow the more successful forecasters (Tetlock, 2005) and note that nothing is impossible and that things will not follow any simple trajectory. But it does seem that the new technological changes may have a greater effect on work than any previous ones. We do not suggest that these changes will be straightforward. Looking around the world, we see little evidence that robotisation and AI will make any significant changes to the way that society is structured. Indeed, the evidence that we have so far suggests that it will enable the rich and powerful to become even more rich and powerful, increasing the inequalities in society. It can also be argued that the increased opportunities for globalisation that the new technology presents are and will increasingly put workers, at all skill levels, in the AMEs in direct competition with lower paid workers in a global freelance market, leading to a so-called race to the bottom (Freeman, 2008).

The pressures for labour arbitrage will be exacerbated. On the one hand, work is moving to places where employers can find cheaper labour, usually in countries where employment standards are either very low, non-existent or not enforced. On the other hand, workers in the poorer countries are fighting for work in the richer countries, joining the huge numbers of migrants and refugees, prepared to work for lower wages than the local and to work in tough or even illegal circumstances: refugees, for example, have been reported as being subject to workplace discrimination, inequality, harassment and skill degradation (Dietz et al., 2015; Knappert, Kornau, & Figengul, 2018).

We expect that threat of robotisation and AI will continue and even accelerate the ongoing process of finding ever-cheaper ways of getting work done through, for example, online platforms designed to link gig workers with eventual employers (Semuels, 2018). Work that is geographically mobile will be off-shored to places in the world where standards of employment are more extreme. This, sadly, could lead to incidences like the Rana Plaza disaster, which illustrated the danger of driving employment to effectively unregulated 'offshore' locations (Chowdhury, 2017; Rahim, 2017). There will likely come a point at which robotisation and AI become cheaper for the employer than using human beings, even at these reduced terms and conditions of employment: and they will likely be replaced. For work that is geographically immobile (such as caring, health, hospitality, the extractive industries) there will be a drive, in the developed societies, towards pressing down terms and conditions of employment in an increasingly deregulated economic environment and the abandonment of employment for 'self-employment' – often encompassed in what is being called the 'gig' economy.

By the end of 2017, self-employment in the UK had risen to 15% – easily the highest figure since the Second World War. Since 2010 there had been a 25% increase in non-employer businesses – the nearest the statisticians come to separating out the 'gig economy' – with an almost 50% increase in London (Office of National Statistics, 2018). In the broader OECD, 20–30% of the labour market worked on a freelance basis – over 162 million individuals (McKinsey Global Institute, 2016). We must ask ourselves, is this necessarily a bad thing, or is our reflexive concern wrought from a fear of the new? The evidence is as of now mixed.

The increasing separation of work from fixed, long-term employment will require new skill sets among workers and place greater emphases on skills entrepreneurialism and self-employment (Ross et al., 2017). These requirements will put pressure on certain elements of the labour market. Those with the hard and soft skills necessary for success thrive in this environment, whilst those who do not possess these skills struggle. In a 2016 study by McKinsey Global Institute, gig workers can be divided into four categories. The first two categories, which represent 57% of the gig workers surveyed by McKinsey, actually made an active choice to work in the gig economy:

- Free agents – those who actively choose gig work and derive their income from it;
- Casual earners – those who use gig work for supplemental work and do so by choice;
- Reluctants – those who derive their primary income from gig work but would prefer a traditional job; and
- Financially strapped – those who do gig work to make the ends meet.

In two surveys covering 11,000 low-income and middle-skilled workers (1,000 respondents in each of 11 countries – Brazil, China, France, Germany, India, Indonesia, Japan, Spain, Sweden, the UK and the USA) and of 6,500 business leaders (at least 800 respondents in each of eight countries – Brazil, China, France, Germany, India, Japan, the UK and USA) conducted by Harvard Business School and the Boston Consulting Group for the "Managing the Future of Work" project in 2018, it is the emergence of gig/freelance work which replaces their work that appears to concern workers most and not robotisation nor AI. Researchers found that the workers were in fact much more positive towards technology development and the future of work than their business leaders gave them credit. In nine out of 11 countries, excepting France and Japan, large majorities thought that they – and not government or their employer – were responsible for equipping themselves to meet the needs of a rapidly evolving labour market (Fuller, et al., 2019).

Surveyed business leaders demonstrated anxious sentiments as to how they can find and retain the employees with the right competencies and what should they do with those whose skills are obsolete. Surveyed workers were more optimistic and focused more on the opportunities and benefits that the future of work holds for them. They opined a greater willingness to embrace change and learn new skills. They were more adaptive and optimistic than their leaders recognise and thought that automation and AI could improve the quality of their working lives by removing "dirty, dangerous, or dull" tasks and giving them greater flexibility and self-directed work (Fuller et al., 2019). We are, at present, in the midst of these developments and that is the focus of our book. It is important to at least attempt to understand the changes we are experiencing. What we are sure of is that the world of work is changing and that it will be different a few years from now. With the help of experts in the field we explore the changes that are currently underway. We restrict our analysis largely to the impact in the developed countries (the worldwide impact would require another, much larger, book). We use the framework of changes in time, changes in place and changes in space, to help interpret the changes we are seeing on a cross section of work and employment that we anticipate will resonate with the reader. We believe (with Fleming, 2018) that both the positive and the negative scenarios of the effects of the new technologies are overblown, but nonetheless there are clear trajectories in the world of work. What we have seen in the first decades of the 21st century indicates that the traditional work patterns and practices of the 20th century are increasingly under challenge.

Whilst many books are currently examining these changes, in this work we are looking to explore the more subtle aspects of this new work environment through the change in the relationship between work and employment and how such changes are impacting on where, when and how work is done. Taking this approach, we believe, enables a more nuanced understanding of how work is changing in the AMEs. We see technology as the conduit in providing the connection to work regardless of time, place or space, threatening some work, allowing more interesting and extreme work to take place or more invasive and exploitative work practices.

Changes to contractual relationships are perhaps the most visible and the most important of the changes that we see in the developed countries. In many ways the changes are moving us away from the employment relationship, where regular labour is exchanged for payment, back towards the kind of relationships that occurred before the first industrial revolution, where either work was done for the individual and their family or the outcome of the work was sold, reflecting the kind of relationship that predominates today in much of the less developed world. So we see the rise of self-employment. More than a small proportion of this is 'fake': the individuals concerned continue to work in the same places, at the same tasks, and under the same managers, but now, rather than an employment contract and a wage they are paid through piecework or on a 'contract for services', responsible for their own tax arrangements, their own insurance, and their own health and safety. This is best exemplified by the rise of the platform economy, or the 'gig' economy as it is popularly known, where people do and get paid for individual tasks, which they try to 'batch up' to provide themselves with sufficient income. The separation of work and employment also means this new economy is underpinned by reduced employment regulation that provides the opportunity for exploitation of labour, including long working hours and wage theft. The frames the first section of the book exploring these themes of unregulated work and *time*. As a result of the separation of work and employment and with regulations, for many people now, their days are not divided into work time and personal time. Work has become all-pervasive. ICTs, such as mobile phones, mean that some people at least have become addicted to the technology, answering emails on the train, in the car (at serious risk to their survival and that of those round them), at dinner and during family gatherings – they are never 'off'. But that raises a question. In many cases people in an increasingly deregulated economy are working ever-longer hours, sometimes as the result of combining three or four jobs or sources of payment good for the quality of (working) life?

A side-effect of technological developments is that work is now done in more locations (*spaces*) for longer periods due to technology and deregulation. Some of this work is being carried out in extreme conditions, beyond those where people used to be able to work, helped by new transport possibilities, new communications, new shelters and even new clothing that have combined with new technologies to turn once inhospitable areas into workplaces. Thus, as we strive to deal with climate change and search for resources, there are now people working in the Antarctic for up to a year at a time. War zones always used to be places where work (other than some trading of goods or bodies) was rarely found. In the last half century, the demands of the technological age for global news and the drive to alleviate suffering mean that there are in nearly all war zones reporters and aid workers trying to carry out their tasks in the most dangerous of conditions. Even in less extreme situations, and going back centuries, there have been and are people in the emergency services who are expected almost as a matter of course to put themselves in danger to help others.

We also explore the changing space in which work is done. The kind of changes that we have noted so far mean that people, particularly those in the 'gig' economy or working without employment contracts, may be working directly on internet platforms, or they may be contract drivers, nurses, security guards, maintenance workers, cleaners. They are not employed, they have no allocated place of work, so they work at home, in their car, the local café or at another person's premises. If work is becoming disconnected from employment, then it is also becoming even more disconnected from 'workplaces'.

One response to the changing space in which work is done has been increased monitoring of workers, but that is a trend that has not been limited to self-employed workers; it is also common for employees in a workplace. Electronic monitoring and surveillance have also been made possible by technological change and represent a major step up from the supervisor 'keeping an eye on' the workers. The extreme level and intensity of electronic monitoring and surveillance of the workforce both inside and outside the work space have never been so pervasive or wide-ranging, and have been found to have a negative effect on those under such scrutiny – 24/7. When asked in our research about why management indulges in these increasingly extreme forms the answer is often, "because we can".

As globalisation becomes more pervasive, to cut cost many organisations outsource their work from the AMEs. In doing so there is the opportunity to distance themselves or provide space from the consequences of the cost savings they achieve through – poor-quality employment standards and often extreme work conditions (Haak-Saheem & Brewster, 2017) and a phenomenon of the oddly named 'modern slavery' (Crane, 2013). The worst excesses of these 'sweatshops' were seen in the Rana Plaza collapse of a garment factory in Dhaka, Bangladesh, in 2013, with the death of 1,100 workers, unable to escape from the building. Retailers with such famous brands as Primark, Zara, Mango, Wal-Mart and Benetton had outsourced their work to the site (Butler, 2015; Chowdhury, 2017). They denied any responsibility, but all contributed to a fund for survivors. Indeed, much of the current discussion of the internal aspects of corporate social responsibility faulters on the rocks of non-employment and outsourcing (Rahim, 2017).

The book concludes with a discussion by the editors about the current issues and uncertainties around work and possible ways forward. We hope you enjoy the challenges and ideas put forward by our highly respected contributors on the variety of work, the range of different kinds of work and the impact this will have in various times, places and spaces, and we encourage others to focus their research on work.

References

Asian Development Outlook 2018: How Technology Affects Jobs (2018). The Asian Development Bank (April).

Bey, M. (2016). Between geopolitics and technology. *Stratfor.com* (September 27). Retrieved from https://www.forbes.com/sites/stratfor/2016/09/27/between-geopolitics-and-technology/#12f8d2c73542

Borland, J. (2017). Workers are actually feeling less insecure in their jobs. *The Conversation*, August 1.

Bostrom, N. (2014). *Superintelligence: Paths, Dangers, Strategies.* Oxford. Oxford University Press.

Butler, S. (1872). *Erewhon.* Taken from 1996. Ware, Herts: Wordsworth Classics edition.

Butler, S. (2015). Benetton agrees to contribute to Rana Plaza compensation fund. Retrieved from http://www.theguardian.com/business/2015/feb/20/benetton-agrees-contribute-rana-plazacompensation-fund, accessed 20 February 2015.

Chalmers, J., & Quigley, M. (2017). *Changing Jobs: The Fair Go in the Machine Age.* Carlton, VIC: Redback.

Cho, J., & Kim, J. (2018). Identifying factors reinforcing robotization: Interactive forces of employment, working hour and wage. *Sustainability (forthcoming).*

Chowdhury, R. (2017). The Rana Plaza disaster and the complicit behavior of elite NGOs. *Organization, 24*(6), 938–949.

Crane, A. (2013). Modern slavery as a management practice: Exploring the conditions and capabilities for human exploitation. *Academy of Management Review, 38*(1), 49–69.

Dell and IFTF. (2017) *The Next Era of Human-Machine Partnership.* Dell-IFTS: Institute for the Future.

Dietz, J., Joshi, C., Esses, V. M., Hamilton, L. K., & Gabarrot, F. (2015). The skill paradox: Explaining and reducing employment discrimination against skilled immigrants. *International Journal of Human Resource Management, 26*, 1318–1334.

Engelbert, C. (2017). Job stealing robots? Millennials see hope, fear in automation. *The Conversation* (March 22).

Fleming, P. (2018). Robots and organization studies: Why robots might not want to steal your job. *Organization Studies.* doi:10.1177/0170840618765568

Freeman, R. (2008). The new global labor market. *Focus, 26*(1), 1–6.

Frey, C., & Osbourne, M. (2017). The future of employment: How susceptible are jobs to computerisation? *Technology, Forecasting and Social Change, 114*, 254–280.

Friedman, T. (2016). *Thank You for Being Late: An Optimist's Guide to Thriving in the Age of Accelerations.* New York: Allen & Unwin.

Fuller, J. et al. (2019). Your workforce is more adaptable than you think. *Harvard Business Review* (May–June Issue).

Haak-Saheem, W., & Brewster, C. (2017). 'Hidden' expatriates: International mobility in the United Arab Emirates as a challenge to current understanding of expatriation. *Human Resource Management Journal, 27*(3), 423–439.

Hao, K. (2019). The AI gig economy is coming for you. *MIT Technology Review* (May 31).

Harari, Y. H. (2016). *Homo Deus: A Brief History of Tomorrow.* London: Vintage Books.

Hirt, M. (2018). If you're not building an ecosystem, chances are your competitors are. *McKinsey & Company* (June 12). Retrieved from https://www.mckinsey.com/business-functions/strategy-and-corporate-finance/our-insights/the-strategy-and-corporate-finance-blog/if-youre-not-building-an-ecosystem-chances-are-your-competitors-are

Knappert, L., Kornau, A., & Figengul, M. (2018). Refugees' exclusion at work and the intersection with gender: Insights from the Turkish-Syrian border. *Journal of Vocational Behavior, 105*, 62–82.

Launchbury, J. (2017). 'A DARPA perspective on artifical intelligence' [Power Point slides]. Retrieved from https://www.darpa.mil/attachments/AIFull.pdf

Marx, K. (1973). *Grundisse der Kritik der Politschen Ökonomie (Fundamentals of Political Economy Criticism).* London: Penguin Books (translation Martin Nicolaus).

McKinsey Global Institute (2016). *Independent work: Choice, necessity and the gig economy.* San Francisco. Retrieved from https://www.mckinsey.

com/featured-insights/employment-and-growth/independent-work-choice-necessity-and-the-gig-economy

McKinsey Global Institute (2017). *Jobs lost, jobs gained: Workforce transitions in a time of automation.* San Francisco. https://www.mckinsey.com/~/media/mckinsey/featured%20insights/Future%20of%20Organizations/What%20the%20future%20of%20work%20will%20mean%20for%20jobs%20skills%20and%20wages/MGI-Jobs-Lost-Jobs-Gained-Report-December-6-2017.ashx

Meehl, P. (2013). *Clinical vs. Statistical Prediction: A Theoretical Analysis and a Review of the Evidence* (latest edition; first edition 1954). Brattleborough, VT: Echo Point Books & Media.

Milner, H., & Solstad, S. (2018). *Technology diffusion and the international system.* Working Paper. Princeton. Retrieved from https://scholar.princeton.edu/sites/default/files/hvmilner/files/technology-diffusion.pdf

Office of National Statistics (2018). *Statistical Bulletin: UK Labour Market.* May 2018. London: ONS.

Partnership on AI (2019). *Compendium synthesis: AI, labor, and economy case studies.* Retrieved from https://www.partnershiponai.org/wp-content/uploads/2019/04/Compendium-Synthesis.pdf

Rahim, M. M. (2017). Improving social responsibility in RMG industries through a new governance approach in laws. *Journal of Business Ethics, 143,* 807–826.

Rayner, J. (2018). *Blue Collar Freyed: Working Men in Tomorrow's Economy.* Carlton, VIC: Redback.

Ross, P., Ressia, S., & Sander, E. (2017). *Work in the 21st Century: How Do I Log In?* Bradford: Emerald.

Saunders, J., & Mogensen, K. (2017). *Working in the Age of Hyper Agility.* Copenhagen: Copenhagen Institute for Futures Studies.

Schwartz, J., Hatfield, S., James, R., & Anderson, S. (2019). *What is the Future of Work: Redefining Work, Workforces, and Workplaces.* Deloitte.

Semuels, A. (2018). The online gig economy's 'race to the bottom'. *The Atlantic* (August 31). Retrieved from https://www.theatlantic.com/technology/archive/2018/08/fiverr-online-gig-economy/569083/

Shea, G., & Gunter, R. (2016). *Your Job Survival Guide, a Manual for Thriving in Change.* Upper Saddle River, NJ: FT Press.

Susskind, R., & Susskind, D. (2015). *The Future of the Professions: How Technology Will Transform the Work of Human Experts.* Oxford: Oxford University Press.

Techno wars: An earlier sunny mood about technology and innovation has given way to pessimism (2016). *The Economist* (October 20).

Tetlock, P. E. (2005). *Expert Political Judgment: How Good Is It? How Can We Know?* Princeton, NJ: Princeton University Press. ISBN 9780691128719.

Vorhies, W. (2017). The three ages of AI – Figuring out where we are. *Data Science Central* (May 9). Retrieved from https://www.datasciencecentral.com/profiles/blogs/the-three-ages-of-ai-figuring-out-where-we-are

2 The 'Gigification' of Work in the 21st Century

Alex Veen, Sarah Kaine,
Caleb Goods and Tom Barratt

What is the Gig Economy?

The rise of the so-called digital gig economy is disrupting existing industries (Schumpeter, 1950), commodifying domestic forms of work (Flanagan, 2018), and creating new services (Srnicek, 2017a). It has been heralded as empowering and unleashing entrepreneurial workers (Mulcahy, 2017), as an expression of post-capitalism (Peticca-Harris et al., 2018) and conversely as 'neoliberalism on steroids' (Murillo et al., 2017): Its disruptive nature is exemplified by the Uber platform, which was founded in 2009 and by 2018 had a market value of over US$60 billion (Goldstein, 2018). In this relatively short period of time, it has established a global presence and disrupted existing taxi industries across both developed and developing countries (Dudley et al., 2017), destroying existing jobs while simultaneously generating labour market alternatives for a swathe of workers (Abraham et al., 2018; Berger et al., 2018; De Stefano, 2016b; Graham et al., 2017; Kenney and Zysman, 2016).

What sits behind these new forms of work? The emergence of work in the 'gig economy' has been driven by new developments in information technologies and computing power (Howcroft and Bergvall-Kåreborn, 2018; De Stefano, 2016b; Gandini, 2018; Peticca-Harris et al., 2018). These advancements have been utilised by capital to create novel solutions to persistent organisational challenges, namely, the division of labour and the challenge of obtaining worker effort (Puranam et al., 2014). Platforms are intermediaries which create services that match and organise exchanges between workers and consumer via their 'digital-ecosystem' (Peticca-Harris et al., 2018). Thus, in theory at least, platforms create transparent instantaneous interactions between workers and end-users. Critical to this matching are autonomous operating systems that rely upon big data. Also central to the novelty of these new organisational forms and solutions is the blurring of organisational boundaries. For instance, the relationship between the platform and the worker performing gigs 'on the platform' is commonly based on arm's-length contracting which is routinely designed via triangular forms of engagement (Rubery et al., 2018), so that the worker's relationship is with the end-user or client rather than with the organisation. In many of these relationships it is the end-user that pays the worker; and the worker pays the platform for its matching services. Moreover, in the food-delivery segment of the gig economy there are quadrilateral forms of engagement with organisational boundaries being further blurred between platforms, workers, restaurants and customers. Although these organisation solutions are novel, platforms also rely upon very traditional solutions to resolve challenges created by divisions of labour and the need to obtain worker effort, namely, the use of piece rate payments and the classification of workers as contractors.

There are polarised views as to the implications of this emerging form of work. Indeed, some (Finkin, 2016; Stewart and Stanford, 2017) suggest that the use of centuries-old management strategies, such as piece rates and contracting relations, renders this work unexceptional. As outlined above, and in line with others (Gandini, 2018; Healy et al., 2017; Peticca-Harris et al., 2018), we find that there is indeed novelty in the work and organisational forms that encompass the gig economy that are worthy of deeper scholarly attention. To date, the vast majority of research has focused upon some of the more distinctive features of the work, for example, the use of algorithms to manage major facets of the work (Rosenblat and Stark, 2016; Zwick, 2018) or how these emerging forms of work could, or should not, be regulated (Cherry, 2016; De Stefano, 2016b; Stewart and Stanford, 2017). The focus of this chapter is on unpacking the main aspects and complexities that surround this growing phenomenon. First, we explore what gig work looks like in the two major streams of the gig economy, differentiating between cloud-based and on-demand services. Second, we critically evaluate what it is like to be a gig worker. Third, we identify some of the most significant negative and positive aspects of these forms of work and the implications that they present for developed societies in particular.

Types of Gig Work – What Does Work Look Like in the Gig Economy?

Digitalised gig work is described by a range of terms, and has been defined in various ways. As with other areas of management, a lack of concept clarity bedevils our attempts to draw conclusions from the extant research. However, if we take the US Bureau of Labor Statistics (2018) definition of 'electronically mediated jobs' as "short jobs or tasks that workers find through websites or mobile apps that both connect them with customers and arrange payment for the tasks" then we can identify two broad categories of gig work: cloud-based 'crowd-work' and 'work-on demand systems' (De Stefano, 2016b).

The gig economy has been widely referred to as 'the sharing economy' (Sundararajan, 2016), but this utilises a narrow notion of 'sharing'

(Hamari et al., 2016; Schor and Attwood-Charles, 2017). All words come with intellectual baggage, and this terminology could be viewed as a way of obscuring reality by creatively branding as 'sharing' efforts to monetise assets or skills. Useful attempts have been made to construct typologies to capture the phenomenon (De Stefano, 2016b; Forde et al., 2017; Howcroft and Bergvall-Kåreborn, 2018). In this chapter, we use the term 'gig work' in line with the approach of Stewart and Stanford (2017). They argue that there are four basis characteristics which typify gig work:

- first, work is driven by customer demand and therefore work schedules are messy;
- second, those who undertake the work provide some or all of the capital required to undertake the work (e.g. car and mobile phone);
- third, work is paid at a piece rate; and
- fourth, the work is organised and/or facilitated by an intermediary or platform such as Uber or Amazon Mechanical Turk.

The two categories of cloud-based and on-demand gig work are largely differentiated by the type and location of work undertaken – with the common element being that the work is accessed through an online platform. Cloud-based crowd-work is usually undertaken in the worker's home. Even within the cloud-based categories there are differences in the types of tasks offered through these platforms (Huws, 2018; Huws et al., 2018). Platforms such as Amazon Mechanical Turk, Microworkers and JobBoy generally, though not exclusively, offer 'microtasks', which are a "broad range of small tasks in an open-call, to a large and undefined crowd, which are usually reimbursed by a small monetary reward per each piece of work they perform" (Naderi, 2018: 1). In contrast, platforms like Upwork or Freelancer facilitate more professional and craft types of work which rely upon the expertise or 'talent' of those who sell their services via these platforms. Table 2.1 provides a sample of different cloud-work platforms. It highlights the diversity in services that are mediated through these platforms. It further reveals that, depending on the respective services which are offered, workers' skill requirements will vary – ranging from low-skilled highly repetitive work to high-skilled highly autonomous work. As a consequence, there is considerable variability within this segment of the gig economy with respect to the quality of work (Kalleberg and Dunn, 2016). Moreover, the table shows that worker remuneration is set in varied ways, with some platforms dictating the price of labour, whilst, in others, end-users set take-it-or-leave it rates. In some cases, workers are able to command specific prices for their labour. Although gig work is frequently portrayed as precarious low-quality work, as Tables 2.1 and 2.2 and other research (e.g. Huws et al., 2018) highlight, such simple portrayals of

Table 2.1 Cloud-work platforms

Platform name	Country of origin	Self-description	Tasks performed	Skill levels and worker requirements	Pay-setting
Amazon Mechanical Turk	USA	'MTurk offers developers access to a diverse, on-demand workforce through a flexible user interface or direct integration with a simple API. Organizations can harness the power of crowdsourcing via MTurk for a range of use cases, such as microwork, human insights, and machine learning development'. https://www.mturk.com	Any task that can be completed using a computing device connected to the internet	Low skilled Must be over 18 years of age and have access to a computing device connected to the internet	By requestor https:www.mturk.com/pricing
Microworkers	USA	'Crowd source your micro jobs' https://www.micro workers.com	Variety including: surveys, reviews, moderation of images, transcription, etc.	Low skilled. Must be over 18 years of age and have access to a computing device connected to the internet	Company puts in the number of minutes a worker needs to finish the job and the number of positions they are willing to pay for. The page automatically displays the total cost of the campaign for them to make adjustments, if necessary.

Platform	Country	Tagline	Tasks	Skill level	Pricing
Clickworker	Germany	'Data powered by Crowd Intelligence, fast, accurate, global' https://www.clickworker.com	Variety including: Creation of texts; Data categorisation; Copy editing; Proofreading; Web research; Surveys; Mystery; Photography; App testing.	Low skilled. Access to a computing device connected to the internet	By platform https://www.clickworker.com/pricing/
UpWork	USA	'Get it done with a freelancer. Grow your business through the top freelancing website. Hire talent nearby or worldwide' https://www.upwork.com	Variety including: Web development; programming; design; writing; accounting and consulting; sales and marketing	Mid-to high. Variety of qualifications depending on task/project	Paid by the hour or fixed price as negotiated with the freelancer. On fixed-price jobs, Upwork uses an escrow service to release funds as pre-set milestones are met. https://www.upwork.com/i/how-it-works/client/
Fiver	Israel	'Find The Perfect Freelance Services For Your Business' http://www.fiverr.com	Variety including: Graphics & Design; Digital Marketing; Writing & Translation; Video & Animation; Music & Audio; Programming & Tech; Business; Lifestyle	Mid-to high Variety of qualifications depending on task/project	Set by the freelancer, paid the fixed price as negotiated with, with in-build opportunities for upselling. https://buyers.fiverr.com/en/article/how-fiverr-works

Table 2.2 On-demand service provision platforms

Platform name	Country of origin	Self-description	Tasks performed	Skill level	Pay-setting
Uber	USA	'Move the way you want' https://www.uber.com	Point-to-point transport	Low; Driver's Licence and Car required	By platform
Deliveroo	UK	'Your favourite restaurants, delivered fast to your door'. https://deliveroo.com.au	Food ordering, delivery and tracking	Low skilled. Bicycle or Motor vehicle licence	By platform
Airtasker	Australia	'Get your to-do list done' https://www.airtasker.com	Variety of tasks including: Business and Administration; Cleaning; Delivery and removals; Furniture assembly; Handyman; Marketing and design; Home services and gardening	Variable depending on the task	Client posts payment offered for task but may revise it as necessary
Glamazon	Australia	'Book a beauty professional to your door https://glamazon.com.au	Hair dressing and beauty services	Appropriate salon qualifications	By platform
Mable	Australia	'The comfort of choosing your own support team' https://mable.com.au/	Aged care and disability support services including: Nursing; travel; domestic assistance; personal care	Variable depending on the task	By worker
Care.com	USA	'Great care starts here' https://www.care.com/	Every facet of care: childcare; special needs care; elderly care; pet care; housekeeping and more	Variable depending on the task	By worker
Helpling	UK	Find your cleaner online! https://www.helpling.com/	Domestic cleaning services	Low skilled, domestic cleaning work	By platform

these emergent forms of work as either 'good' or 'bad' are highly problematic and also disregard how the emergence of these atypical forms of work fits within other labour market developments such as the rise of precarious work (Standing, 2016).

In contrast to cloud-work platforms, on-demand service provisions (sometimes called work-on-demand systems) have been defined as "involving more traditional, physical or 'real world' tasks and jobs" (Stewart and Stanford, 2017) that generally occur outside the worker's home. Some examples of platforms that facilitate work on-demand include Airtasker, Handy, Uber, Ola, Mable and Home Care Heroes which provide property and home maintenance, point-to-point transport as well as personal care services. Table 2.2 provides a selected overview of the types of work on-demand platforms that operate across a range of sectors. Critical to workers' ability to partake in these forms of work is not solely their access to the internet, but frequently also their capacity to source other relevant types of assets. Platforms and other intermediaries offer workers different opportunities to lease or purchase these assets (Splend Pty Ltd, 2019; Uber Technologies Inc., 2018), exposing them to production-related risks. In contrast to traditional employment, however, these workers, while carrying such financial burdens, have limited guarantees for ongoing work, can be unilaterally terminated by platforms at any time and have limited recourse to pursue workers' rights (Stewart and Stanford, 2017).

The growth of cloud-work and on-demand service provision is a symptom of a broader fissuring of work (Weil, 2014), which has seen the "employment relationship broken into pieces often shifted to subcontractors, third-party companies or … to individuals who are treated as independent contractors" (Weil and Goldman, 2016). Gig work, with its discrete tasks and tenuous attachment to consumers and platform providers, represents fissuring at the extreme and raises questions about expectations of work as a place where social needs are met, and social capital is built (we explore this in more detail in a later section).

The spatial characteristics of both types of gig work have important implications for the experience of work and opportunities for gig workers to voice issues related to their work, negotiate better conditions and collectively organise. In particular, cloud-work atomises individual workers, who may be undertaking discrete parts of a much larger project independently over the internet, without ever communicating with others. While micro-tasks do generally require human judgement (e.g. labelling specific objects in photos), they tend to be 'invisible labour' (Scholz, 2017). Some micro-task workers have developed very active online forums that have allowed them to share reviews of sites and particular customers and take part in a virtual community (see, e.g. Turkopticon or TurkerView). Moreover, as part of the labour process these platforms further seek to exercise considerable control over the performance of the work, including worker conduct (Gandini, 2018; Peticca-Harris et al., 2018). Through the design of the 'apps' that workers use to undertake the work, the platforms are able to monitor such things as their screen time and keyboard strokes (see Chapter 9). On-demand services are different in that they tend to be public facing with a real-time interaction between the worker and the customer and often include extensive opportunities for monitoring delivery times, customer feedback (and 'the customer is always right') and the intensity of the worker's activities (Gandini, 2018; Peticca-Harris et al., 2018).

While Tables 2.1 and 2.2 provide an example of the types of services that platforms offer, they do not show the often extreme competition in numerous sectors among the platforms. Many platforms enter into markets with an understanding that profitability is unlikely in the short or even medium term. Much activity in the gig economy has been generated by speculation. Specifically, platforms have sought to finance their activities through attracting venture capital. Some of the largest, most well-known platforms that have been operating for a decade or so have yet to turn a consistent profit in their global business. Uber is a case in point. While it has been valued at US$62 billion, it has only had two quarters of net profit since it began in 2009 and both of these were due to sales of internal businesses (CBS News, 2018). Other ride-sharing platforms have been similarly reliant on venture capital's capacity to keep investing in the face of an increasingly competitive market (Barratt et al., 2018). Although competition between platforms is appealing for customers in the short term, it also raises questions about the long-term sustainability of the industry with obvious implications for workers including further competition on price which flows through to rates of pay and working conditions.

What is 'Gig' Work Like for Workers?

The different forms of gig work, whether cloud-work or on demand, retain some similarities with each other for workers. In particular, this work has been set up using arm's-length arrangements which see platforms engage workers as contractors rather than engaging them directly as employees (Cherry, 2016). This distinction is significant as it increases the precarity of workers, as they have no employer and, unlike traditional contractors, often have little to no capacity to negotiate the terms of hiring out of their own services. Gig platforms therefore do not provide workers with the security that has traditionally been associated with employment and the welfare state (Standing, 2016: 14).

The classification of gig workers as contractors means that the workers bear the risks inherent in the labour market. Workers are reliant on consumer demand in order to generate their income (Stewart and Stanford, 2017); however, there are further factors that influence workers' ability to earn income, depending on the particular form of gig work. For example, in some on-demand platform work, such as Uber, workers are dependent on the platforms to allocate them work. This means, due to the piece-rate nature of their remuneration, they are unable to control how many pieces they are allocated and, in turn, how much they can earn. Other on-demand platforms, such as Airtasker, allow consumers to determine which workers perform the requested tasks on the basis of price and limited information such as posted skills, star ratings from other consumers and task completion rates. As workers are not employees, they have to organise their own legal and fiscal compliance; have little or nothing in the way of safety protection, health benefits or pension arrangements. Thus, a driver involved in an accident may find themselves in legal trouble for driving too many hours without a break, still being liable to repay a car leasing company and be unable to work, thus losing all their income whilst they rack up costs.

Cloud-work allows workers to accept tasks online, where the requester sets the number of positions available, lists the price and tasks to be performed. This leaves workers dependent on the presence of consumer demand, inter-worker competition and processes of task allocation, meaning the income they can generate is both variable and uncertain. When this uncertainty is coupled with the requirement to provide their own capital, then again limited occupational health and safety protections (depending on the jurisdiction) and the need to provide one's own insurance and retirement savings (Healy et al., 2017), this effectively transfers the risks of employment onto these workers.

This transfer of risk means that work in the gig economy becomes less socially regulated and increasingly market-regulated (Peck, 1996; Kalleberg and Dunn, 2016). This market regulation means that the desirability of these jobs is dependent on workers' labour market power (Wood et al., 2018a). For example, in the food-delivery sector of the Australian gig economy, one study encountered an overwhelming majority of workers were temporary migrants, constrained by their visa conditions in their ability to find work and outside the protections of the Australian welfare state (Goods et al., 2019). This weak market position limited these workers' ability to support themselves financially. For example, some food-delivery workers were found to be relying upon charities such as soup kitchens (original interview material of the authors). Moreover, low pay rates and income uncertainty can make low-skilled gig workers take risks, sometimes with extreme consequences, with one ride-sharing passenger in Australia being killed as a result of the negligent driving of one Uber driver who had worked for 21 consecutive hours (McPhee, 2018).

Another aspect of gig work which alters workers' experience of work is the capacity for the work to be managed by algorithms, where direction and supervision is done by machines rather than humans (Rosenblat and Stark, 2016). The growth of 'big data' and monitoring of gig workers means that decisions such as which workers are 'fired' (or precisely, since they are not employees, not given any further work) and who works at what times can be made by self-learning algorithms. This results in the rules of work being increasingly made by analysts and programmers rather than managers (Schildt, 2017). The nature and form of these algorithms can thus become central to the experience, and performance, of work as workers react differently to algorithms as to managers (Schildt, 2017). In the case of Uber, this has resulted in constant monitoring of performance, limited workplace support, low transparency between platform and worker and 'automatic' worker disciplinary processes (Mohlmann and Zalmanson, 2017). Some algorithms continuously relate each worker's performance to benchmarks set by other workers, so that there is a subtle and sometimes almost invisible, but very real, process of continuing work intensification: algorithmic kaizen. Despite the increased significance of algorithmic management in the gig economy, there remains managerial input into the design and use of algorithms, meaning that algorithmic management must be considered a part, rather than the totality, of how rules are made within the gig economy.

There have also been attempts by platforms, the most high profile of which is Uber ride-sharing (Scheiber, 2017), to entice workers to engage in work via gamification (Woodcock and Johnson, 2018). The capacity to be remunerated for intrinsically enjoyable activities means that there is the opportunity for gig work to represent 'playbour', where play and labour are combined (Howcroft and Bergvall-Kåreborn, 2018). There is also the ability for capital to make work game-like to try and entice labour effort using psychological tricks (Rosenblat and Stark, 2016; Scheiber, 2017), which can be characterised as gamification-from-above (Woodcock and Johnson, 2018). This is particularly significant as a means of securing cooperation where arm's-length relationships restrict platforms' ability to direct and closely supervise workers. There is also, however, evidence of gamification-from-below (Woodcock and Johnson, 2018), where workers incorporate elements of play as a mechanism for coping with work (original interview material of the authors).

Worker Entrepreneurs or a New Underclass of Precarious Worker – What are the Implications of Digitally Enabled Platform Work for Workers and Society?

There are positive implications for workers primarily occupying what we characterise as the higher skilled end of the gig spectrum, that is, work skills that are in high demand, specialised and not easily transferable. In many ways this form of work, which can be found on platforms such as 'Upwork', is no different to the well-paid 'freelancing' work that predates the gig economy. The intermediaries that operate in this space have, via their 'digital-ecosystem', simply created large marketplaces where these skilled freelancers or entrepreneurs can be more easily located (De Stefano, 2016b; Finkin, 2016; Huws et al., 2018; Lehdonvirta, 2018; Pongratz, 2018; Wood et al., 2018a, 2018b). There are, however, some negative implications for these workers, for instance, as platforms mediate, and therefore largely set the rules of the game between workers and consumers, workers have reported a loss of autonomy (McDonald et al., 2018).

Conversely, for workers in the 'on-demand' segment of the gig economy, one of the major recorded positives was flexibility. As an example, our research on food-delivery and ride-sharing services in Australia highlights that for some gig workers choosing 'when' and 'where' they worked was one of the primary benefits of engaging in gig work rather than more traditional forms of employment (Goods et al., 2019; Kaine et al., 2017) – with some recent research in the UK context suggesting that ride-share partners with Uber have higher levels of life satisfaction than other London workers (Berger et al., 2018). The temporal flexibility (Cooper and Ellem, 2008) associated with these forms of work organisation are frequently highlighted by platforms (e.g. Uber, 2018a, 2018b) as one of the primary benefits of the work, allowing workers to fit their work around other life commitments such as studying or caring. The benefits of flexibility in the gig economy are, however, messy and reflective of the type of service provided. Demand for delivery-food, for example, is shaped by the eating habits of consumers, meaning that demand for these services primarily occurs for small parts of the day, or in fact the evening, and more often on weekends. As Lehdonvirta (2018) highlights, while cloud-workers appear to have high levels of temporal flexibility, these workers' dependence on end-users for future work as well as positive reviews on performed tasks entails that the flexibility of their work is also considerably constrained. Thus, whilst from the outside the gig economy can appear hyper-flexible, economic and social realities structure the working lives of gig workers and often result in gig workers having to fit their lives around the work and not the other way around, as often purported by the platforms.

A significant drawback of gig work is the lack of economic security provided by the work. Albeit subjected to considerable critique from unions and other labour organisations for adopting an overly managerialist approach with little concern for worker 'choice' and 'voice' (Bales et al., 2018; Nolan, 2018), the recent Taylor review on modern working practices underscores the insecurity and one-sided flexibility faced by gig workers. Workers' economic insecurity is driven by the contractual arrangements used by platforms, including independent contractor status and zero-hour contracts (Adams and Prassl, 2018) – leaving particularly the low-paid, women and migrants vulnerable to exploitation (van Doorn, 2017). This exposing of workers to 'the higgling of the market' (Higgins, 1907), with few guarantees of continued work, raises questions about the desirability of some of the platforms currently in operation. This, coupled with the circumvention of, or operating "in the shadow of" (Howcroft and Bergvall-Kåreborn, 2018: 10), existing employment relations regulation across the developed world has allowed platforms to engage workers to perform tasks in a manner in which the terms and conditions of work are determined by markets; markets that, due to un-employment- and under-employment, put downward pressure on payments and on working conditions. Similarly, while the growth of the cloud-based gig economy has provided economic opportunities to workers from across the globe, Graham et al. (2017) highlight the fact that cloud-based workers are exposed to 'layered vulnerability' including a lack of bargaining power, discrimination, re-intermediation and constrained opportunities for value-chain upgrading. As the 'gigosphere' grows, there is also an increasing shift into white-collar industries (Mulcahy, 2017), with platforms taking advantage of wage differentials to shift these tasks to lower-wage countries (see Chapter 10). Thus, while the focus here, and the focus of some of the platforms, has been on lower skilled work, the gigosphere is expanding its reach into more skilled services as well (Kessler, 2018; Prassl, 2017).

Workers try to respond to, and cope with, these economic challenges and barriers by, for example, operating on multiple services (Goods et al., 2019; Graham et al., 2017; Wood et al., 2018a), in the on-demand segment referred to as 'multi-apping'. At the same time, there has also been a rise in more collective responses to the sub-par working conditions in some segments of the gig economy. Over the 2016–2018 period, for instance, there was an increasing manifestation of different forms of collective action and protest for better working conditions in the UK, the USA and continental Europe (Johnston and Land-Kazlauskas, 2018), with workers for Deliveroo and Uber engaging in different forms of action. This includes the successful campaigns by the Independent Drivers Guild in New York for better rates and market restrictions (Greenhouse, 2016; Johnston, 2018). In the UK, various protests were organised by the Independent Workers Union of Great Britain (IWGB), which also launched a successful legal action against Uber to reclassify ride-share partners as workers (Employment Appeal Tribunal, 2017). It further organised country-wide protests against poor working conditions and seemingly arbitrary 'dismissals' by Deliveroo, a major food-delivery platform (Johnston and Land-Kazlauskas, 2018). In early 2018 thousands of Uber ride-share partners across Australia also engaged in a log-off protest (The Guardian, 2018), while protests against poor working conditions in the food-delivery sector were held in Sydney and Melbourne (Afshariyan, 2018; Smiley, 2018).

Gig workers in on-demand services are thus increasingly resorting to more traditional means to combat some of the exploitative features of these new forms of work organising, engaging in grassroots campaigns (Staunton, 2018) and instigating litigation on behalf of workers. These attempts were, however, met with varied results across the developed world, with court cases yielding different outcomes within the same jurisdiction, depending on the particular platform, service and legal institutions. Some courts and tribunals have deemed gig workers to be falsely self-employed and others have upheld them as independent contractor – albeit with serious reservations about the entrepreneurial spirit of this breed of contractors (in the Australian context cf. Fair Work Commission, 2018a, 2018b). Traditional unions are also increasingly seeking to respond to the challenges posed by the gig economy, with some engaging with platforms directly to encourage forms of self-regulation across industries (Patty, 2017; Unions New South Wales, 2016). Hampering workers' ability to unionise and engage in collective action, however, are existing anti-trust and cartel laws which prevent these workers' from engaging in collective action and bargaining. Across most developed economies existing competition laws prevented supposed entrepreneurs from fixing market prices, a critical issue increasingly raised by different legal scholars (Biasi, 2018; De Stefano, 2016a; Lobel, 2017). In the European context (ETUC, 2018), for instance, this has already resulted in politicians debating whether existing directives should be amended to allow this new class of workers to engage in social dialogue.

Conclusion

The primary beneficiaries of the emerging gig economy have been consumers, who now have access to a wide array of low-cost services. The other primary beneficiaries have, of course, been the entrepreneurs who set up or own the platforms who have become millionaires overnight. For venture capital and institutional investors the anticipated returns of the gig economy are in a sense still to materialise (Srnicek, 2017a, 2017b), with existing investment decisions frequently made on the speculation of future returns. The gig economy has further provided new, frequently relatively flexible, work opportunities for those were traditionally excluded from the labour market, like older workers, migrants, disabled workers and women with caring responsibilities – yet at the same its current form has the potential to exacerbate some of their existing challenges (van Doorn, 2017). Cloud-based work further provides workers in the developing world with an opportunity to connect into the global economy, whilst at the same time exposing peers in the global-north to a race-to-the-bottom competition on wages (Graham et al., 2017). As Gratton (2015: 34) predicted, exposure to globalised markets means for workers in the developed world that there are "more people available to engage in skilled work – and some of them can work harder, faster, or better, or cheaper".

Moreover, the rosy picture for consumer and entrepreneurs skips over some of the broader challenges and consequence that the gig economy raises for contemporary society. What are our expectations of paid work? At a minimum paid work should allow individuals to reproduce themselves in a safe and sustainable manner; and yet with the hyper fragmentation of work brought about by the gig economy these basic principles are breaking down. Moreover, while consumers understandably appreciate the explosion of low-cost convenient services some costs are being pushed onto the wider society. For example, in the food-delivery sector workers explain how their lack of employment status leads them to pass on costs associated with work-related injuries to the national social insurance system rather than appropriate worker compensation scheme, with those who had no access to these either working through injury or making bogus claims on other insurance policies like their travel insurance (Goods et al., 2019). These costs, and who bears them, need to be considered in understanding the wider social implications of the gig economy.

While there is continued debate about the size of the gig economy, the pace of its development, aided by technological advancement, is likely to accelerate. With new gig platforms appearing in almost every industry gig work may 'punch above its weight' in terms of impact on existing industries and the work that takes place within them. That is, while the numbers of gig workers may still be far overshadowed by regular employment (Peetz, 2018), the downward pressure on labour standards gig work creates makes it an area requiring close monitoring. Moreover, as more traditional organisations such as banks and public institutions (Maciag, 2018) look to engage 'gig workers' to supplement a smaller, permanent workforce – it could be that the gig economy is the new frontier of outsourced work creating yet another layer of labour market segmentation to be navigated by organisations, policy-makers and workers themselves.

References

Abraham KG, Haltiwanger JC, Sandusky K, et al. (2018) Measuring the gig economy: Current knowledge and open issues. NBER Working Paper No. 24950, National Bureau of Economic Research.

Adams A and Prassl J. (2018) Zero-hours work in the United Kingdom. Conditions of Work and Employment Series No. 101, International Labour Organization.

Afshariyan N. (2018) Deliverude: Food-delivery riders protest unfair work and below average pay. *ABC*. ABC.

Bales K, Bogg A and Novitz T. (2018) 'Voice' and 'Choice' in modern working practices: Problems with the Taylor review. *Industrial Law Journal* 47: 46–75.

Barratt T, Veen A, Goods C, et al. (2018) As yet another ridesharing platform launches in Australia, how does this all end? *The Conversation*, Parkville, Victoria.

Berger T, Frey CB, Levin G, et al. (2018) Uber Happy? Work and Well-being in the "Gig Economy", *Economic Policy,* eiz007.

Biasi M. (2018) 'We Will All Laugh at Gilded Butterflies.' The Shadow of Antitrust Law on the Collective Negotiation of Fair Fees for Self-Employed Workers.

CBS News. (2018) Uber, valued at $62 billion, still loses money on its rides. *CBS News.*

Cherry MA. (2016) Beyond misclassification: The digital transformation of work. *Comparative Labor Law Journal & Policy Journal* 37: 577–602.

Cooper R and Ellem B. (2008) The Neoliberal State, trade unions and collective bargaining in Australia. *British Journal of Industrial Relations* 46: 532–554.

De Stefano V. (2016a) Non-standard work and limits on freedom of association: A human rights-based approach. *Industrial Law Journal* 46: 185–207.

De Stefano V. (2016b) The rise of the "Just-In-Time Workforce": On-demand work, crowdwork, and labor protection in the "Gig-Economy". *Comparative Labor Law and Policy Journal* 37: 471–504.

Dudley G, Banister D and Schwanen T. (2017) The rise of uber and regulating the disruptive innovator. *The Political Quarterly* 88: 492–499.

Employment Appeal Tribunal. (2017) Aslam v Uber BV [2017] IRLR 4.

ETUC. (2018) Council of Europe recognises bargaining rights of self-employed: Now EU should follow. *European Trade Union Confederation*, Brussels.

Fair Work Commission. (2018a) Klooger v Foodora Australia Pty Ltd [2018] FWC 6836.

Fair Work Commission. (2018b) Pallage v Raiser Pacific Pty Ltd [2018] FWC 2579.

Finkin M. (2016) Beclouded work, beclouded workers in historical perspective. *Comparative Labor Law and Policy Journal* 37: 603–618.

Flanagan F. (2018) Theorising the gig economy and home-based service work. *Journal of Industrial Relations* 00: 1–22.

Forde C, Stuart M, Joyce S, et al. (2017) The social protection of workers in the collaborative economy. *Report for European Parliament Employment and Social Affairs Committee.*

Gandini A. (2018) Labour process theory and the gig economy. *Human Relations* 00: 1–18.

Goldstein M. (2018) Is uber finally growing up? *Forbes.* Forbes Media.

Goods C, Veen A and Barratt T. (2019) "Is your gig any good?" Analysing job quality in the Australian platform-based food-delivery sector. *Journal of Industrial Relations* 61: 502–527.

Graham M, Hjorth I and Lehdonvirta V. (2017) Digital labour and development: Impacts of global digital labour platforms and the gig economy on worker livelihoods. *Transfer: European Review of Labour and Research* 23: 135–162.

Gratton L. (2015) Reshaping work for the future. *CEDA Report Australia's Future Workforce.* CEDA, 32–37.

Greenhouse S. (2016) On demand, and demanding their rights. *The American Prospect*, Washington.

Hamari J, Sjöklint M and Ukkonen A. (2016) The sharing economy: Why people participate in collaborative consumption. *Journal of the Association for Information Science and Technology* 67: 2047–2059.

Healy J, Nicholson D and Pekarek A. (2017) Should we take the gig economy seriously? *Labour & Industry* 27: 232–248.

Higgins J. (1907) Ex parte H.V. McKay.

Howcroft D and Bergvall-Kåreborn B. (2018) A typology of crowdwork platforms. *Work, Employment and Society* 00: 1–18.

Huws U. (2018) Eating us out of house and home: The dynamics of commodification and decommodification of reproductive labour in the formation of virtual work. *International Journal of Media & Cultural Politics* 14: 111–118.

Huws U, Spencer NH and Syrdal DS. (2018) Online, on call: The spread of digitally organised just-in-time working and its implications for standard employment models. *New Technology, Work and Employment* 33: 113–129.

Johnston H. (2018) Workplace Gains beyond the Wagner Act: The New York Taxi workers alliance and participation in administrative rulemaking. *Labor Studies Journal* 43: 141–165.

Johnston H and Land-Kazlauskas C. (2018) *Organizing On-demand: Representation, Voice, and Collective Bargaining in the Gig Economy.* Geneva: ILO.

Kaine S, Veen A, Goods C, et al. (2017) 'The way they manipulate people is really saddening': Study shows the trade-offs in gig work. *The Conversation.* Melbourne: The Conversation Media Group Ltd.

Kalleberg AL and Dunn M. (2016) Good jobs, bad jobs in the gig economy. *Perspectives on Work* 20: 10–14.

Kenney M and Zysman J. (2016) The rise of the platform economy. *Issues in Science and Technology* 32: 61–69.

Kessler S. (2018) *Gigged: The Gig Economy, the End of the Job and the Future of Work.* New York: St. Martin's Press.

Lehdonvirta V. (2018) Flexibility in the gig economy: Managing time on three online piecework platforms. *New Technology, Work and Employment* 33: 13–29.

Lobel O. (2017) The gig economy & the future of employment and labor law. *USFL Review* 51: 51.

Maciag M. (2018) More governments turning to gig economy for help. *Governing*, Folsom, CA

McDonald P, Williams P and Robyn M. (2018) Working the gig economy: The use (or not) of digital platforms in photography. *International Labour Process Conference.* Buenos Aires.

McPhee S. (2018) Uber driver guilty over passenger's death. *News.com.au.* News Pty Ltd.

Mohlmann M and Zalmanson L. (2017) Hands on the wheel: Navigating algorithmic management and uber drivers' autonomy. *ICIS.* South Korea.

Mulcahy D. (2017) *The Gig Economy: The Complete Guide to Getting Better Work, Taking More Time Off, and Financing the Life You Want*, New York: American Management Association.

Murillo D, Buckland H and Val E. (2017) When the sharing economy becomes neoliberalism on steroids: Unravelling the controversies. *Technological Forecasting and Social Change* 125: 66–76.

Naderi B. (2018) *Motivation of Workers on Microtask Crowdsourcing Platforms*, Cham: Springer International Publishing.

Nolan P. (2018) Good work: The Taylor review of modern working practices. *Industrial Relations Journal* 49: 400–402.

Patty A. (2017) Airtasker and unions make landmark agreement to improve pay rates and conditions. *The Sydney Morning Herald*. Sydney: Fairfax.

Peck J. (1996) *Work-Place: The Social Regulation of Labor Markets*, New York: Guilford Publications.

Peetz D. (2018) Workers' compensation doesn't cover gig workers – here's a way to protect them. *The Conversation*.

Peticca-Harris A, de Gama N and Ravishankar MN. (2018) Postcapitalist precarious work and those in the 'drivers' seat: Exploring the motivations and lived experiences of Uber drivers in Canada. *Organization* 00: 1–24.

Pongratz HJ. (2018) Of crowds and talents: Discursive constructions of global online labour. *New Technology, Work and Employment* 33: 58–73.

Prassl J. (2017) *Humans as a Service*. Oxford: Oxford University Press.

Puranam P, Alexy O and Reitzig M. (2014) What's "New" about new forms of organizing? *Academy of Management Review* 39: 162–180.

Rosenblat A and Stark L. (2016) Algorithmic labor and information asymmetries: A case study of uber's drivers. *International Journal of Communication* 10: 3758–3784.

Rubery J, Grimshaw D, Keizer A, et al. (2018) Challenges and contradictions in the 'Normalising' of precarious work. *Work, Employment and Society* 32: 509–527.

Scheiber N. (2017) How uber uses psychological tricks to push its drivers' buttons. *New York Times*. New York: New York Times Company.

Schildt H. (2017) Big data and organizational design – the brave new world of algorithmic management and computer augmented transparency. *Innovation* 19: 23–30.

Scholz T. (2017) *Uberworked and Underpaid: How Workers are Disrupting the Digital Economy*, Cambridge, UK: Polity Press.

Schor JB and Attwood-Charles W. (2017) The "sharing" economy: Labor, inequality, and social connection on for-profit platforms. *Sociology Compass* 11: e12493.

Schumpeter JA. (1950) *Capitalism, Socialism and Democracy*, New York: Harper and Row.

Smiley S. (2018) Three quarters of food-delivery riders earn less than minimum wage, union says. *ABC News*. ABC.

Splend Pty Ltd. (2019) *Want Complete Peace of Mind? Flexible Car Access for On-Demand Rideshare Drivers*. Available at: https://www.splend.com.au/.

Srnicek N. (2017a) The challenges of platform capitalism: Understanding the logic of a new business model. *Juncture* 23: 254–257.

Srnicek N. (2017b) *Platform Capitalism*, Cambridge: Polity Press.

Standing G. (2016) *The Precariat: The New Dangerous Class*, London: Bloomsbury Publishing.

Staunton B. (2018) Grassroots action prominent in the platform economy, *Open Democracy*, London.

Stewart A and Stanford J. (2017) Regulating work in the gig economy: What are the options? *The Economic and Labour Relations Review* 28: 420–437.

Sundararajan A. (2016) *The Sharing Economy: The End of Employment and the Rise of Crowd-based Capitalism*, Cambridge: MIT Press.

The Guardian. (2018) Uber drivers log off in Australia-wide protest against low fares. *The Guardian*. Guardian News and Media Limited.

Uber. (2018a) Submission to the senate select committee on the future of work and the worker. *Senate Select Committee on the Future of Work and Workers*. Canberra.

Uber. (2018b) *White Paper on Work and Social Protection in Europe*. Available at: https://ubernewsroomapi.10upcdn.com/wp-content/uploads/2018/02/Uber-White-Paper-on-Work-and-Social-Protections-in-Europe.pdf.

Uber Technologies Inc. (2018) *Need a Car? Vehicle Solutions Providers could Help You Get a Vehicle in a Matter of Days*. Available at: https://www.uber.com/en-AU/drive/vehicle-solutions/?ds_rl=1249734&utm_source=google&utm_medium=cpc-brand&utm_campaign=search-google-brand_10_-99_au-national_d_all_acq_cpc_en_bmm&adgroup_name=GE%3EDR%3EUber%3EPure%3EGeneric%3EBMM&utm_term=%2Buber&kw=%2Buber&campaign_id=71700000018201859&cid=71700000018201859&adgroup_id=58700002066907734&adg_id=58700002066907734&kw_id=p16328901176&kwid=p16328901176&ad_id=256951161342&ext_id=17505623714&ran=2607896290200771998&lint_id=&lphy_id=1000286&pos=1t1&dev=c&net=g&match=b&placement=&target=&gclid=CjOKCQiAg_HhBRDNARIsAGHLV50UYCzMx6H8ugiAaHpOLRB4spKtkQZOK0-6r4QdVL9PeAgLUDwVD_caAjuREALw_wcB&gclsrc=aw.ds.

Unions New South Wales. (2016) *Innovation or Exploitation: Busting the Airtasker Myth*. Available at: https://d3n8a8pro7vhmx.cloudfront.net/unionsnsw/pages/3135/attachments/original/1474529110Unions_NSW_Report_into_Airtasker.pdf?1474529110.

US Bureau of Labor Statistics. (2018) *Labor Force Statistics from the Current Population Survey*. Available at: https://www.bls.gov/cps/electronically-mediated-employment.htm.

van Doorn N. (2017) Platform labor: On the gendered and racialized exploitation of low-income service work in the 'on-demand' economy. *Information, Communication & Society* 20: 898–914.

Weil D. (2014) *The Fissured Workplace: Why Work Became So Bad for So Many and What Can Be Done to Improve It*, Cambridge: Harvard University Press.

Weil D and Goldman T. (2016) Labor standards, the fissured workplace, and the on-demand economy. *Perspectives on Work*, Champaign, IL.

Wood AJ, Graham M, Lehdonvirta V, et al. (2018a) Good gig, bad big: Autonomy and algorithmic control in the global gig economy. *Work, Employment and Society* 00: 1–20.

Wood AJ, Lehdonvirta V and Graham M. (2018b) Workers of the Internet unite? Online freelancer organisation among remote gig economy workers in six Asian and African countries. *New Technology, Work and Employment* 33: 95–112.

Woodcock J and Johnson MR. (2018) Gamification: What it is, and how to fight it. *The Sociological Review* 66: 542–558.

Zwick A. (2018) Welcome to the gig economy: Neoliberal industrial relations and the case of Uber. *GeoJournal* 83: 679–691.

3 Extreme Working Hours

Peter Holland and Xiaoyan Liang

Introduction

In recent years the issue of the perfect work-time has been debated. Much has been made of the Swedish experiment to reduce the working day to 6 hours (Savage, 2017) and focusing on the job fitting the person. Nevertheless, even in the face of increasing evidence of occupational health and safety problems associated with extended working hours, more organisations (including multinational corporations [MNCs]) have been pushing for extended working hours. This chapter explores the literature on extended or extreme working hours and why, in the face of the evidence, such practices are being extended. It then examines three case studies across different industries which lacked any pilot study to justify the extension of hours, or assess the fatigue and risk implication in high risk and dangerous industries. In the light of increasing deregulation the cases also highlight the ongoing importance of unions as a countervailing power to stand up to these attempt to challenge key terms and conditions of work.

What Are Extended Hours and Why Are They Growing?

To define extended hours, and shift work which is at the heart of the extended hours culture, is not as easy as it seems initially. With globalisation and technology advancements (see Chapter 1) the notion of what constitutes a normal workday is increasingly unclear. So are the varieties of extended patterns of work. For example, shift work can be permanent day shift, permanent night shift, rotating shift patterns, split shifts, standard shift pattern or compressed shifts including extended hours within each day. A further complexity is offshore work and fly-in-fly-out (FIFO) work patterns, which can involve weeks or months at a time in isolated or remote location far from family and friends where there is little to do other than work. A 'hidden' aspect of extended hours covers on-call or call back work. We define 'extended hours' here as work that starts and/or continues outside the broad view of a 'normal' working day, with 'normal' generally falling into the following categories:

- Paid work day completed between 7 am and 7 pm;
- Work time of no more than 8 hours a day and 40 hours a week; and
- Hours work continuously except for designated breaks (AMWU, 2009).

Several authors have identified (Chatzitheochari & Anber, 2009; Ferguson & Dawson, 2012) the rapid proliferation of extended hours work patterns in many advanced market economies (AMEs). Several factors on their own or in combination can be seen as catalysts in these changing patterns of work. A key influence has been deregulation of work patterns and practices (of course, in the less advanced economies they were never regulated). As Loudoun and Harley (2011) note, such changes are proposed and made under the rubric of increased labour flexibility and the elimination or deregulation of (restrictive) work practices. These changes appear to pay little attention to the health and safety implications of such alterations to working patterns (Holland & Nelson, 2001; Loudoun & Harley, 2011), or indeed person-job fit, even though these patterns of work are linked to increased health issues and fatigue and are emerging increasingly in industries with significant potential for critical incidents. Conversely, in, for example, their study of the move from 8 to 12 hours shifts in the mining industry in Australia, Nelson and Holland (2001) found that no manager could point to productivity gains from extended shifts. Indeed the research found that no pilot or trial of such extensive change in working conditions (increasing the working day by 50%) were undertaken and/ or evaluated before-hand. This is a theme we will return to in the case studies in this chapter.

The decline in trade union membership in this period of increased deregulation has also been seen as significant. In many AMEs the union movement has been the main bulwark against the implementation of such work patterns and practices without due negotiation or trialling of such patterns of work. It is increasingly clear that extended work periods have the potential to cause workplace disengagement, fatigue and turnover. What is surprising in the development of these work practices is the apparent lack of consideration of these factors and their impact. This includes impacts on the individuals, as well as their families. So is it ignorance or wilful blindness? (Heffernan, 2010). Whilst it is beyond the scope of this chapter to explore the internal decision-making of managers in pushing such work practices, it is worth noting that the case studies explored in this chapter are of multinational organisations which it would be argued have the time, capacity and resources to carry out due diligence on these work practices.

Worker Well-Being – the Link between Extended Hours and Health

Given the debate and the increasing focus on human resources (people) as the key organisational asset (Boxall & Purcell, 2016), a major consideration regarding extended work hours is the impact on worker well-being. Meta-analysis research in the 1990s on prolonged work hours by Sparks et al. (1997) found a negative relationship with employees' physical and mental health. Other research has linked prolonged and unsocial work hours to poor lifestyle habits (Maruyama et al., 1995).

Links have also been identified between extended working hours and fatigue. Chatzitheochari and Anber (2009) found over a 1,000 studies at the individual level examining the health consequences of sleep patterns, age-related disorders, health issues and mortality (see also Basner et al., 2007; Speigal et al., 1999). At the organisational level and public safety context, extended work hours and sleep deprivation impact on performance and have been linked to mistakes and errors (Dembe, 2009). Major catastrophes such as the Exxon Valdez oil tanker accident and Chernobyl nuclear power plant meltdown have been linked to sleep deficiency (Coren, 1998). Yet still there appears to be an expansion of these work patterns and practices. Boourdouxhe and Toulouse (2001), in a study of film technicians, found that working extended hours increased the risk of accidents and aggravating musculoskeletal injuries. This supports Dembe's (2005) large-scale study of US workers which found those working extended hours more likely to suffer from on-the-job injuries. For those undertaking overtime, this rose by 61%; evening shift carried an increased chance of 38% and night shift 31%, compared to standard day shift.

What has emerged from this research is the issue of the so-called 'healthy worker' effect (Pearce et al., 2007), where people who can sustain these extended work patterns are generally fitter, stronger and healthier than the normal population and have a lower proportion of health issues. They might be described as a resilient 'survivor' cohort. So one effect of extended work hours will be a potential for indirect discrimination as they will potentially force older employees or those with physical conditions or with demanding family responsibilities to give up their jobs. As Quinlan et al. (2010) point out, research has yet to completely disentangle the impact of working hours from ageing and other variables. What evidence there is indicates overall negative outcomes.

Work-Life Balance

One of the less explored aspects of the impact of extended working hours and shift patterns is on work-life balance where the family has to cope with the work and sleep patterns of those working these hours.

Such hours can have an adverse outcome on work-life balance and, in particular, on 'normal' family life (Peetz & Murray, 2011) – see Chapter 5. As with age, people working under these conditions can self-select out because of these issues, increasing turnover. As Peetz and Murray (2011) found in their research:

> High labour turnover, rather than enabling employees to match hours and preferences appears simply to be a result of extensive employee dissatisfaction and poor job quality arising from working hours arrangements. It weeds out many employees whose families cannot cope with the working arrangements, but does not overcome the problems they create. There are adverse implications for work-life balance.
>
> (p. 26.)

These findings support research by Costa (2003) who points out that the inability to conform to socially valued time schedules produces a sense of alienation from the wider community, which may have marked negative effects on the individual. Whilst the virtues of being home for extended time periods are highlighted as a key advantage for employees, the fact remains that employees are also absent for significant lengthy time periods, be it daily, weekly or monthly, compared to the normal patterns of work. This potentially isolates them from family, friends, organisations and institutions. Parkes et al. (2005) described the personal impact on families of employees working on the North Sea oil rigs as 'intermittent husband absence', which describes the emotional impact of repeated partings and reunions for these families. Research on FIFO workers indicates similar family and health issues (Haslam-Mckenzie, 2016). Again, Quinlan et al. (2010) point to the need for more research.

The Economic Argument

Increasing or extending working hours has often been linked with increased efficiency for both the employee and the organisation, but most of the focus has been on the organisation. Issue identified include less downtime due to fewer shift change-overs with potentially reduced shifts from 3 x 8 hours to 2 x 12 hours (Baptise, 2007; Nelson & Holland, 2001). This can also reduce overheads (Hart, 2004). For employees a compressed working week potentially allows them more leisure time. However, as Caruso et al. (2006) point out, longer working hours have been associated with transport accidents, workplace injuries and accidents, lower productivity, higher turnover and increased health problems and family conflict. Indeed Baptise (2007) argues that business-focused performance indicators have obscured other important indicators such as injury, health and employee well-being. This is supported by Guest (2002), who argues that the lack of support for worker well-being can be assumed to be linked to the fact that workers are not an end in themselves but a means to an end, or part of the production process. The irony in this approach is highlighted by Renwick (2008), who noted that employee well-being can be linked to greater employee satisfaction, commitment to more stable workforce and improved business performance. However, it is more likely that the deregulation of work and workplace in many AMEs has allowed extended work hours to develop unchecked, based on little more than assumption of productivity improvements. The case studies below are illustrative of MNCs attempting to extend working hours, in the face of employee resistance supported by their union or any evidence to support productivity gains. So with the economics of such changes largely unproven, but the consequences of such changes clearly identified, should we be looking at the ethical argument for such change?

The Ethics of Extended Work-Time

Looking at extended or extreme working hours from an ethical perspective can allow a more nuanced assessment of the impact of such work patterns and practices from the individual, organisation and societal perspectives. By exploring these issues from a variety of perspectives we take a pluralist approach. This allows us to examine extended working hours using several classical ethical theories including egoism, utilitarianism and deontology.

Egoism and utilitarianism are both consequential theories which judge the morality of an issue based on the consequences it generates: in the former case, consequences for the decision makers under question and, in the latter, consequences for all parties whose interests might be affected.

Egoism suggests that an action is morally right if all decision makers in a given situation freely decide to pursue either their short-term desires or long-term interests (Crane & Matten, 2016). Applying this theory to the issue of extended working hours, we would have to evaluate whether the decision makers involved (i.e. employees and their employers) freely pursue their desires or interests. This certainly applies to employers who makes extended working hours part of their employment contracts with employees to ensure either continuity of their business or maximisation of efficiency. Even if employers do not write the clause in the contract, if they psychologically coerce their employees into working extended hours, they may still stand to gain from engaging in this practice. As for the employees, it could be argued that they may be quite happy to work extended hours forgoing time away from family for appropriate remuneration. If this were the case, an egoistic perspective would deem extended working hours morally acceptable. However, accruing research demonstrates that the employees, supported by their representative (often trade unions), are not supportive of these work patterns and practices, particularly in the long term (Mountain, Quon, Dodek, Sharpe, & Ayas, 2007; Wali et al., 2013). Research continues to indicated that their physical, emotional and social well-being are compromised as a result of these long-term work patterns (Dembe, Erickson, Delbos, & Banks, 2005; Raediker, Janßen, Schomann, & Nachreiner, 2006; Wirtz & Nachreiner, 2010). Hence, it is questionable whether the majority of employees are freely pursuing their own desires or interests by engaging in extended work patterns. In such a case, from an egoistic perspective, extended working hours would be immoral. From an employer's perspective, the perceived gains of efficiency (often structural, i.e. less shift changes) need to be juxtaposed with the evidence of the detrimental impact of such work practices on its workforce and long-term organisational performance.

Utilitarianism, or the 'greatest good principle' states that an action is morally justified if it brings about the greatest good for the greatest number of people affected by the action (Crane & Matten, 2016). Differing from egoism, it looks at not only the outcomes for the decision makers, but also the collective welfare that is produced by the action. This collective welfare would be calculated with what we call cost-benefit analysis. An action is deemed morally correct if it generates the highest aggregate economic value (i.e. utility) for all parties involved, regardless of the negative impact it has caused. In other words, 'the ends justifies the means'. If we apply utilitarianism theory to extended working hours, we need to identify all parties affected, and analyse the potential utility to them involved in either participating in extended working hours or not engaging in extended working hours. Table 3.1 demonstrates a simple balance sheet. After analysing all the positive and negative effects for the parties involved, we can add up the pleasure and pain for 'engaging in extended work shift' and 'not engaging in extended work shift' respectively. Adopting a utilitarian perspective, our analysis shows 'not engaging in extended work shift' is the morally preferable action as it generates the most pleasure for most parties, whilst under 'engaging in extended work shift', the pain for most parties dominates the analysis.

Deontology is a moral philosophy derived from the work of the German philosopher Immanuel Kant (1724–1904) who, contrary to consequential theorists, believed that morality of an issue or action is not subject to the particularity of a certain situation, neither should it be subject to its consequences. For Kant, morality is defined by a set of rationally deduced a priori moral rules, which must be applied consistently across situations without any exception He termed this set of rules a 'categorical imperative', which is comprised of three principles. First, "Act only according to that maxim whereby you can at the same time

Table 3.1 A utilitarian analysis of extended work shifts

Actors involved	Engaging in extended work shifts		Not engaging in extended work shifts	
	Pleasure	*Pain*	*Pleasure*	*Pain*
Employee	Monetary compensation	Sleep deprivation Fatigue and burnout (Raediker et al., 2006) Cognitive function, mental alertness (Wali et al., 2013; Wirtz & Nachreiner, 2010) Absence from important family events Guilt (Peetz & Murray, 2011) Increase mistakes, accidents and decreased productivity (e.g. Dembe et al., 2005; Nicholls, Bren, & Humphreys, 2004)	More time for self-care Better physical and emotional well-being Better work-life balance	Less financial reward potentially more financial pressures
Family and Social Fabric	Extended time for family and social events with expanded time off	Cope with absence of loved ones Cope with return of loved ones Disappointment, worry, concern and missing (Murray & Peetz, 2011; Parkes et al., 2005)	More normal family life More opportunities to connect with friends More quality time	Less financial options for investing in family
Organisations	Continuity of service Efficiency maximisation	Legal affairs Financial loss from fatigue-induced professional mistakes Reputation damage High turnover	More satisfied and 'safe' working employees Less mistakes/ risks Better reputation as employer Attract and retain quality staff	Not meeting customer/market demands Competitive edge
Society	Continuity of service and increased income flowing into the community	The impact of the mistakes and the burnout of these workers and resulting medical support and potential loss of life (Ref)	More active community members, less stress on families and health and welfare systems	Les income and tax for community investment

will that it should become a universal law" (Kant, 1994, p. 421). Second, "Act in such a way that you treat humanity, whether in your own person or in the person of any other, never merely as a means to an end, but always at the same time as an end" (Kant, 1994, p. 429). The third practical principle follows [from the first two] "...Act in accordance with the maxims of a member legislating universal laws..." (Kant, 1994, p. 438). Taken together, they form the basis of moral judgement. Applying Kant's moral 'test' to the issue of extended working shift, we develop the following insights.

Based on the first principle of universality, the question to ask is whether we would want everybody in every part of the world, regardless of age, gender, physical capability, profession and other characteristics, to engage in extended working hours? Obviously, not everybody can and not everyone is willing to. Hence, most of the people would not like this to be a universal law consistently applied, which suggests that extended working shifts are morally objectionable. Based on the second principle of human dignity, the question to ask is whether employees freely and autonomously decide to engage in extended or extreme working hours. Employees being pressured into accepting employment terms with these working hours would mean that they are merely used as a means to the employer's end, rather than as an end in themselves, which would entail respect for their desires, human needs and dignity. Hence, extended working shift is morally questionable by the measure of the second principle. Based on the third principle, the practical test, the question to ask is whether every other rational being, including your family, friends and strangers, would condone the action, and apply the same rule. It seems doubtful that all other rational human beings would accept extended working hours as a general principle to follow.

There are other ethical perspectives (e.g. virtue ethics, feminist ethics, post-modern ethics) which would not favour engaging in extended working shift either. But for the purpose of this chapter, the three classical ethical theories are authoritative enough to draw an ethical conclusion; i.e. engaging in extended working shift is morally questionable from an egoistic, utilitarian and deontological perspective.

Case Studies of Extended Work Hours

Case Study One: TransportCo

Background

TransportCo is a wholly owned subsidiary of a multinational corporation and operates public transport systems globally. It is also involved in transport consultancy and contracting services to governments around the world. One of its mission statements is to promote safe and ethical practices. In this context, it states that upholding safety is an absolute pre-requisite for all stakeholders.

The Issues

The organisation intended moving from 8 to 12 hours shifts for employees who work on safety and scheduled maintenance. The workforce had a three rotating shift system of 8 hours, Monday to Friday, with some work (fault rectification) done on the weekends and paid as overtime. The new proposal was for two 12 hours shifts, in which the workforce would alternate from day to night shift three times a year and included Saturday working. This would also include weekends. The underlying reasons given for these changes were to increase the efficiency of the work, and an increase in compensation was factored in to take account of the changes. The workforce, supported by their unions, opposed the changes on the grounds of safety and the unsocial work hours disrupting their personal lives and upsetting work-life balance.

The Analysis

Superficially, the changing work patterns from normal hours to alternating extended shift patterns showed only a minor change in the number of hours worked per week, with apparent increased compensation for employees. However, the key issue that appears in this case, which is also reflected in research, is that the only increase in productivity appears to be in the reduction of one shift change-over per day. It was difficult to see how any sustainable increase in productivity would be achieved beyond that.

However, in adopting these shift patterns, the length of the working day would be increased by 50%. Interviewees referred to the long-term effects on employees, noting that older workers found it increasingly difficult to work these shifts (Bohle et al., 2009; Costa, 2003, 2005; Costa & DeMila, 2005; Kandelaars et al., 2006; Nelsen & Holland, 2001). In profiling the workforce the average worker was aged in their mid-40s, and the work environment largely manual work. The issues raised are that whilst, in the short-term, the effects of these shift patterns may not be seen, over a longer period of time issues such as fatigue towards the end of shifts and changed work and rest patterns affect the capabilities of workers. As such, workers self-select out (Peetz & Murray, 2011), creating the 'healthy worker' effect (Pearce et al., 2007).

That is, those who can sustain these unnatural work patterns remain – the resilient 'survivor' cohort. These work-patterns therefore discriminate against the 'normal' worker and family and social patterns.

The work environment involves the use of industrial equipment. This requires on-going concentration. The development of extended working hours (12-hour period) increases the potential for accidents and injuries to the workforce (Dembe, 2005). Second as a maintenance workforce for a public transport system, the potential for major accidents and catastrophes could also increase, and the links between fatigue and major accidents are well documented (Basner et al., 2007; Chatzitheochari & Anber, 2009; Dembe, 2009). In addition, research by Holland and Nelson (2001) found that workers returning after injury found a 12-hour shift difficult to cope with. Major issues related to work-strain resulted in worker compensation claims. In addition, shift work starting at 6 pm and 6 am would affect the work-life balance, leisure and the sleep patterns of this largely blue-collar, male, middle-aged workforce. Again whilst these may not be seen initially, the long-term consequences might be increased stress on the worker and the family. These are not good combinations for employees working with industrial machinery and public safety. What was also concerning about these new work patterns was the opportunities for employees to work extra hours during the week. This erosion of recuperation time has the potential to add to the health and safety issues noted above.

It is also important to note that in the context of the safety of the workforce and the public, no undertaking was made for the development of a pilot study to gather information on a variety of health, safety and employment issues. It is difficult therefore to understand how the organisation would make an informed assessment of the impact of these work changes, or the impact on employees around these matters. Such a study would have allowed for monitoring and gathering information on issues such as employee fatigue. This is just one example of the many issues that the organisation needs to consider with these changed work patterns.

The Outcome

It is clear that extended working time has inherent risk for the individual, for the organisation and for the society which is not in line with TransportCo's mission statements to promote safe and ethical practices as an absolute pre-requisite for all stakeholders.

It is the obligation of employers to provide a safe workplace for all employees and visitors in many AMEs. Reconciling a safe workplace culture with this type of work within the requirement of the framework for occupational health and safety (OH&S) legislation is in this case difficult to justify. A key aspect of this type of legislative framework is that employer liability extends to employees' actions and/ or omissions, regardless of their state of mind.

In the event, the dispute was resolved in favour of the workforce and the work patterns were maintained as three 8-hour rotating shift from Monday to Friday with overtime for emergency or unscheduled work at the weekends.

BeveridgeCo

Background

BeveridgeCo is a subsidiary of a multinational corporation providing a wide range of alcoholic and non-alcoholic beverages globally. Part of its Health and Safety mission statement is a commitment to a safe workplace, as preventing harm is critical to the organisation's success. Its policies in this area are more substantial than other organisations and state that improving the health, safety and well-being of staff and maintaining safe plant and equipment and improving employee health are organisational priorities.

The Issue

BeveridgeCo intended to move its workforce at its manufacturing plant from a standard three-shift 8-hour work period to 12-hour shifts, 6 days a week. In attempting to prevent these changes, which the workforce did not want, negotiations led to a dispute and then industrial action, in which BeveridgeCo locked-out the workforce.

The organisation intended moving from 8-hour shifts 5 days a week (Monday to Friday) to 12-hour shifts, Monday to Thursday, day and night, and Thursday to Saturday day and night of employees in the production plant, to improve efficiencies of production. Specifically BeveridgeCo management argued that the change in shift patterns would increase capacity utilisation through lower labour utilisation costs and through less change-over of production teams. The workforce and unions opposed the changes on the grounds of unsocial work hours disrupting their personal life and work-life balance, as they moved from standard work hours to non-standard hours.

Issues of safety became a focal point. Whilst BeveridgeCo undertook modelling to assess the return on investment, there was no pilot study undertaken to assess the impact upon the workforce of these major changes to work patterns. The workforce profile was blue-collar, semi-skilled, middle-aged, males. As a manufacturing plant the workers were using industrial equipment: again, we note that the links to fatigue, sleep patterns, ageing and injury are well established (Basner et al., 2007; Chatzitheochari & Anber, 2009; Dembe, 2009). The increase in the working day by 50% combined with unsocial hours provided a classic workplace terrain for older workers to be forced out of employment by these work patterns.

The Outcome

The fact that pilot studies and overall risk assessment were not undertaken by BeveridgeCo was an important consideration in the prevention of the move of the workforce to the proposed 12-hour-shift patterns. It was clear that BeveridgeCo had not taken the health, safety or well-being of its workforce into account when attempting to change the work patterns at its manufacturing plant – in line with its own mission statement. The dispute was resolved in favour of the workforce.

EnergyCo

Background

EnergyCo is a subsidiary of a multinational energy produces and suppliers. Within EnergyCo's core values are statements that 'safety is more than a priority, it is a core value including a deep ethical commitment to employees and their families'.

The Issue

The issue in the case of EnergyCo is slightly different but draws upon the same matters of management pushing the limits of work patterns and practices in an environment using heavy machinery and with the potential for critical incidents. In this case the push by management was to increase the 12-hour work shifts from 7 days on and 7 days off to 14 days on and 14 days off. The argument was that overall the hours per 28-day cycle would not change, but the efficiency saving would allow a reduction in cost arising from the reduced change-over of shift teams.

The response by the workforce and their representatives was that whilst there was no change in the actual hours over a 28-day cycle, for these FIFO workers and their families these changes would result in them being away from home for half a month at a time. In addition, the increase in fatigue is effectively doubled with a move from 7 to 14-day shifts. Again the workforce in this case is middle-aged, blue-collar men who would according to the research find it increasingly difficult to cope with and manage these work patterns, in particular the doubling of cumulative fatigue (Basner et al., 2007; Chatzitheochari & Anber, 2009; Dembe, 2009; Holland & Nelson, 2001).

Once again, research on FIFO workers' life styles and the impact on their families was not taken into account. The stress of separation is an unavoidable aspect of such work and taking the span of time away from the family and friends from one week to half a month exacerbates the problems. The inability to conform to socially valued time can produce a sense of alienation from the family and the wider community (Costa, 2003). This increasing isolation through extended time away can create socially significant isolation for the individual.

There is also, again, the issue of the so-called 'healthy worker' effect (Pearce et al., 2007). Workers who can sustain these unnatural work patterns are generally fitter, stronger and healthier than the normal population with a lower proportion of health issue. As such these new patterns leave a more resilient 'survivor' cohort. Even this cohort, if they have families may also be forced to self-select out. This indicate that there is an expectation that such work practice will potentially force current employees to give up their work, a point further exacerbated by the age profile of this workforce: blue-collar and middle-aged.

Employees become less tolerant of shift work with age (Kandelaars et al., 2006): older employees' performance declined faster during night shifts than their younger counterparts.

The Outcome

The extension of 12 hours shift patterns from 7 to 14 days was strongly resisted by the workforce and their representatives. The fact that no studies were undertaken of the impact of these changes on workers or their families, combined with no overall risk assessment, was an important consideration in the prevention of the subsequent change of shift-patterns. It was interesting that EnergyCo relied on custom and practice as the argument for the change in work patterns across its (global) organisation. It is clear that the company's management had not considered the health, safety or well-being of its workforce when attempting to change the work patterns as its own mission statement indicated that it should. As such the dispute was resolved in favour of the workforce who were prepared to resist the changes and were strongly supported by their representative unions.

Ethical Perspective Summary

The three cases demonstrate that assumptions underpinning organisations' disposition to shift work appear to be largely unproven. All three companies proposed work patterns with the premise of efficiency gain, which could either be an egoistic argument, involving the parties concerned to be freely pursuing their short-term desires or long-term interests, or a utilitarian argument. However, in reality, in all three cases, there is little evidence supporting changes in work patterns and practices that will benefit either the organisations in question or the employees working for them. Contrarily, employees' interests could be greatly compromised, which consequently, might lead to a drop in organisational productivity and increased turnover.

If there were a utilitarian argument underpinning all three case companies' shift work proposals, then it could be argued that extended work patterns do indeed guarantee continuity of production and services, which might benefit the greatest number of people. However, utilitarianism entails a more thorough cost-benefit analysis; the morally justifiable action is the one that brings about the greatest net benefits or the lowest net costs. This begs the following questions of our three case MNC organisations: have all parties whose interests this decision might impact being considered? Have all possible costs and benefits (across individual, organisational and societal levels) being considered? How do these organisations calculate economic benefit? More importantly, how do they calculate the health cost of their employees, their emotional happiness, well-being and the social cost, noting their own mission statements? It is unlikely that the three organisations could conduct accurate measurement of such wide-ranging costs and benefits, given that it is impossible to assign an undisputable economic value to an individual's physical and emotional well-being. Hence, the proposed decisions are not justifiable using utilitarianism principles either. Thus, we draw the conclusion that the three cases in which the organisations attempt to implement extended work shift are not morally defensible.

Conclusion

There has been an increasing push in recent years to extended working hours, across a variety of industries. This can include the move from 8 to 12 hours shifts, or the extension of shifts over a longer period, i.e. one to two weeks at work. The focus on this chapter explores the impact of these changes on the employees, their family and community. The findings highlight major concerns about how in the context of sustained evidence work patterns and practices are being extended in an increasingly deregulated environment. The case studies of three organisations in heavy industry are illustrative of these concerns. In their mission statements health and safety are given priority and placed at the forefront of their management practices. However, the strong push for extended working hours with little evidence of any significant improvement casts doubt on this rhetoric. In industries with significant potential for critical incidents, employees are the ones being asked to modify their biological rhythms rather than the organisations modifying the work to better adapt to the capacity of the workers (Bohle & Quinlan, 2000, p. 236). In all three cases, the bulwark of strong unions prevented these changes in an increasingly deregulated environment. It is of concern that despite the negative evidence regarding extended work patterns the push continues.

References

Australian Manufacturers and Workers Union (AMWU) (2009). *Health and Safety Guidelines for Shiftwork and Extended Working Hours.* AMWU. Melbourne.

Baptiste, N. (2007). Tightening the link between employee wellbeing at work and performance: A new dimension of HRM. *Management Decision, 6*(2): 284–309.

Basner, M., Fomberstein, K., Razavi, F., Banks, S., William, J., Rosa, R. & Dinges, D. (2007). American time use survey: Sleep time and its relationship to waking activities. *Sleep, 30*(9): 1085–1095.

Bohle, P. & Quinlan, M. (2000). Time to call it quits: The safety and health of older workers. *International Journal of Health Services, 40*(1): 23–41.

Bohle, P. & Tilley, A. (1989). *Managing Occupational Health and Safety: A Multidisciplinary Approach* (2nd Ed). Melbourne: MacMillan.

Boxall, P. & Purcell, J. (2016). *Strategy and Human Resource Management.* Basingstoke, England: Palgrave MacMillian.

Caruso, C., Bushnell, T., Eggerth, D., Heitmann, A., Kojola, B., Newman, K., Roger, R., Sauter, S. & Vila, B. (2006). Long working hours, safety and health: Towards a National Research Agenda. *American Journal of Industrial Medicine, 49*(11): 930–942.

Chatzitheochari, S. & Arber, S. (2009). Lack of sleep, work and the long hours culture: Evidence from the UK time use survey. *Work, Employment and Society, 23*(1): 35–48.

Costa, G. (2003). Shift work and occupational medicine overview. *Occupational Medicine, 2*(1): 83–88.

Costa, G. (2005). Some considerations about ageing, shift work and work ability. In G. Costa, W. Goddard and J. IImarimen (eds). *Assessment and Promotion of Work Ability, Health and Well-being of Ageing Workers*. Elsevier: San Diego, CA: 67–72.

Costa, G. & DeMila, L. (2005). Ageing and shift work: A complex problem to face. *Chronobiology International, 25*(2): 165–181.

Crane, A. & Matten, D. (2016). *Business Ethics: Managing Corporate Citizenship and Sustainability in the Age of Globalization*. Oxford: Oxford University Press.

Dembe, A. (2005). The impact of overtime and long work hours on occupational injuries and illnesses: New evidence from the US. *Occupational and Environmental Medicine, 63*(9): 588–597.

Dembe, A. (2009). Ethical issues relating to health effects of long working hours, *Journal of Business Ethics, 84*(2): 195–208.

Dembe, A. E., Erickson, J. B., Delbos, R. G. & Banks, S. M. (2005). The impact of overtime and long work hours on occupational injuries and illnesses: New evidence from the United States. *Occupational and Environmental Medicine, 62*(9): 588–597.

Ferguson, S. & Dawson, D. (2012). 12-h or 8-hr shifts? It depends. *Sleep Medical Reviews, 16*(6): 519–528.

Guest, D. (2002). Human resource management, corporate performance and employee wellbeing: Building the worker into HRM. *Journal of Industrial Relations, 44*(1): 335–358.

Hart, R. (2004). *The Economics of Overtime Working*. Cambridge, UK: Cambridge University Press.

Haslam-Mckenzie, F. (2016). *Labour Force Mobility in the Australian Resource Sector*. Singapore: Springer.

Heffernan, M. (2010) *Wilful Blindness: Why We Ignore the Obvious at Our Peril*. London: Simon & Schuster.

Holland, P., Allen, B., & Cooper, B. (2013). Reducing burnout in Australian nurses: The role of employee direct voice and managerial responsiveness. *International Journal of Human Resource Management*, 24(16): 3146–3162.

Holland, P., Cooper, B., Pyman, A. & Teicher, J. (2012) Trust in management: The role of employee voice arrangements and perceived managerial opposition to unions. *Human Resource Management Journal*, 22(4): 377–391.

Holland, P., Pyman, A., Teicher, J. & Cooper, B., (2011). Employee voice and job satisfaction in Australia: The centrality of direct voice, *Human Resource Management*, 50(1): 95–111.

Kandelaars, K., Baulk, S., Fletcher, A., Eitzen, G., Roach, D. & Dawson, D. (2006). Observations of age-related differences in neurobehavioral performance in a 12-hour shift system. *Sleep and Biological Rhythms* 4(2): 171–174. May 2006

Kant, I. (1994). *Ethical Philosophy: Grounding for the Metaphysics of Morals* (J. W. Ellington, Trans. 3rd ed.). Indianapolis and Cambridge: Hackett Publishing Company (Original work published 1785).

Knutson, A. (2003). Health disorders and shift work. *Occupational Medicine*, 53:103–108

Loudoun, R. & Harley, B. (2011). Industrial relations, decentralisation and the growth of 12- hours shifts in Australia. *Journal of Industrial Relations*, 43(4): 402–421.

Maruyama, S., Kohno, K. & Morimoto, K. (1995). A study of preventative medicine in relation to mental health among middle-management employees: Effects of longer working hours on lifestyles, perceived stress and working-life satisfaction among white-collar middle management employees, *Japanese Journal of Hygiene*, 50(4): 849–860.

Mountain, S. A., Quon, B. S., Dodek, P., Sharpe, R., & Ayas, N. T. (2007). The impact of housestaff fatigue on occupational and patient safety. *Lung, 185*(4), 203–209.

Nelson, L. & Holland, P. (2001). Assessing the impact of twelve hours shifts: An evaluation by ten companies and union officials. *Labour & Industry*, 12(2): 97–113.

Nicholls, A., Bren, L., & Humphreys, N. (2004). Harvester productivity and operator fatigue: Working extended hours. *International Journal of Forest Engineering, 15*(2), 57–65. doi:10.1080/14942119.2004.10702497

Parkes, K. R., Carnell, S. C., & Farmer, E. L. (2005). 'Living two lives' perceptions, attitudes and experiences of spouses of UK offshore workers. *Community, Work and Family, 8*(4), 413–437.

Pearce, N., Checkoway, H. & Kriebel, D. (2007). Bias in occupational epidemiology studies. *Occupational and Environmental Medicine*, 64:562–8.

Peetz, D. & Murray, G. (2011). You get really old, really quickly: Involuntary long hours in the mining industry. *Journal of Industrial Relations*, 53(1): 13–29.

Pyman, A., Holland, P., Teicher, J. & Cooper, B. (2010). Industrial relations climate, employee voice and managerial attitudes to unions: An Australian study. *British Journal of Industrial Relations*, 48(2): 460–480.

Quinlan, M., Bohle, P. & Lam, F. (2010). *Managing Occupational Health and Safety* (3rd). Palgrave-Macmillian. Melbourne.

Raediker, B., Janßen, D., Schomann, C., & Nachreiner, F. (2006). Extended working hours and health. *Chronobiology International, 23*(6), 1305–1316. doi:10.1080/07420520601096245

Renwick, D. (2008). The origin of employee wellbeing in Brazil: An exploratory analysis. *Employee Relations, 31*(3): 312–321.

Savage, M. (2017, February 8). What really happened when Swedes tried six-hour days? *BBC News*, Retrieved from https://www.bbc.com/news/business-38843341.

Sparks, K., Cooper, C., Fried, Y. & Shirom, A. (1997). The effects of hours of work on health: A meta-analysis review. *Journal of Occupational and Organizational Psychology*, 70(4):391–408.

Spiegal, K., Knitson, K., Leproult, R., Tasali, E. & Van Cuter, E. (2005). Sleep lose. *Journal of Applied Psychology*, 99(5): 2008–2019.

Wali, S. O., Qutah, K., Abushanab, L., Basamh, R. a., Abushanab, J., & Krayem, A. (2013). Effect of on-call-related sleep deprivation on physicians' mood and alertness. *Annals of Thoracic Medicine, 8*(1), 22–27.

Wirtz, A., & Nachreiner, F. (2010). The effects of extended working hours on health and social well-being—A comparative analysis of four independent samples. *Chronobiology International, 27*(5), 1124–1134.

4 Wage Theft and the Challenges of Regulation
Reinventing an Old Form of Exploitation

Julian Teicher

Wage theft is gaining increasing media attention in countries such as Australia and the USA and some states in Europe due in part to the provocative re-naming of a set of exploitative labour practices. In Australia revelations of exploitative labour practices involving wage theft have become routine with one recent case involving a chain of upmarket restaurants owing 500 current or former employees approximately AU$8 million. (https://www.theage.com.au/national/victoria/george-calombaris-underpayment-woes-not-over-as-more-workers-come-forward-20190719-p528yi.html). While the story is familiar, in that the culprit was in the food industry and many victims were migrants, some elements are pertinent to this chapter. The employer was a corporation operating in a profitable market niche, and the underpayments were longstanding and diverse, including denial of paid breaks and unpaid overtime. Such cases underscore that wage theft cannot be dismissed as simply resulting from human error, the complexities of the regulatory system (Hallett 2018) or slender profit margins in competitive markets. Historically, exploitative labour practices such as these were a powerful force fostering the collective organisation of workers and enabling them to exercise effective voice in workplaces and in the political sphere. With union membership at historically low levels in many developed countries along with the emergence of business models which look as if they are designed to thwart traditional employment regulation, wage theft has become more prevalent in countries such as the USA and Australia.

In simple terms wage theft is underpayment of wages, but it is much more: it involves taking advantage of vulnerable workers by intentionally or recklessly failing to provide mutually agreed or legally required financial benefits to workers. Wage theft includes compelling workers to provide their services for additional unpaid hours including working through breaks, 'working off the clock' and unpaid overtime, in effect a form of modern slavery. It also includes withholding gratuities, payment of piece rates in place of time-based wages, and compelling workers to purchase items like uniforms and accommodation by direct deduction. Workers suffer these abuses for reasons including ignorance of their entitlements, unwillingness or inability to enforce their rights, acceptance that underpayment is the norm, gaps in regulatory frameworks and insufficient or inadequate enforcement by responsible government authorities.

While wage theft is longstanding, the term has entered public discourse only recently and is confined to a small number of developed economies where the concept of the employment relationship and the associated framework of employment rights are most developed. Thus, it has been observed (ILO 2016) that the two conditions that underpin wage theft, precarious employment and non-standard employment are prevalent in developing countries but tend to be encapsulated in the prevalence of informal and disguised employment. In several developed countries wage theft is closely connected to political campaigns seeking more effective regulatory responses to the exploitation of vulnerable groups of workers (see, e.g. https://www.abc.net.au/triplej/programs/hack/i-cant-wait-for-wage-theft-to-be-criminalized/11409886; https://www.teenvogue.com/story/what-to-do-wage-theft-explainer). These campaigns typically emphasise that wage theft is routinely treated as 'a minor infringement like a parking fine unlike offences against property'. As Hallett (2018: 21–22) observes:

> Popularized in the last decade by labor activists and progressive scholars, the term recognizes that when workers are not paid the minimum wage or overtime, their employers are in effect committing a form of theft. It is intentionally provocative in its characterization of common employer behavior as a crime.

Hallett further argues that these forms of theft that impact the poor have historically been considered less seriously than property crimes which are more likely to be against more affluent group in society. As well as drawing wider attention to the systematic exploitation of vulnerable workers, the wage theft label prompts us to reflect on the need for novel approaches to securing compliance. Attaching criminal sanctions has some attraction as a way of changing societal attitudes to wage theft, but it does not confront the inadequacy of a model which largely relies on victims to initiate enforcement and recovery of debts

This chapter focuses on Australia, a liberal market economy where wage theft has become a common business practice. Other closely related aspects of worker vulnerability such as lack of employee voice and the absence of the legal rights that come with employment are not considered directly. In this regard it is widely recognised that location in precarious employment is rarely a conscious choice and usually results from membership of certain demographic groups or location in particular regions, industries and occupations that facilitate employers engaging in wage theft. The chapter first outlines the various dimensions of wage theft and in the second section identifies the circumstances in which wage theft is most likely to occur. The third section considers the challenges of improving compliance and reducing wage theft.

Dimensions of the Problem

Wage theft takes diverse and novel forms but typically involves paying less than the minimum wage or failing to pay a component of wages. Some of the more egregious forms occur when an employer

- fails to pay any wages at all for reasons of purported insolvency, something which is often a feature of sub-contracting chains;
- deliberately misclassifies workers as independent contractors;
- requires employees to work 'off-the-clock'; or
- requires workers to pay recruiting fees or makes other illegal deductions from their wages such as for work-related equipment (Boba 2009).

When concerns about wage theft are raised publicly, it is often suggested that rather than being systemic, wage theft is unintentional or is a response to the pressures of competition. While there is doubtless some truth to these arguments in some cases and this will be influenced by the complexity of regulation and the resources firms have available for compliance, these arguments tend to be overstated. In the Australian case it was noted that errors are always in one direction (Australian Senate 2017). In the USA that argument for wage underpayments was challenged by the finding that in California between 2008 and 2011, 83% of workers with a court order for recovery of unpaid wages received nothing (https://www.labor.ucla.edu/wage-theft/).

In Australia various practices have been identified including requiring migrant workers in agriculture to pay for accommodation provided by the labour hire companies that recruited them and falsely classified them as independent contractors. Another widespread abuse involved coercion and fraud in which international students employed in franchised 7-Eleven convenience stores were required to work more than the 20 hours per week permitted under the terms of a student visa. The workers were compelled to repay wage payments for more than 20 hours by making deposits into the franchisee's bank account or risk having their visa breach reported to the immigration authorities by the very people who had pressured them into these work practices.

Wage theft is widespread in the USA with almost two million workers receiving less than the minimum wage and this affects most low-wage workers at some point in their working lives, particularly women, minorities and immigrants without workers' rights (Hallett 2018). A 2009 study of 4,000 workers in the three largest cities, Chicago, Los Angeles and New York, found that in the week prior to the survey, 26% had received less than the minimum wage and 60% were underpaid by more than one dollar per hour. In addition, 76% of respondents worked over 40 hours per week and were not paid for all their overtime as required by the *Fair Labor Standards Act*. Off the clock violations were also common:

> About one-quarter of workers surveyed (22 percent) stated that they had worked before and/or after their regular shifts in the previous work week and were thus "at risk" for off-the-clock violations. Of these "at risk" workers, 70 percent did not receive any pay at all for the work they performed outside of their regular shift.
>
> (Bernhardt et al. 2009: 22)

Similar figures were reported in 2018 survey of hourly paid workers by the US Bureau of Labor Statistics, which found that 58.5% of all wage and salary workers were hourly paid and 1.28 million (1.6%) were paid below the prevailing minimum wage of $7.25 per hour (https://www.bls.gov/opub/reports/minimum-wage/2018/home.htm). Women and younger workers were more likely to report being paid below the minimum wage with 61.6% of all hourly paid women and 41.8% of those aged 16–24 years in this category. Complementing these findings, a research project focusing on collective actions lodged by workers for wages violations by large corporations found that over the period 2000–2017, 4,220 cases were identified where wage theft led to large corporations paying a penalty. Walmart was the top-ranked corporation paying wage theft penalties of almost US$1.49 billion (https://www.goodjobsfirst.org/sites/default/files/docs/pdfs/wagetheft_report.pdf).

The extent of wage theft in the USA is not entirely unexpected in view of the less regulated nature of the labour market. More surprising is the extent of wage theft in Australia, a country with over a century of detailed and comprehensive employment regulation through federal and state arbitral tribunals. Despite continuing legislative change driven by neo-liberal ideology the *Fair Work Act 2009* prescribes a comprehensive safety net of minimum wages and conditions. While few categories of workers are excluded from this framework, a committee of the Senate inquiry found that "employers in some industries are underpaying workers with such impunity that the question of an effective floor is almost redundant" (Australian Senate 2017: 59). Nationally it is estimated that one in two hospitality workers are being underpaid, with similar figures applicable in the retail, beauty and fast food sectors. The Hospitality industry employs mostly vulnerable, low-skilled workers, with 60.7% having no post-school qualifications. The Senate enquiry reported that compliance was highest at 69% in Accommodation, taverns and bars, whereas in Restaurants, cafes and catering compliance was 42% with most errors relating to wage entitlements. In the Takeaway food group only 33% were found to be fully compliant with most "errors relating to underpayment of wages, incorrect payslips and incorrect or non-payment of weekend penalty rates" (Australian Senate 2017: 61).

A less visible form of wage theft in Australia is underpayment of compulsory superannuation contributions. This increased by AU$300 million to AU$5.94 billion over the two years ending 2015/16 with the number of victims rising by 220,000 to 2.98 million or about one-third of eligible workers (https://www.industrysuper.com/assets/FileDownloadCTA/1a6826792b/Unpaid-Super-Getting-Worse-While-Nothing-Is-Done-FINAL.pdf). Similar to other forms of wage theft, age is a key risk factor for underpayment of superannuation contributions and workers aged 20–29 had a 39.7% probability of underpayment. Other risk factors are earning under $30,000 per annum, being a part time or casual worker and working in a manual job. While it is arguable that some underpayments arise from errors by employers in determining their obligations, the data are further evidence that wage theft in Australia is now so widespread that it is normalised.

The widespread nature of wage theft and the seeming irrelevance of minimum standards in Australia have been identified by Thornthwaite (2017). First, workers on various forms of migrant work visa including temporary worker, working holiday and international student visas employed in horticulture have been underpaid either by farmers or by the labour hire contractors operating on their behalf. In one case Fijian workers on seasonal work visas as part of a programme to help Australia's Pacific neighbours received zero wages after the deduction of 'costs' for accommodation and the like. Similarly, international students have been found to be working in restaurants and cafes for less than two-thirds of the minimum wage.

Second, in the retail sector convenience store, operators and major retail chains including 7-Eleven, Caltex, Coles and Woolworths routinely underpaid direct employees, such as shop assistants, and workers lower in the supply chain, such as trolley collectors, and cleaners were also frequently underpaid. Similarly, fast food operators such as KFC, McDonalds and Hungry Jacks have been identified as underpaying their workers. As in the USA the franchising model, particularly in fast food and retailing, has drawn unfavourable attention. As noted, a major media investigation of the 7-Eleven chain revealed widespread wage theft by franchisees and a lack of vigilance by the franchisor. In Australia franchising is large and growing rapidly, accounting for 79,000 operating franchisees and more than 470,000 direct employees and turnover is estimated at $146 billion (https://s3-ap-southeast-2.amazonaws.com/wh1.thewebconsole.com/wh/1401/images/Franchising-report-2016.pdf). The size of franchising in itself suggests both the challenge of enforcement and suggests the need to consider how the model itself can be more effectively regulated rather than focusing on franchisee behaviour alone. Third, the on-demand economy which uses job platforms like Uber and Deliveroo and job auction sites like Airtasker is drawing increasing attention. A key issue with job platforms is whether the business model rests on circumventing employment obligations by creating the appearance of independent contracting. In regard to job auction sites Thornthwaite (2017: 262) observes that workers are presented as "being engaged in the 'share' or 'community' economies, a specious characterisation as their work has nothing to do with sharing or community and everything to do with the market". Workers bid against each other to quote a rate for completing a job "which may magnify the prospects of their real wage falling below legal minima".

While there is a tendency to attribute increasing wage theft to the rise of the on-demand economy, the extent of this problem is unclear for two main reasons. First, as is often the case with exploitative employment arrangements, the victims are often unaware of their rights or are unwilling or unable to voice their concerns. Problems of under-reporting and enforcement are compounded by the virtuality of the platforms used and even the form in which information is collected and stored may impede transparency. Second, there is some shifting of older forms of work onto platforms: for example, household maintenance, gardening and removal services which have often been undertaken by self-employed people. As workers in the on-demand economy are either categorised as independent contractors or simply as users of an online platform, conventional tests of whether a person should be classified as an employee are problematic. Typically, the determination of employment status in Australia (and other advanced economies) requires an assessment of whether a worker is 'dependent' on a single employer.

Fourth, a classic form of underpayment is 'cash-in-hand' arrangements. In November 2016, the Australian Tax Office estimated that 1.6 million businesses with a turnover of up to $15 million were paying workers cash-in-hand so avoiding taxation, superannuation and workers' compensation payment obligations. Cash-in-hand payment of workers demonstrates most of the worst characteristics of precarious employment; specifically, low pay and the various forms of insecurity including exposure to unsafe work and working practices (Burgess & Campbell 1998; Campbell & Burgess 2018). Cash-in-hand employment is common among casual workers in the retail, hospitality, cleaning and trade-related occupations

Fifth, labour hire companies have come under increasing scrutiny. In the state of Victoria, a recent Government Inquiry into the Labour Hire Industry and Insecure Work (Industrial Relations Victoria 2016) found substantial evidence of 'rogue' labour hire agencies which systematically engaged in breaches of payment regulation and other forms of regulation such as occupational health and safety. Labour hire abuses often include 'sham contracting' arrangements in which workers are deliberately mis-classified as contractors despite lacking the autonomy of contractors. These arrangements are commonplace in bicycle delivery services, call centres and charity collectors including Amnesty International and Wesley Mission. In a potentially important decision, the national workplace tribunal, the Fair Work Commission, ruled that a Foodora bicycle delivery 'contractor' was an employee. While the case was continuing the company went into voluntary administration citing "significant external challenges" (https://www.abc.net.au/news/2018-11-16/foodora-loses-unfair-dismissal-case-fair-work-commission/10506470).

Explaining Wage Theft

It is important to identify the factors that enable wage theft and the reasons for the increasing prevalence of wage underpayments. This process begins with the identification of vulnerable groups of workers and the dimensions of these groups. The second step is to examine changing business models that facilitate wage theft. Finally, it is necessary to consider the reasons for the changing attitudes of business managers to meeting their wage payment obligations.

Vulnerable Workers

Wage theft and other manifestations of precarity are typically found among workers with low education levels, youths, and migrants: people who are reluctant to report exploitation or lack awareness of their employment rights. The situation may be further complicated by a lack of resources to pursue legal remedies and representation insecurity all of which underscore the importance of effective enforcement and compliance mechanisms, an issue which we consider in the following section.

Youth

Among younger workers a key factor in wage thefts is that they "are not always familiar with the law, and may be hesitant to report exploitative practices for fear of losing their jobs" (Australian Senate 2017: 75). In one Australian case a petrol station worker was required to pay for petrol when a driver filled their tank and left without paying. More commonly workers receive an hourly payment below the minimum wage or are paid cash in hand. Young workers in regional and rural areas of Australia are especially vulnerable due to the fact that low job vacancy rates are the norm (Australian Senate 2017: 62). In turn, young workers are reluctant to report exploitation because employers sometimes threaten to use 'word of mouth' to damage their future employment prospects, a potent threat in small towns.

Migrant Workers

Migrant workers are vulnerable for reasons including fears of deportation but also because they "do not fully understand their rights in relation to receiving the same wages and entitlements of Australians employed in the same job" (Australian Senate 2017: 64). The *Report of the Migrant Worker Taskforce* (Australian Government 2019: 26) provided a compelling account of the causes of vulnerability of migrants on temporary visas including nurses and international students in particular:

> There are a number of vulnerabilities to workplace exploitation that are common among migrant workers, including limited English language skills, lack of awareness of Australian workplace laws and fear of visa cancellation, detention and removal from Australia. Peer and community or family expectations, norms within cultural groups, as well as economic settings in visa workers' home countries can also influence their decisions regarding low paid work.

In horticulture the Working Holiday Maker visa has been described as "synonymous with unscrupulous labour hire companies, exploitation and abuse" (Australian Council of Trade Unions 2017: 22). Instances of wage theft here include sham contracting, underpayment, debt bondage and employers demanding payment by employees in return for visa extensions. According to the Fair Work Ombudsman there is systematic exploitation of the Working Holiday Visa programme with visa holders from Asia (largely non-English speaking) being particularly vulnerable:

> The FWO regards 417 visa workers as especially vulnerable due to the difficulties in understanding and exercising their entitlements because of age and language barriers. In particular, their vulnerability is increased if they choose to undertake an 88 day placement, because of the remoteness of their working location and their dependence on employers to obtain eligibility for a second year visa.
>
> (Fair Work Ombudsman 2016: 3)

It is significant that this programme has grown rapidly and is large by international standards. In 2016 Working Holiday visas accounted for almost 11% of the workforce aged 15–24 with more than 100,000 visas being granted, whereas similar schemes in Canada and the considerably larger labour market of the UK account for only 20,000 workers. Unsurprisingly, there is a large overlap between exploitation of migrant workers and use of sham contracting arrangements. In one example, a Korean holiday maker was recruited for warehouse work via a website.

His contact arranged for him to receive an ABN number which in effect meant that he was being treated as a contractor. He was paid a flat $20 per hour cash-in-hand from which was deduced accommodation and transport, both of which he was compelled to use. A Senate committee (2017: 62) described this as a "form of modern day slavery".

Often neglected in discussion of wage theft is the situation of illegal workers, non-citizens who are working without a visa or working in breach of their visa conditions. By virtue of their legal status and lack of employment rights these workers are almost inevitably victims of wage theft and other abuses. Estimates of the total number or people in this category are incomplete; however, in 2017 this was estimated there were nearly 63,000 overstayers (Australian Government 2019). There are no data on other illegal entrants in the workforce.

International Students

Australia is a major destination for international students with more than half a million people being enrolled in universities, private colleges, English language courses and schools. In 2018 they accounted for almost 477,000 of the 880,000 temporary visa holders in Australia. Most international students work to support themselves, most are paid below the minimum wage and some hold multiple poorly paid jobs. Compounding the complexity for international students as migrants and young people is visa conditions limiting working hours. As described above, there is abundant evidence that employers have compelled international students to work in excess of the allowable maximum hours while systematically underpaying them (Australian Government 2019; Australian Senate 2017: 67). Surveys suggest that the rate of payment below the minimum wage is at least 25% and as high as 60% with cash-in-hand being widespread (Australian Government 2019: 34).

Changing Business Models

The second step in this exposition is to consider changing business models including sham contracting, labour hire, franchising and platform economy applications.

Sham Contracting

Sham contracting arrangements, deliberately mis-classifying employees as self-employed, constitute wage theft as the contracts aim to deny workers the entitlements arising from relevant employment relations laws including minimum wages, annual and sick leave and superannuation entitlements. A sham contractor is economically dependent on a single employer and has limited discretion over how and when they work. In Australia there has been increasing use of independent contractors over the last three decades, much of it involving sham contracting. According to the Australian Bureau of Statistics (ABS 6333.0 2018) there are over one million independent contractors in a total employed workforce of 12.6 million with 26% engaged in the construction industry and 20% in Administration and support services. As 37% of independent contractors claimed not to have sole authority over their work, it can be concluded that sham contracting is widespread in certain industries and occupations. The major construction industry union has "suggested that between 26% and 46% of so-called independent contractors in their industry are engaged on sham contracts" (ACTU 2018: 18). Cleaners, construction workers, beauticians, call centre workers and drivers are "among a growing and under researched group of workers engaged as independent contractors" (Victorian Government 2019). Significantly, workers under sham contracts often work alongside workers doing similar or the same work but are remunerated differently, a practice which has led some to ask whether "it should be allowable for a person to be treated differently to an employee when they are remunerated wholly or principally for their personal labour or skills" (ACTU 2017: 24).

Labour Hire

Originally labour hire was isolated and specialised, typically providing skills on an as-needed basis or to fill temporary gaps in an organisation, but over recent decades labour hire arrangements have grown rapidly and become widespread. According to the Productivity Commission, labour hire work grew at an average of 15.7% between 1990 and 2002 and over the same period the proportion of labour hire workers in workplaces with more than 20 employees rose from 0.8% to 3.9% (Productivity Commission 2002). Consequently, Australia is near the top of Organisation for Economic Co-operation and Development (OECD) rankings.

The contemporary business rationale for the growth of labour hire is straightforward; essentially, it is a core-periphery strategy intended to minimise costs and shift risks on to the workforce. Labour hire is too often part of a layered sub-contracting arrangement in which successful tenderers engage a company to provide workers to deliver the contracted services. These arrangements are distinguished by the fact that the sub-contract workforce does not usually possess specialised expertise and is subjected to the worst features of precarious employment. The required knowledge and skill rests with the host company.

In Australia, labour hire is common in horticulture and cleaning. Horticulture work locations are often remote, making scrutiny of wage theft and other forms of exploitation difficult. In the case of cleaning and other tasks, elaborate chains of contracts have been used to distance workers from the ultimate employer in the process enabling wage theft in a similar manner to offshore outsourcing in the clothing manufacture (see Chapter 10). As the case of the Woolworths supermarket chain demonstrates, wage theft along the supply chain can occur without a conscious intention by the host company and co-exists with sham contracting. The workplace regulator, the Fair Work Ombudsman (James 2016), observed wage theft was in effect a governance failure:

> Once again we find a big established company at the top of a chain that involves worker exploitation, reaping the benefit of underpaid labour while failing to keep sufficient watch on what its contractors are paying the workers.

Host companies save on staffing costs by using labour hire workers who are frequently employed as independent contractors and almost invariably receive inferior pay and conditions to other workers performing the same or similar work.

Franchising

This model provides a specific regulatory challenge because it creates a multitude of smaller businesses which are in a contractual relationship with the franchisor and are subject to varying degrees of operational control. Typically, franchisors have little day-to-day control over individual franchises and the fragmented nature of their business makes misconduct more difficult to identify. It is sometimes argued also that the business model underpinning franchising is premised on the underpayment of workers so that a required amount of gross profit can be remitted to the franchisor as occurred with the 7-Eleven convenience stores which were exhaustively examined by the Migrant Workers Taskforce (Australian Government 2019) and the Fair Work Ombudsman (Australian Government Fair Work Ombudsman 2016). As noted, these enquiries found systematic exploitation of international student by taking advantage of fears of deportation for breaching visa conditions in relation to working hours and of ostracism by the local ethnic community. Similar to sham contracting arrangements the Fair Work Ombudsman (Australian Government 2016) observed that the franchisor seemingly promoted compliance but did not adequately detect or address non-compliance. It is significant that 7-Eleven had "very high levels of control across their network" (Australian Government 2016: 32), a finding that suggests that the company was at best negligent in allowing wage theft and other abuses to develop.

A Declining Culture of Compliance

While there is detailed evidence that wage theft is an increasing problem in Australia, there is a dearth of historical data on the nature, extent and patterns of wage theft (Howe, Hardy & Cooney 2014). A small number of studies particularly Bennett (1994), Goodwin and Machnochie (2007), and Goodwin and Machnochie (2011) argue that non-compliance has been significant and persistent, and that enforcement was limited. Considering the overall compliance regime, however, throughout the 20th century unions made a major contribution to enforcement. This role was progressively undermined by legislative changes designed to decentralise and individualise employment relations beginning in the 1980s.

Historically, inspection enforcement efforts concentrated on small, provincial and non-unionised workplaces as larger organisations were likely to employ employment relations specialists. The shortcomings of this regime were partly offset by the fact that the system of employment regulation (detailed specification of wages and conditions by industrial tribunals) was predicated on the existence of strong unions. Registered unions among other things had the right to inspect the time and wages records of all employees in a workplace and played a role of ensuring compliance at least in relation to their members (Howe, Hardy & Cooney 2014).

This regime of compliance however was progressively undermined beginning in the late 1980s. Australia shifted from an arbitral model in which worker entitlements were contained in industrial awards to one based on enterprise agreements. This dramatically complicated the task of enforcement due to the proliferation of agreements with differing terms. This had two main consequences: more resources were required to keep abreast of changing wages and conditions provisions; and employee uncertainty led to increased complaints forcing inspections to shift to a reactive approach (Goodwin & Machnochie 2011). The strains on the enforcement system caused by the shift to enterprise bargaining were exacerbated by later legislation restricting unions' rights to inspect time and wages records to members and requiring unions wishing to enter premises to investigate suspected breaches to provide both 24 hours' notice of entry and particulars of the suspected breach (Goodwin & Machnochie 2011). Cumulatively, legislative changes have undermined the culture of compliance that existed in Australia in the process making underpayment of wages 'more acceptable'.

Reducing Wage Theft

The prevalence of wage theft rivals and even surpasses other categories of theft that receive considerably more public attention and law enforcement resources. The experience of Australia demonstrates that wage theft is widespread and not confined to small businesses that lack the resources or specialised staff to ensure the correct classification and payment of employees. In the USA, Hallett (2009: 97) comments that employers steal more wages from workers each year than is stolen in "bank robberies, convenience store robberies, street and highway robberies, and gas station robberies combined". Wage theft is, by many accounts, one of the most common offences committed in the USA and Australia, but until recently its existence has been largely normalised.

The reasons why people comply with laws is the subject of continuing discussion. Compliance with laws in any society is at least partly a reflection of culture but also of the traditional economic conception, that is, an assessment of the probability of being apprehended and punished. The connection between the economic and cultural approaches to compliance is that where the perception of apprehension declines, the culture of compliance is gradually eroded as was outlined above. It follows that an important part of the response to wage theft is improved enforcement mechanisms, that is, the certainty and severity of punishment, but precisely what this involves exactly is unclear. In recent times this has received increasing consideration from academics, practitioners and policy makers from which we can discern the features of an effective compliance regime.

Reliance on workplace inspections and the routine issuing of penalties has practical difficulties. Specifically, not all breaches are wilful or even neglectful. Employment regulation is usually complex, and many employers do not have the requisite resources to ensure compliance. Governments must also juggle political priorities and practicalities, so blanket inspection of workplaces is unlikely to be an efficient use of scarce resources. Similarly, a strict liability in response to wage theft would be resisted by business organisations as oppressive and a disincentive to small business. Similarly, a complaints-based regime of enforcement is flawed for several reasons, especially that victims are unlikely to complain primarily due to acceptance of their situation, ignorance and concerns about repercussion. Also, it has been demonstrated that the incidence of complaints in an industry is not a reliable predictor of the extent of regulatory breaches (Australian Government Migrant Worker Taskforce 2019; Hallett 2018). These considerations prompt enforcement agencies to adopt a model of strategic compliance or responsive regulation (Ayres & Braithwaite 1992; Weil 2007). The essence is that regulation is not only about the relations between the state and business and that to avoid regulatory capture regulators must respond to multiple stakeholders in crafting regulation; regulation must be sensitive to context including culture and history; and that effective regulation involves a pyramid beginning with the least coercive and least costly strategies at the base. The Australian case highlights the challenges of enforcement. The workplace regulator uses the enforcement pyramid that takes into account the seriousness and deliberateness of employer behaviour in the process being criticised for being more a mediator than a regulator (Parker 2019). Recognising the increasing incidence of wage theft by large employers the Fair Work Ombudsman encourages businesses to self-report with the assurance that they will be required to enter into enforceable undertakings and in some cases to make a 'contrition payment'.

Wage theft is rarely an isolated phenomenon but occurs in conjunction with tax evasion, breaches of immigration laws, fraudulent business practices, deliberate bankruptcy (to avoid liabilities), and breaches of environmental and occupational health and safety laws. Consequently, improved enforcement involves collaborative approaches involving multiple agencies in identifying inspection targets, undertaking inspections, collecting and analysing data, and undertaking enforcement. In Australia, for example, a common practice for companies that engage in wage theft is to go into liquidation to avoid liabilities such as paying wages. Such firms typically breach multiple laws by failing to keep adequate records for tax or employment purposes, breach occupational health and safety laws, and deliberately mis-classify workers as independent contractors.

Certain business models create abundant opportunities for wage theft including through failure of the franchisor or the head contractor to properly supervise the business practices of franchisees or sub-ordinate contractors. In the Australian context, this has given rise to proposals for more extensive regulation of franchise operations to ensure that franchisors carefully monitor franchise operations and also to ensure that the franchisor profit margin does not force franchisees to cut costs and underpay workers in order to meet their obligations (Australian Government Migrant Worker Taskforce 2019). Similarly, two Australian states have introduced labour hire licencing schemes to which make it an offence for an organisation to engage an unregistered labour hire provider and these organisations are required to report annually on their operations. The schemes aim to remove the scope for unscrupulous operators to undercut wages and conditions by creating a 'level playing field'.

Creation of a crime of wage theft is often proposed and is presently under consideration by the Australian Government. The attraction of criminal sanctions is most likely to be its effect on changing community attitudes, and the imposition of penalties is likely to be reserved for the most egregious cases of wage theft, that is cases in which the behaviour in question is deliberate rather than neglectful (Australian Government Migrant Worker Taskforce 2019). There are also considerable challenges for regulators in deciding the individuals in an organisation who should be subject to criminal liability. It is also relevant that this would be a departure from the norm in employment regulation in that breaches are treated as civil offences.

Conclusion

The concept of wage theft arose primarily from the work of activists initially who were concerned at the fact that low paid workers in the USA suffered from both low minimum wages and the willingness of many employers to undercut even this limited form of protection. Similar concerns are increasingly being raised in Australia, a country which historically had a highly regulated system of employment relations. Whether legislators will respond to the increasing challenge of wage theft by criminalising a range of behaviours is unclear; however, there is now increasing media and government attention to these once widely accepted abuses of vulnerable workers. Running through these discussions is the considerable challenge of implementing an effective regime of compliance.

While the resources available for enforcement are almost inevitably insufficient in view of the competing priorities of governments, the extent of these deficiencies has been exacerbated by the growth of wage theft. Additional resources for inspection and enforcement would assist in reducing wage theft, but alone this is unlikely to be an optimal response to systematic and deliberate breaches. The best known of these models involve a combination of extended supply chains, mis-classifying employees as contractors, franchising arrangements with insufficient central monitoring and instances of modern slavery including migrant visa breaches.

Resource constraints and the challenges posed by systematic wage theft and the associated illegal activities necessitate regulators adopting strategic approaches (responsive regulation). By definition compliance systems need to be designed for the situation and there is no single solution. To varying degrees responsive regulation emphasises achieving voluntary compliance through educational and facilitative approaches before moving to traditional enforcement. Use of the enforcement pyramid is sometimes criticised as placing too much emphasis on education rather than penalising illegal behaviour and as an inadequate response to businesses designed around non-compliance. A particular challenge is 'phoenixing' or the practices of serially establishing and liquidating businesses to avoid legal obligations. More generally, the adoption of business models designed to take advantage of vulnerable workers has prompted some regulators to adopt a whole-of-government approach. This follows from the fact that systematic wage theft is almost inevitably accompanied by a range of other illegal behaviours such as tax and business fraud and breaches of environment, immigration and health and safety laws. While these businesses usually minimise or falsify employment and financial records, inter-agency co-operation enables sophisticated data matching and enhanced chances of successful prosecutions.

References

Australian Bureau of Statistics (2018). 6333.0 – Characteristics of employment, Australia, August 2018, https://www.abs.gov.au/AUSSTATS/abs@.nsf/DetailsPage/6333.0August%202018?OpenDocument

Australian Council of Trade Unions (2017). *The incidence of, and trends in corporate avoidance of the fair work act 2009, senate education & employment references committee, submission.* https://www.actu.org.au/our-work/submissions/2017/the-incidence-of-and-trends-in-corporate-avoidance-of-the-fair-work-act-2009

Australian Council of Trade Unions (2018) *Wage theft: The exploitation of works is widespread and has become a business model,* ACTU submission, https://www.actu.org.au/media/1385221/d170-wage-theft-in-australia-the-exploitation-of-workers-is-widespread-and-has-become-a-business-model-actu-submission-15-august-2018.pdf

Australian Government (2019). *Report of the Migrant Workers Taskforce,* Commonwealth of Australia, https://www.ag.gov.au/industrial-relations/industrial-relations-publications/Pages/report-migrant-workers-taskforce.aspx.

Australian Government Fair Work Ombudsman (2016). *A report of the fair work ombudsman's inquiry into 7-Eleven, identifying and addressing the drivers of non-compliance in the 7-Eleven network.* April, Commonwealth of Australia. https://www.fairwork.gov.au/about-us/access-accountability-and-reporting/inquiry-reports#7-11

Australian Senate (2017). *Corporate avoidance of the fair work act 2009.* Standing Committee on Education and Employment. https://www.aph.gov.au/Parliamentary_Business/Committees/Senate/Education_and_Employment/AvoidanceofFairWork/Report

Ayres, I. & Braithwaite, J. (1992). *Responsive regulation, transcending the de-regulation debate.* New York: Oxford University Press.

Bernhardt, A. et. al. (2009) *Broken laws, unprotected workers,* https://www.nelp.org/wp-content/uploads/2015/03/BrokenLawsReport2009.pdf

Boba, K. (2009). *Wage theft in America.* New York: New Press.

Burgess, J., & Campbell, I. (1998) The nature and dimensions of precarious employment in australia, *Labour & Industry,* 8(3), 5–21. doi:10.1080/10301763.1998.10669175

Campbell, I. & Burgess, J. (2018). Patchy progress? Two decades of research on precariousness and precarious work in Australia. *Labour & Industry,* 28(1), 48–67.

Fair Work Ombudsman (2016). *Inquiry into the wages and conditions of people working under the 417 working holiday visa program.* https://www.aph.gov.au/Parliamentary_Business/Committees/Joint/Foreign_Affairs_Defence_and_Trade/ModernSlavery/Final_report/section?id=committees%2Freportjnt%2F024102%2F25425#footnote9target

Goodwin, M. & Machnochie, G. (2007). Unpaid entitlement recovery in the federal industrial relations system: Strategy and outcomes 1952–95. *Journal of Industrial Relations,* 49(4), 523–544.

Goodwin, M. & Machnochie, G. (2011). Minimum labour standards enforcement in Australia: Caught in the crossfire? *Economic and Labour Relations Review,* 22(2), 55–80.

Hallett, N. (2018). The problem of wage theft. *Yale Law & Policy Review*, 37(1), 93–152.

Hardy, T. & Howe, J. (2009). Partners in enforcement? The new balance between government and trade union enforcement of employment standards in Australia. *Australian Journal of Labour Law*, 22(3), 306–336.

Howe, J., Hardy, T. & Cooney, S. (2014). *The transformation of enforcement of minimum employment standards in Australia: A review of the FWOIs Activities from 2006–2012*. Melbourne: Centre for Employment and Labour Relations Law, Melbourne Law School.

Industrial Relations Victoria (2016). *Victorian government inquiry into the labour hire industry and insecure work final report.* https://s3.ap-southeast-2. amazonaws.com/hdp.au.prod.app.vic-engage.files/3615/5685/9019/IRV-Inquiry-Final-Report-.pdf

Industry Super Australia (2019). *Unpaid super: Getting worse while nothing is done.* https://www.industrysuper.com/assets/FileDownloadCTA/1a6826 792b/Unpaid-Super-Getting-Worse-While-Nothing-Is-Done-FINAL.pdf

International Labour Organisation (2016). *Non-standard employment around the world.* Geneva: International Labour Office.

James, N. (2016). You see no evil when you hold your hands over your eyes. https://www.fairwork.gov.au/about-us/news-and-media-releases/archived-media-releases/2016-media-releases/june-2016/20160625-wooliestcopeed#

Parker, S. (2019). Address by the fair work ombudsman 2019 Annual National Policy-Influence-reform Conference. https://www.fairwork.gov.au/about-us/news-and-media-releases/2019-media-releases/june-2019/20190603-aig-pir-media-release

Thornthwaite, L. (2017). The living wage crisis in Australian industrial relations. *Labour and Industry*, 27(4), 261–269.

Weil, D. (2007). Crafting a progressive workplace regulatory policy: Why enforcement matters. *Comparative Labor Law and Policy Journal*, 28(2), 101–130.

5 Working at the Edge of the World

Kimberley Norris, Peter Holland,
Rob Hecker and Xiaoyan Liang

Introduction

Technology and knowledge have pushed the boundaries of where, when and how we work to extreme environments. Few can be much more extreme than the Antarctic. Increasingly, high-skilled worker (scientists) and operational support teams are spending longer time periods in this environment as they research major issues such as climate change. It is one thing to prepare and manage a workforce for such extreme working conditions. It is another to explore the way new technologies are impacting on the workforce physically isolated from home and family. The chapter looks at the complexities of managing a workforce in such an extreme environment in the technology-intensive 21st century, which are arguably making the ability to manage work and non-work life potentially more difficult.

Working in the Extremes

When it comes to extreme working environment, there are few places in the world that can match the Antarctic. As Norris, Paton and Ayton (2010) point out, temperatures range between –10°C and –60°C. The air temperature results in minimal precipitation, so that the Antarctic has been described as the world's largest desert (King & Turner, 1997). Added to this are fierce winds that have been recorded at speeds of over 300 kilometres per hour. A key point Norris et al. (2010) make is that it is impossible to sustain life without technology, a theme that we shall return to in the context of 21st-century technology. A further characteristic identified by Suedfeld and Weiss (2000) is that the signing of the Antarctic Treaty in 1961 has negated territorial claims, the continent was officially disarmed and resource extraction prohibited. Those now living and working there are concerned primarily with scientific research and different nations work side-by-side in relative harmony. The post-treaty has seen sustained investment in scientific research on the continent. As Suedfeld and Weiss (2000) note:

> The principles of openness and international cooperation have survived well ... In spite of periodic wrangling concerning the renewal of the treaty, complaints from countries that would like to exploit the

sub-ice mineral riches of the area or fish its marine biota and the semi
discreet moves of some nations to strengthen a possible claim to territory suzerainty. Amity reigns; it has been suggested that universal
peace could be established by moving the boundary of the Antarctic
Treaty north by 10 degrees of latitude every year or every decade.

(p. 9)

The impact on humans working in this hostile environment is extensive
and ongoing and in terms of best practice many research organisations
are continually striving to improve the lifestyle, health and well-being
of those working in the Antarctic. Research continues to explore the
physical, social and psychological aspects of working in this extreme
environment. Indeed, research on working in Antarctica can also provide evidence of effective human resource management (HRM) policies
and practices for other extreme or remote working environments such
as deep-sea drilling, mining and space travel. Using Antarctic exploration and living as an analogue for space travel has been a long-held research approach (Burke & Feitosa, 2015; Suedfeld & Weiss, 2000). For
example, NASA and Monash University (Australia) studied expeditioners' circadian rhythms in a programme to assess sleep, circadian phase,
cognitive functioning behavioural and health and safety in isolated and
confined environments (AAD, 2012). As the Station Manager noted "It's
a very small community and it's very confined and it's a prolonged isolation without any access to external support. So it's about the closest
thing you've got to a nine-month mission to Mars" (Catalyst, 2015). As
such, increasing research on factors influencing expeditioner's employment experience in Antarctic has attempted to integrate the individual,
interpersonal and organisational influences (Norris et al., 2010).

The Individual Perspective

Research (Francis et al., 2002; Lugg, 2000) has identified a range of
physical systems including reduced cardiovascular fitness and diminished levels of immunity. Social and psychological stressors from this
prolonged period in extreme and confined conditions include limited
privacy and, critically, absence of family and social support (Sudfeld &
Steel, 2000). As Norris et al. (2010) have identified, issues associated
with prolonged isolation from family and friends have been well documented for over 50 years. Such isolation has been associated with an
increased risk of developing or exacerbating mood or adjustment disorders, personality disorders and substance abuse (Palinkas, Houseal &
Miller, 2000; Strange & Youngman, 1971).

Researchers have thus consistently addressed issues of physical, social
and psychological isolation and adaptation to the environment, which
are the most challenging aspects of working in Antarctica, influenced by

a combination of factors – not least technological (Decamps & Rosnet, 2005). Whilst positive responses to the Antarctic environment have been reported, often associated with critical incidents resulting in enhanced teamwork and camaraderie (Moult, Norris, Payton & Ayton, 2015; Suedfeld & Steel, 2000; Wood, Hysong, Lugg & Harm, 2000), the negative impact cannot be underestimated. Typical negative reactions include declines in mood and cognitive performance (Palinkas, Suedfeld & Steel, 1995) and sleep quality (Palinkas et al., 2000), as well as increased anxiety (Lugg, 2000), aggression (Palinkas, Glogower, Dembert, Hansen & Smullen, 2004) and somatic complaints (Palinkas & Suedfeld, 2007). A widely reported psychological response to working in Antarctica is the 'winter-over syndrome' (Palinkas & Suedfeld, 2007). This syndrome is characterised by alterations in mood, irritability and hostility, increases in psychosomatic complaints, insomnia, fatigue, cognitive impairment and occurrences of mild hypnotic states termed 'long eye' or 'Antarctic stare', and has been described as having similar impacts on functioning as subclinical depression (Palinkas & Suedfeld, 2007). As the name suggests, 'winter-over syndrome' is most likely to occur during the Antarctic winter when travel to and from the continent is made more difficult (and sometimes impossible) by dangerous weather conditions and extending ice sheets. As a result, the isolation associated with this environment is reinforced physically, socially and psychologically. Thus, reliance on technology for survival and communication with the outside world takes on an even larger importance.

Compounding these difficulties is the absence of coping resources that would normally be relied upon in challenging circumstances. For example, people cannot simply escape the stressor by getting away for the weekend, or go for a run. These types of activities require extensive planning, as well as favourable weather conditions, to ensure that a seemingly everyday activity does not result in serious injury, or even death. Moreover, it's not as simple to communicate with friends and loved ones to whom you would normally turn for social support – most of these people will be thousands of kilometres away and only reachable via limited and restrictive email or telephone calls and social media. This necessitates identifying and using alternative coping methods, which can be difficult in such an isolated, confined and sparse environment.

The Interpersonal Perspective

Working in Antarctica necessitates living and working in close confines with others not of one's own choosing, and without hope of 'reprieve' from their organisation. Compounding this is the fact that there is limited, if any, physical demarcation between work and non-work spaces within the Antarctic environment, with many spaces fulfilling multiple functions such as both recreation and work facility. Furthermore, social interactions are conducted within these same constraints, with the same group of individuals not of one's own choosing, until resupply – the changeover period in which a station is equipped with resources and personnel for the coming employment period. Even then, the new social milieu is staffed with individuals with whom an individual may not normally choose to interact. As such, the Antarctic environment offers limited social novelty compared to routine environments, and a restricted cohort from whom to draw social interactions and resultantly, social support.

The quality of social interactions in an extreme and unusual environment such as Antarctica is influenced by the perceived control over social experiences within that environment (Suedfeld & Steel, 2000). Factors that may influence the level of perceived control in this regard include the availability of communication technologies such as email and Skype as well as voluntary face-to-face interpersonal interactions, both of which are limited in Antarctica due to the limited band width and the need to relay significant amounts of data and research. Such social factors deviate markedly from voluntary interactions that are possible in most other environments and present many unusual social and psychological challenges (e.g. interacting as a matter of necessity rather than choice) (Suedfeld & Steel, 2000). In and of itself, this poses unique challenges to human performance that are not encountered in the majority of routine work environments.

Further compounding these challenges is a shift in the broader sociocultural landscape whereby a growing majority of adults conduct at least some of their social interactions in an online environment, through social media outlets such as Facebook, Instagram, Snapchat and other platforms. Recent estimates suggest that more than two billion people worldwide are active on Facebook; more than 400 million people use Instagram every day; and nearly two billion people use Snapchat every day (Salinas, 2018). What's more, there is an expectation that such resources should be available as and when desired, and many are routinely accessed in a work context, regardless of whether such behaviour is sanctioned. In many ways, these online social media platforms are considered ubiquitous and as such a necessity in advanced market economies, rather than a privilege. If social media is viewed as a necessity, restrictions placed on accessibility run the risk of being interpreted as punitive or a form of deprivation which can lead to a range of negative psychological outcomes including anxiety, depression, panic and fear-of-missing-out (Przybylski, Murayama, DeHaan & Gladwell, 2013). Importantly here, the identified declines in mental health are not due to the absence of social media per se, but instead result from the meaning placed on this absence by the individual.

More recently, researchers have identified that social media use in and of itself has become a coping resource that people engage in to manage different forms of stress (Snyder & Ford, 2013), leading many to argue that social media platforms offer a viable and important mechanism for accessing social support in times of need (Naslund, Grande, Aschbrenner & Elwyn, 2014). The importance and effectiveness of traditional face-to-face social support as a coping resource is well documented (Carver & Conner-Smith, 2010). The efficacy of social media in providing such social support outlets is beginning to be examined, with some researchers (Naslund et al., 2014) demonstrating efficacy in this regard – particularly for individuals for whom face-to-face interactions are not viable, for situations in which people wish to retain a degree of privacy or anonymity, or health conditions that limit the ability to leave the home (including anxiety disorders and physical impairments). The utility of social media in meeting social support needs when direct face-to-face interactions are not possible has relevance in many situations beyond those mentioned above, to include situations in which people are geographically dislocated due to work demands, such as when deployed overseas or working in extreme environments such as Antarctica.

At present, Antarctica expeditioner's access to social media platforms whilst working 'on the ice' varies, with some national programmes offering varying levels of contact and others offering none at all. Reasons for not providing access are often pragmatic in nature – restricted or limited bandwidth necessitates prioritisation of mission goals above social interactions, and issues of equity mean that if such access cannot be provided to all expeditioners it is provided to none. The majority of National Antarctic Programmes have developed social media policies that outline the level of access that can be afforded, and in some instances, provide guidelines as to the posting of content – a practice which is consistent with many other organisations that provide social media policies with which their staff are expected to comply. Despite National Programmes clearly disclosing these limitations to successful applicants, reports suggest that many expeditioners underestimate the impacts of such restricted access, and experience frustration at such restrictions being placed on them. What's more, a number of these individuals attempt to thwart the system by accessing social media through non-sanctioned methods in an attempt to have their social media needs met. The issue of equity between stations as a factor should also not be underestimated. As noted, there are close and constant ties between the stations so if one has less restriction on information and communication technologies (ICTs), this can also cause tension for those restricted as it can be perceived as a punitive policy.

The Organisational Perspective: The Supportive Role of HRM

The importance of these challenges cannot be underestimated as the number and duration of expeditions to Antarctica continues to increase. The total winter population is approximately 1,000 people, which increases to over 5,000 during the summer period. Thirty countries support at least one facility in Antarctica and 20 of these have a year-round presence (COMNAP, 2017). A key aspect of these expeditions is the extended period of time people are exposed to this environment. The level and intensity of the human resource management programmes, policies and practices for the successful recruitment, selection, preparation and management of individuals for these major expeditions to the most extreme continent in the world is critical, because external help or evacuation in the event of an incident or emergency may be impossible. As noted, people need to be able to get on and work in highly functioning teams. An early example of the extreme challenges faced in such a remote environment was illustrated in the case of the station doctor at a Russian Antarctica base. Upon developing severe appendicitis, he operated on himself to save his life while instructing his friends what to do if he lost consciousness. As one of the current Australian doctors on-station commented "I think me getting injured is one of my big worries. I think, 'Who's going to look after me?' … Surprisingly appendicitis is actually quite common in Antarctica compared to the general community" (Station medical officer). All Australian doctors now going to Antarctica have their appendices removed before becoming an expeditioner as a preventative measure. Another example of the extreme medical challenges that can occur in Antarctica pertains to the case of Dr Jerri Lin Nielsen, who was forced to diagnose and treat her own breast cancer until an evacuation was possible, with the support of a machinist and welder who were trained in basic medical support. It is safe to say that these types of additional duties are unlikely to be encountered in many routine work environments.

Extreme interpersonal conflicts 'on-station' are rare, but do occur. Other well-documented incidents include a chef serving up 'hair pie' to an expeditioner who had complained they had found a single hair on their plate the night before (remembering that chefs are key people on-station, are highly valued team members vital for station health and morale and take their role very seriously). Another station chef began serving up unpalatable meals to the station workforce after a love affair with a co-worker finished; the workforce were deeply unhappy with this behaviour and through a series of negative behaviours directed towards him, 'encouraged' him to appropriately resume the role for which he was employed. In an extreme case at Russia's Vostok station in 1959, a scientist murdered his chess opponent with an axe following losing a game to this colleague. Unsurprisingly, chess was subsequently banned at Russian Antarctic stations. As these vignettes indicate, the management of the workforce is a critical role, to ensure minor issues do not become major incidents.

In contrast to these challenges, there are also incidents of highly effective and cohesive station dynamics. For example, male members of wintering crews may collectively decide to grow their beards as a sign of identity and group membership. Unique station and continent-based language and communication patterns can also emerge – one Australian station developed a method of verbal communication based on clicks as opposed to words (a sort of variation on Morse-code, if you will). Thus, effective HRM principles that facilitate development of a highly functioning group can and do make an important contribution to station life and culture.

The role of HRM is therefore not only to enable the specific person-job fit but the ability to select people who can cope with the demanding physical, psychological and social aspects of working in such an extreme environment (Decamps & Rosnet, 2005). As noted, critical aspects of these assignments include issues such as 'wintering over' where there is no option to leave for up to 9 months and the assignment may exceed 12 months (3 months of which are in total darkness). In such situations, people must be able to function effectively not only in their own job but, critically, as part of a team. As such, HRM must be cognisant of the role of the three key 'abilities' in Antarctica (task ability, sociability and emotional stability), and how they play out in policies that shape selection, training and development, support and retention. Task ability refers to an individual's capacity to effectively perform the role for which they are employed. Sociability refers to an individual's capacity to effectively work and cohabit with a range of individuals not of their own choosing. Emotional stability refers to an individual's ability to remain psychologically robust and emotionally stable despite the challenges inherent in the Antarctic environment (Norris et al., 2010; Taylor, 1969). To be unable to meet performance expectations on any one of these three abilities can have marked impacts on the individual and team in both the short and long term, with consequences including increased psychological distress, ostracism from the larger work group, and failure to achieve expected work goals. In Antarctica context, the ramifications of this are even more extreme, in that these impacts are not left 'on the ice' but instead impact at all levels even after leaving the continent, whilst incomplete work tasks are then an additional burden upon those who are undertaking the next deployment cycle.

It is important to also note in the context of organisational practices that research has found positive outcomes from the experiences of working in Antarctica, including:

- perceived increased self-reliance derived from not having ready access to resources afforded in more routine work environments (Palinkas, 1991) and separation from routine sources of social support;
- self-efficacy developed through opportunities to demonstrate their capabilities in challenging circumstances (Kahn & Lean, 1994), thereby leading to increased trust in such abilities and perceived aptitude;

- self-development (Mocellin & Suedfeld, 1991) in both work-related tasks (i.e. performing their role in an extreme environment) as well as in personal realms such as tolerance;
- new skills development with many expeditioners undertaking projects in non-work time that allow them to learn a new skill-set such as photography, woodwork, cinematography or creative writing;
- team-building skills facilitated by the necessity to live and work in close proximity with colleagues and rely on them for the most basic work interactions such as completing assigned tasks through to life-saving situations that can and do occur due to the hostile environment such as field injuries or medical emergencies (Suedfeld, 2002); and
- a sense of accomplishment associated with having survived, and in many cases thrived, in one of the most extreme and unusual workplaces on Earth. This sense of accomplishment can remain with the expeditioner long after the experience ends (Oliver, 1991; Suedfeld & Steel, 2000).

Considering the number of staff rotating through national Antarctic programmes, demonstrating positive experiences of Antarctic employment outcomes facilitated by sound HRM practice is significant in the long-term attraction and retention of the next-generation workforce. To achieve this, HRM specialists are involved in all stages of the Antarctic employment experience: pre-departure preparation, absence (i.e. when the expeditioner is 'on the ice'), and reunion and reintegration post-return (Norris et al., 2010). Further, due to researchers identifying the interactive influences of individual, interpersonal and organisational factors on the Antarctic employment experience (Norris et al., 2010), HRM specialist involvement often spans these three domains. In fact, this process is akin to that undertaken by expatriates going on major assignments. As Norris et al. (2010) note, in this context, there are four phases to the expeditions.

The first phase is the *pre-departure* phase, which includes, for example, training in undertaking their work role in an environment that poses additional challenges to basic activities (such as repairing communications equipment in high winds and freezing conditions), as well as training in additional skills such as fire-fighting, and developing basic medical support for the doctor on the base.

The second phase is the *absence/deployment period*. This is the phase most people refer to when thinking of Antarctic employment, and is when the expeditioner is physically in Antarctica. Research on this period shows a mixed response to when people are more vulnerable to negative psychological and physiological health (Norris, Paton & Ayton, 2008; Palinkas & Browner, 1995), although many expeditioners lament the further restriction placed on activities and absence of sunlight during the middle of winter. However, Wood et al. (2000) found overall the expeditioners report positive experiences more than negative experiences during the deployment period.

The third period is the *reunion phase* – the time at which expeditioners have left Antarctica and returned to their normal place of residence. This involves reuniting with friends and family, and for some, returning to routine employment. For many, this phase is not highly reflective of routine life in that most have not yet returned to paid employment, and larger than normal amounts of time are spent 'catching up' with friends and family who have not been seen for many months. As such, it is often referred to as 'the honeymoon phase'. This time can also involve negotiating a balance between spending time with colleagues and friends from Antarctica whom you may not see again for some time, and spending time with family and friends whom often expect this time to be dedicated to them. Some expeditioners have also described not feeling completely relaxed during this time, trying to gently re-insert themselves into family and friendship units that have learned to function without their presence. Negotiating this phase can be challenging, however, as Norris et al. (2010) note, this phase has not been well documented or researched and would benefit from targeted focus in this regard to better inform HRM and intervention principles.

The final, *reintegration*, phase spans the reunion and successful readjustment to the expeditioner's previous life (Busuttil & Busuttil, 2011), and only commences once the initial 'honeymoon' of the reunion phase has passed. This phase often involves recommencing previous paid employment or commencing or seeking new paid employment opportunities that need to be balanced with non-work commitments. It also signals greater reintegration into family and friendship networks, with either resumption of previous roles or renegotiated roles in these domains (e.g. an expeditioner who undertook a lot of the cooking duties prior to deployment may find their partner does not wish to relinquish this role upon their return, or an expeditioner may not resume financial responsibilities that were conducted in their absence, or they may find that home improvement activities have been assumed by another family member). As research on expatriation from and international HRM perspective has also noted, family members also have a period of adjustment and then readjustment and issues to deal with, as for the expatriate it can feel to them that they have hit the pause button on life and home and it can start again on their return (Dowling, Festing & Ingle, 2017). It is during this stage of mutual readjustment that some expeditioners will feel more able to make informed decisions about if, and when, they will return to Antarctica for work in the future. However, as Norris et al. (2010) note, there needs to be more research into this area as an important aspect of the support services provided by human resources.

Underlying all these phases is the work-family interface. However, research exploring the family during expatriation, which we consider an Antarctic assignment to be, have often been seen as something outside the transactional relationship of employee and employer (Haslberger & Brewster, 2008; Riusala & Suutari, 2000). As argued by Lämsä, Heikkinen, Smith and Tornikoski (2017) and, specifically in the case of separation from family by Haak-Saheem and Brewster (2017) and McNulty and Brewster (2019), this is a major oversight and underestimates the disruption and potential impact these assignments have on the expeditioner and their family. This is supported by Makela, Suutari and Mayerhofer (2011) who argue family issues represent a key concern and challenge for expatriates across many professions and play a critical role in the success or failure of the assignment and their subsequent willingness to return for future assignments. It is therefore argued that a more relational approach should be taken, and the family should be seen as a key stakeholder in the process and on the impact of expeditioners' experience and the potential for the expeditioners to return for further assignments. Interference between the work and family domain has been associated with, from the employee side, decreased productivity, poor moral, employee retention and a host of general social, emotion and psychological problems (Norris et al., 2010). For the family, issues of distress, marital tension and decreased family satisfaction all combined to increase the stress and therefore the impact of working in Antarctic. However, assignments can be a positive and enhancing experience for the individual and the family if the individual, interpersonal and organisational factors of adjustment and adaption are properly managed (Norris et al., 2010), and that requires further research. In taking this holistic approach to developing and applying notions of 'well-being' to the social functioning of the expeditioners and their family, the relationships between the organisation, expeditioner and their family needs to be based on quality relationships.

The Constructive and/or Destructive Role of Technology in the 21st Century

The interface between work and family roles has significant implications for Antarctic employees (Norris et al., 2010), so every decision made with regard to work and family relations can have a major impact on the individual and families' well-being. In this context, the changing nature of technology has the potential to enhance or compound these environmental challenges, in particular, the psychosocial stressors of separation from, and restricted communication with, family and friends. Advances in technology in this century have enabled '24/7' interconnectivity. However, the decisions and policies regarding the connectivity of Antarctic bases vary, for a variety of reasons. The impact of these decisions on the well-being of the expeditioners can be profound.

Our research indicates that problems exist in the use of technologies such as the internet which are magnified by the extreme context and isolation. Frustrations are often externalised to the Head Office, which is both positive in terms of protecting the station-level dynamics, but detrimental in creating additional tensions between those working 'on the ice' and those providing oversight to such work thousands of miles away. This is compounded by the ubiquitous nature and use of 21st-century information and communications technologies and the fact that expeditioners are federal government employees, theoretically working a standard day of around 8 hours. Not to have access to, or being restricted in the opportunity to use, channels such as social media to communicate with family and friends like 'normal' employees in their down periods may create additional tensions.

There is ongoing potential for issues and challenges outside the workplace (i.e. with family and friends back home) to impact performance on the job. For example, situations in which a family member has unexpectedly become ill can detract from the psychological resources available to perform in extreme and unusual environments, which already place additional stressors on cognition and emotion regulation. Restricted access to social media in cases such as these can have a substantial negative effect. There have also been instances in which expeditioners on the ice have spent large portions of each day trying to connect to support people at home, and this can cause some intolerance from fellow station members who feel that they are not contributing to the work or station culture due to this divided time.

Expeditioners, especially those in leadership roles, will have teleconferenced video meetings with head office personnel but do not have the same opportunity for visual communications with family and friends. These perceptions that access is available, but the opportunities are restricted, can cause tensions, as expeditioners feel that the technological capacity is there, but they are being unfairly restricted from using them which creates further tension between head office (polices makers) and the station. As noted, in a generalised sense, expeditioners, like employees in general, see social media as part of everyday life and expect the same access despite the arguments about limited bandwidth available in Antarctica and the necessity to prioritise work-related tasks.

The future will see more Generation Y and millennial expeditioners who are much more likely than older employees to use social media in the workplace and more likely to use it for both work and personal activities (Holland, Cooper & Hecker, 2016). The current instructions to Australian expeditioners is "peer-to-peer file sharing applications or internet video and voice applications, including Skype, are NOT permitted ... mobile phone and/or tablet ... will be able to use mobile devices to a limited degree" (AAD, 2016) – this is more restrictive than some other stations manned by other national Antarctic programmes, and, therefore, issues of inequity continue to simmer.

Conclusions

Research has generated substantial knowledge in terms of our understanding of how humans function under extreme conditions. Those who adapt best have realistic expectations pertaining to both the work and non-work components of the roles. They are able to work under situations with limited access to resources, and are able to psychologically compartmentalise work from non-work tasks without engaging in avoidance strategies. Despite this, as the duration and frequency of assignments associated with extreme working conditions increase and more people undertake return assignments, the challenge for HRM is to continually achieve the best fit and best practice to ensure the successful and effective location of these teams, in what are extreme conditions of work in the aspects of environment and human relations. The advances in technology are also bringing unique pressures to those working in Antarctic and those managing the expeditioners thousands of miles away who return to their families after their working day.

The focus of this chapter has been to understand the contextual issues of working in Antarctic and associated issues of family and other relationships and to understand the relationship with emerging challenges such as new communication technologies of the 21st century and how it is impacting the individual, interpersonal and organisational factors of expeditioners, their family and the organisation. Such insights provide further knowledge on developing effective assignments and proactive strategies and targeted interventions to enhance the experience of employees in extreme environments.

References

Australian Antarctic Division (AAD) (2012). *NASA study.* Retrieved from http://www.antarctica.gov.au/living-and-working/stations/casey/this-week-at- casey/2011/this-week-at-casey-29-july-2011/2. Viewed May 2018.
Australian Antarctic Division (AAD) (2016). *Expeditioners handbook 2016– 2020.* Hobart: Commonwealth of Australia.
Burke, C. S. & Feitosa, J. (2015). *Team culture issues for long-duration exploration missions.* Houston, TX: NASA.
Busuttil, W. & Busuttil, A. (2011). Psychological effects on families subjected to enforced and prolonged separation generated under life threatening situations. *Sexual and Relationship Therapy,* 16, 207–228.
Carver, C. S. & Connor-Smith, J. (2010). Personality and coping. *Annual Review of Psychology,* 61, 679–704. doi:10.1146/annurev.psych.093008.100352
Catalyst (2015). *Polar people.* Sydney: Australian Broadcasting Corporation.
COMNAP (2017). *Antarctic station catalogue.* Christchurch: The Council of Managers of National Antarctic Programs.
Decamps, G. & Rosnet, E. (2005). A longitudinal assessment of psychological adaptation during a winter-over in Antarctica. *Environment and Behaviour,* 37, 418–435.

Dowling, P. J., Festing, M. & Ingle, A. (2016). International human resource management (7th ed). Melbourne: Cengage.

Francis, J., Gleeson, M., Lugg, D., Clancy, R. Ayton, J., Donovan, K., McConnell, C, Tingate, T., Thorpe, B.`& Watson, A. (2002). Trends in mucosal immunity in Antarctic during six Australian winter expeditions. *Immunology and Cell Biology*, 80, 382–390.

Haak-Saheem, W. & Brewster, C. (2017). 'Hidden' expatriates: International mobility in the United Arab Emirates as a challenge to current understanding of expatriation. *Human Resource Management Journal*, 27(3), 423–439.

Haslberger, A. & Brewster, C. (2008). The expatriate family: An international perspective. *Journal of Managerial Psychology*, 23(3), 324–346.

Holland, P., Cooper, B. & Hecker, R. (2016). Use of social media at work: A new form of employee voice? *International Journal of Human Resource Management*, 27(21), 2621–2634.

Kahn, P. & Leon, G. (1994). Group climate and individual functioning in all women's Antarctic expedition teams. *Environment and Behavior*, 26, 669–669.

King, J. C. & Turner, J. (1997). *Antarctic meteorology and climatology*. Cambridge: Cambridge University Press.

Lämsä, A., Heikkinen, S., Smith, M. & Tornikoski, C. (2017). The expatriate's family as a stakeholder of the firm: A responsibility viewpoint. *International Journal of Human Resource Management*, 28(2), 2916–2935.

Lugg, D. (2000). Antarctic medicine. *Journal of the American Medical Association*, 283, 2082–2084.

Makela, L., Suutari, V. & Mayerhofer, H. (2011). Lives of female expatriates: Work-life balance concerns. *Gender in Management: An International Journal*, 26, 256–274.

McNulty, Y. & Brewster, C. (2019). *Working internationally: Expatriation, migration and other global work*. Cheltenham: Edward Elgar.

Mocellin, J. & Suedfeld, P. (1991). Voices from the ice: Diaries of polar explores, *Environment and Behavior*, 23, 704–722.

Moult, C., Norris, K., Paton, D. & Ayton, J. (2015). Predicting positive and negative change in expeditioners at 2-months and 12-months post Antarctic employment. *The Polar Journal*, 5(1), 128–145.

Naslund, J., Grande, S., Aschbrenner, K. & Elwyn, G. (2014). Naturally occurring peer support through social media: The experiences of individuals with severe mental illness. Using YouTube. *PLoS ONE*, 9(10), 1–9.

Norris, K., Paton, D. & Ayton, J. (2008). The long cold night. Comparing expeditioners and partners experiences during Antarctic absences. *Proceedings from the 47th APS Conference*, Hobart, Australia.

Norris, K., Paton, D. & Ayton, J. (2010). Future directions in Antarctic psychological research. *Antarctic Science*, 22(4), 335–342.

Oliver, D. (1991). Psychological effects of isolation and confinement of a winter-over group at McMurdo station, Antarctica. In Harrison, A., Clearwater, Y. & McKay, C. (eds.), *From Antarctic to outer space: Life in isolation and confinement* (pp. 217–229). New York: Springer.

Palinkas, L. A. (1991). Effects of physical and social environments on the health and well-being of Antarctic Winter Personnel. *Environment and Behavior*, 23, 782–791.

Palinkas L. A., & Browner, D. (1995). Effects of prolonged isolation in extreme environments on stress, coping, and depression. *Journal of Applied Social Psychology*, 25, 557–576.

Palinkas, L. A., Glogower, F. G., Dembert, M., Hansen, K. & Smullen, R. (2004). Incidence of psychiatric disorders after extended residence in Antarctica. *International Journal of Circumpolar Health*, 63, 157–168.

Palinkas, L. A., Houseal, M. & Miller, C. (2000). Sleep and mood during a winter in Antarctica. *International Journal of Circumpolar Health*, 59, 63–73.

Palinkas, L. A. & Suedfeld, P. (2007). Psychological effects of polar expeditions. *The Lancet*, 371, 153–163.

Palinkas L. A., Suedfeld, P. & Steel, G. (1995). Psychological functioning among members of a small polar expedition. *Aviat Space Environment Medicine*, 66, 943–950.

Przybylski, A. K., Murayama, K., DeHaan, C. R. & Gladwell, V. (2013). Motivational, emotional, and behavioral correlates of fear of missing out. *Computers in Human Behavior*, 29(4), 1841–1848.

Riusala, K. & Suutari, V. (2000). Expatriation and careers. Perspectives of expatriates and spouses. *Career Development International*, 5, 81–90.

Salinas, S. (2018). Instagram stories have twice as many daily users as Snapchat's service – And it now has background music. Retrieved from https://www.cnbc.com/2018/06/28/instagram-stories-daily-active-users-double-snapchats.html

Snyder, C. & Ford, C. (2013). *Coping with negative life events: Clinical and social psychological perspectives*. Heidelberg: Springer Science & Business Media.

Strange, R. E. & Youngman, S. A. (1971). Emotional aspects of wintering over. *Antarctic Journal of the United States*, 5, 255–257.

Suedfeld, P. (2002). Applying positive psychology in the study of extreme environments. *Human Performance in Extreme Environments*, 6, 21–25.

Suedfeld, P. & Steel, G. (2000). The environmental psychology of capsule habits. *Annual Review of Psychology*, 51, 227–253.

Suedfeld, P. & Weiss, K. (2000). Antarctica: Natural laboratory and space analogue for psychological research. *Environment and Behavior*, 32(1), 7–17.

Taylor, A. J. W. 1969. Ability, stability, and sociability of Scott Base personnel, Antarctica. *Occupational Psychology*, 43, 81–93.

Wood, J., Hysong, S., Lugg, D. & Harm, D. L. (2000). Is it really so bad? A comparison of positive and negative experiences in Antarctic winter stations. *Environment and Behavior*, 32, 84–110.

6 Working in Danger Zones

Customized Risk Management for Expatriate Occupations

Richard A. Posthuma, Eric D. Smith,
Jase R. Ramsey and Yang Zhang

Introduction

We examine how employers can better manage the risks for expatriates working in danger zones. There are some generally accepted methods for managing expatriates, such as helping them better adjust to their environments through improved pre-departure training, home country leave, etc. However, expatriates working in high-risk environments need extra support to manage their safety and security. Prior research has identified several methods which protect expatriates in such environments (e.g. crisis management, safe houses and evacuation procedures). These techniques are typically recommended for a broad spectrum of expatriates. Nevertheless, people accept expatriate assignments in various locations, industries and positions. Occupational differences in risk management for expatriates have not been extensively studied, however, although occupational differences can be a key factor in expatriate risk management. For example, foreign correspondents seek unique opportunities for self-expression, nurses look to help others and engineers crave challenges where they can use their problem-solving skills. Employees in different occupations desire different levels and types of interaction with the local environment. This can result in occupational differences in the risks that expatriate face. However, these differences also create opportunities for occupation-specific methods for managing both the likelihood and severity of harm from different causes. By recognising the existence of these occupational differences, organisations can tailor their risk management methods to specific occupations. This can reduce expatriate frustrations and increase their acceptance of risk management techniques designed to help improve their safety and security.

Background

Expatriates are people employed by multinational enterprises (MNEs) who leave their home country in order to live and work in another

Support for this research was provided by the Mike Loya Distinguished Chair at the University of Texas at El Paso.

country. MNEs include for-profit businesses, non-profit organisations and government entities. Expatriates are becoming increasingly necessary as organisations spread their international reach. Expatriates are important agents of MNEs because they implement operations, help to control and coordinate organisational activities, transfer knowledge across borders, and impact local economies and people (Bader, 2015; Gannon & Paraskevas, 2017; Suder, Reade, Riviere, Birnik & Nielsen, 2017). For these reasons, the employment of expatriates continues to be a growing trend for MNEs (Brookfield Global Relocation Services, 2015; Kraimer, Bolino & Mead, 2016).

Moreover, expatriates are increasingly being deployed to hostile environments which present threats to their safety or security (Bader, 2015; Fee, McGrath-Champ & Berti, 2017). This often occurs because expatriates are needed in developing countries, which present the best opportunities for businesses, and for non-profit or governmental MNEs expatriates to fulfil their mission. Nevertheless, these developing countries often present higher risks because their institutions can suffer from corruption, they are not fully developed and their environments are generally less secure (Bader, 2015; Posthuma, Ramsey, Flores, Maertz & Ahmed, 2017).

The Hollywood View of Expatriates

The growing use of expatriates has fuelled an interest among Hollywood filmmakers, who depict the excitement, adventure and importance of this type of work. The illustrations of expatriates in film are useful for researchers, as filmmakers often conduct their own research to ensure that the characters and circumstances portrayed are a sufficiently realistic reflection of the world in order for audiences to cognitively accept the films as lifelike (Hathaway, 2013; Leet & Houser, 2003). For example, the film *Jane* depicts Jane Goodall's work with chimpanzees in Tanzania and the social support received from her cameraman husband. *A Private War* shows the history of Marie Colvin, played by Rosamund Pike, a war correspondent who lost one eye in an ambush in Sri Lanka and was, probably, killed by the government of another country she was covering.

Many films that focus on expatriates working in dangerous environments also illustrate some of the challenges of expatriate work assignments. In the film, *Whiskey, Tango, Foxtrot* actress Tina Fey depicts a foreign correspondent in Afghanistan who is sometimes frustrated by her handler's attempts to keep her safe. Her interest is to write unique stories for her publisher about life in a war zone, but to do so, she needs to interact directly with locals. In the film *Medicine Man* actor Sean Connery depicts an eccentric biologist working in the Amazon rainforest searching for a cure to cancer. His interest is in the intellectual endeavour of discovery, but his intellectual focus drove him to engage closely with the rainforest despite potential dangers. This interfered with his obligation to transfer the knowledge he gained back to his funding agency. In *No Escape* actor Owen Wilson depicts an American civil engineer who is holed up with his wife and daughters in a hotel in a Southeast Asian country during a political upheaval. His interest is in helping his corporation bring improved water systems to the region, but he needs to use his problem-solving skills as an engineer to save himself and his family. Jaclyn Smith depicts *Florence Nightingale* in a film of the same name, as the famous nurse who travelled to Turkey to help victims of the Crimean War. Stepping down from her aristocratic upbringing, she encounters unsanitary conditions, yet she overcomes opposition as she advocates for cleanliness and hygiene. Her altruistic efforts helped shape the profession of nursing as it is known today.

These films are not only engaging and entertaining, but they also illustrate the importance of the work of internationally mobile people and the challenges they face. Such films exemplify the psychological and emotional challenges confronting expatriates. Even more so, they underscore the need for effective risk management for expatriates working in danger zones.

Research on Risk Management for Expatriates

The dominant theme in prior research about expatriates has focussed on the predictors and outcomes of expatriate adjustment to work in foreign countries (Bhaskar-Shrinivas, Harrison, Shaffer & Luk, 2005; Hechanova, Beehr & Christiansen, 2003; Kraimer et al., 2016). The concept of adjustment has focussed on expatriates' levels of acceptance and satisfaction with the assignments and the environments within which they are working (Haslberger, Brewster & Hippler, 2014; Hechanova et al., 2003). This includes adjustment to the surrounding culture and people as well as the work that they are performing (Bhaskar-Shrinivas et al., 2005). When expatriates are better adjusted to these factors, their job satisfaction and work performance is higher, and their likelihood of quitting is lower (Bhaskar-Shrinivas et al., 2005; Hechanova et al., 2003). Reduction in turnover is especially important for expatriates because the cost of failure for an expatriate on a foreign assignment is much higher than the turnover cost for a domestic employee. Still, MNEs can significantly improve the success rates of expatriate assignments by managing adjustment through improved pre-screening, pre-departure training, in-country family and social support, etc. (Kraimer et al., 2016).

Recent research recognises that many of the best opportunities for MNEs to accomplish their missions, capture knowledge and expand global reach are found in less industrialised countries (Bader, 2015; Suder et al., 2017). In these countries, many of the institutions designed to facilitate a stable society – the legal system, the police force, health services – are also less developed and less effective (Suder et al., 2017). This results in the environments in which expatriates work being less secure and more unsafe (Bader, 2015; Suder et al., 2017).

Figure 6.1 illustrates this phenomenon. In this figure the horizontal (X) axis represents the degree of danger in a country. The degrees of danger are represented by four categories of countries with 1 being the safest and 4 the most dangerous. There are a number of rankings of danger including those defined by the United Nations: we have chosen to use the categories defined by the US Department of State, Bureau of Consular Affairs. That agency monitors conditions around the world and assigns travel risk ratings to each country and several regions therein. For example, the country of Mexico is rated as a 2 for traveller risk, but within Mexico, the state of Chihuahua near the US border is rated as a 3 due to the threat of crime. These ratings are updated as conditions change. Although these risk ratings are designed for Americans travelling to other countries, the lists provided by other governments, by international organisations like the United Nations and by private agencies and companies tend to be similar, and there is no absolute truth in this area, so that these rankings provide an estimate of the risks that would be faced by nationals of other countries.

Category 1 countries are the safest and for these countries normal (tourist-type) travel precautions are recommended. Australia, Japan, Peru and Poland are among the countries in category 1. Category 2 countries are less safe, and it is recommended that people exercise increased caution when travelling to them. China, France, Germany, Mexico and the Russian Federation are among those in category 2. Category 3 countries are even less safe, and it is recommended that tourists reconsider travelling to these areas and do not do so unless they have a strong requirement to travel there. If they do, they should take extra precautions. Honduras, Nicaragua, Nigeria and Pakistan are some of the countries in category 3. Category 4 countries are the most dangerous. It is recommended not to travel to them. Afghanistan, Iran, Iraq, Libya, Somalia and Yemen are in category 4. For example, in the case of Afghanistan, the US Department of State's website notes "Do not travel to Afghanistan due to armed conflict, terrorism, crime, and civil unrest". Specifically, travel to all areas of Afghanistan is unsafe because of critical levels of kidnappings, hostage taking, suicide bombings, widespread military combat operations, landmines, and terrorist and insurgent attacks, including attacks using vehicle-borne, magnetic or other improvised explosive devices (IEDs), suicide vests and grenades.

In addition to these risk ratings, countries have also been evaluated on the degree to which they have corruption. The relationship between the degree of risk in a country and the degree of corruption therein is illustrated in Figure 6.1. As noted, the horizontal (X) axis represents the degree of danger in each country. The vertical (Y) axis represents the degree to which a country is perceived to engage in corrupt practices. The degree of corruption is measured by the Corruption Perceptions Index (CPI) from Transparency International. This is a publicly available measure that incorporates several different sources of perceived corruption in different countries. A high score on the CPI is good. The higher the CPI score, the less corrupt a country is thought to be. Thus, higher levels on the vertical axis represent less corruption. This graph shows lines for each of the four categories of travel risk rankings. The dot in the centre of those lines is the mean CPI for that country risk category. The top and bottom marks for those lines indicate the 99% confidence interval of the range of CPI scores for countries in each risk category.

The graph shows that for the safest countries (category 1), the CPI scores are much higher, indicating that these countries are also the least corrupt. For the most dangerous countries (category 4), the CPI scores

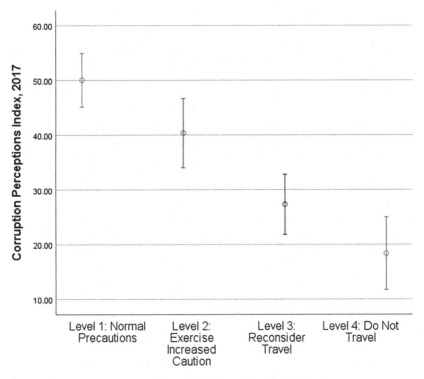

Figure 6.1 The Relationship between Country Risk and Corruption Levels.
Notes: Corruptions Perceptions Index from Transparency International, 2017. Graph Shows Average (mean) Levels (and 99% confidence interval error bars) for countries within each of the four levels of the US State Department, 2018, Travel Advisory Levels. There is a significant relationship between the risk of travel to a country and the amount of corruption therein. The more the corruption, the higher the risk of travel.

are the lowest, indicating that corruption in these countries is much higher. The distributions of CPI scores for country risk categories 2 and 3 fall in between these two extremes. Figure 6.1 indicates that there is a relationship between danger and corruption. The more dangerous the country is, the more corrupt the country is.

For some readers, it may be somewhat surprising to see some European countries in category 2. However, in recent years these countries have experienced incidents of terrorism which could affect the level of risk that travellers face. For example, a lorry smashed into a crowded Christmas market in central Berlin on December 19, 2016, killing 12 people and injuring 49, leaving 18 in a critical condition. The so-called Islamic State (IS) has said one of its "soldiers" carried out the attack.

This figure illustrates how countries that are the most dangerous may have significant problems with developing and maintaining trustworthy institutional systems that could potentially provide safety and security to expatriates. An expatriate's home country may be comparatively safe (category 1) compared to the country they are working in, for example, a category 3 country. In their home country they may have felt confident in calling upon police or private security forces to ensure their safety. However, while working in a category 3 country, the expatriate should exercise increased caution in relying on such institutions to provide for their safety due to the potential that the police or security forces may be compromised or corrupted. For example, the Government of Nicaragua (category 3) is known to be authoritarian, limits freedom of expression and peaceful assembly, represses internal dissent, and monitors and responds to perceived threats to its authority. Armed civilians in plain clothes have "acted as police" and should not be trusted. To further illustrate this relationship, the Appendix to this chapter provides a list of all countries that have both an elevated travel risk level (2, 3, or 4) and a published CPI score at the time of publication. These countries have been sorted from safest to most dangerous.

The corruption and accompanying danger that expatriates may face in some countries have resulted in an acute problem. An example of this was the detention and subsequent prosecution of a senior executive and three colleagues from Rio Tinto's mining operation in China in 2009, who found themselves front and centre in a high-profile tussle between China and Australia. MNEs often struggle to find sufficient numbers of qualified applicants for overseas assignments (Kraimer et al., 2016). One of the main reasons that people turn down foreign assignments is the perceived danger of the country to which they would be going (Kraimer et al., 2016). This can leave open jobs unfilled, thereby impairing the ability of MNEs to expand their reach in some countries. To help solve this recruiting challenge, MNEs need to find ways to manage the risks of working abroad and to alleviate fears, so that people will be more likely to accept such assignments. In response to these issues, recent research has increased the focus on the importance of risk management for expatriates working in hostile environments (Bader, 2015; Posthuma et al., 2017).

Expatriate Risk Management: General Recommendations

Expatriate risk management research has identified several risks that expatriates face, as well as several methods for managing risk in countries with elevated levels of risk (Fee & McGrath-Champ, 2017; Fee et al., 2017; Gannon & Paraskevas, 2017). The risks to expatriates can include terrorism, kidnapping, crime. Risk management practices include country and local environmental risk analysis, information sharing, expatriate screening and training, housing security, crisis management and relocation, among others.

A good first step in analysing appropriate risk management techniques should entail an assessment of both the severity of harm that expatriates could suffer and the likelihood of different types of harm. To do so, data should be gathered from subject matter experts who are familiar with the jobs expatriates perform in addition to industry and geographic differences. The subject matter experts should rate the severity and likelihood of these different kinds of risks. For example, kidnapping in Mexico occurs in border cities such as Juarez, Tijuana and Tampico where street thugs and rogue cab drivers have been known to take foreigners to ATMs in order to withdraw money. Other times, they hold them for a few days until a family member pays a ransom. A subject matter expert on Mexico might suggest using a private driver while doing business in these border towns.

Figure 6.2 represents a *pro forma* hypothetical illustration of the severity and likelihood of different types of risks that expatriates could face in a particular location and industry. The graph shows how MNEs operating in this location and industry could enact an overall risk management plan that addresses risks based on their severity and likelihood. This would include events which are high in severity but less likely. For example, a bombing may be a relatively unlikely event; however, the severity of the harm caused by a bombing can be high. Since the event is unlikely, expatriates may tend to ignore risk management methods designed to help them avoid harm caused by a bombing because they don't think it is likely to occur. Risk management methods can be tailored to overcome this weakness. For example, expatriate security briefings can emphasise the importance of maintaining safety and security practices; expatriates might need to be reminded that they could face discipline if they fail to comply with their employer's recommendations. In this way, the fear of discipline could motivate compliance with safety rules even if the fear of an unlikely but high severity event would not motivate compliance.

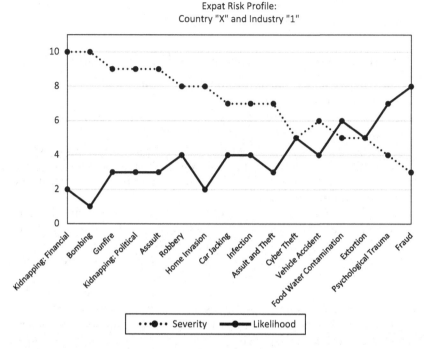

Figure 6.2 Sample Generic Expat Risk Profile for a Particular MNE and Geographic Location: Listing Risks and the Likelihood and Severity of Each.

In addition to the generic and overarching recommendations, recent research has recognised that other contextual factors matter as well. MNEs in different organisations may face institutional pressures to respond differently to the risks faced by expatriates in their own industrial sectors (Fee et al., 2017). The need for these practices is likely to vary depending on the types of risk that are present in different industries, as well as across different countries and regions. Risks faced in mining and natural resources, media, and international aid and development can be quite different. As a result, MNEs in different industries have adopted different risk management practices. For example, when performing expatriate screening, firms in the mining industry focus more on formal crisis qualifications and accreditation, those in the media focus more on inherent 'street smarts' and those in international aid focus more on cultural intelligence (Fee et al., 2017). However, not all expatriates in the same industry perform the same type of work. Therefore, in addition to addressing industry sector differences in risk management practices, adapting risk management practices to specific occupations is also important (Fee et al., 2017). For example, when a dam broke at a mine in Brazil (category 2) in 2018, the response by an engineer and an accountant would be vastly different. The engineer likely focussed on saving as many lives as possible downstream from the dam. The accountant would immediately set aside reserves to cover short- and long-term financial costs associated with the disaster. While both responses are important to enhancing resilience and the continued existence of the firm, they are vastly different in how to respond to the same catastrophe.

Expatriate Risk Management: Occupation-Specific Recommendations

Even within the same organisation, expatriates with different job functions will have diverse interests in the work that they perform (Fee & McGrath, 2017). This is likely to result in differences in the risks that job incumbents face while working in danger zones. Figure 6.3 illustrates the

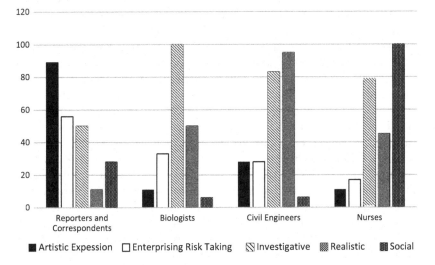

Figure 6.3 Occupational Interest Differences among Expatriate Occupations.

Notes: Job Interest Ratings were prepared by subject matter experts in job analysis as part of the O*Net project. The five factors that were rated were derived from Holland's (1985) model of work environments and personality types. Definitions adapted from O*Net. https://www.onetonline.org/

Artistic Expression occupations involve independent work where employees can perform well without following a clear set of rules.

Enterprising Risk-Taking occupations frequently involve starting up and carrying out projects that can require risk taking.

Investigative occupations frequently involve working with ideas and require an extensive amount of thinking. These occupations can involve searching for facts and figuring out problems mentally.

Realistic occupations frequently involve work activities that include practical, hands-on problems and solutions. They often deal with plants, animals and real-world materials like wood, tools and machinery. Many of the occupations require working outside, and do not involve a lot of paperwork or working closely with others.

Social occupations frequently involve working with, communicating with and teaching people. These occupations often involve helping or providing service to others.

interests that workers tend to have in four representative occupations in which expatriates typically work: Nurse, Foreign Correspondent, Civil Engineer and Biologist. To illustrate the differences between these occupations, we obtained data from the O*Net, which is an official and public source of data related to numerous occupations (Peterson et al., 2001).

These data come from job analysis experts who assess the degree to which people working in different occupations have different interests, skills, etc. Figure 6.3 shows significant differences across occupations. Because of these divergent interests, expatriates in different occupations will engage in different behaviours while working in danger zones. For example, foreign correspondents are most strongly motivated by artistic expression, which can induce them to seek out stories even though doing so may put them in danger of personal harm, such as politically motivated kidnapping. Biologists are most strongly motivated by enterprising endeavours that can lead them to risk their own health, by exposing themselves to infections, for example, as they seek new discoveries. Civil Engineers' motivation to engage in structured problem solving may be a strength when it comes to following logic-based risk management practices, but does not enable them to appreciate the strength of social bonds with locals that could help them obtain useful information and avoid risks. Nurses' desires for social interaction can be a great help in providing them with social support in dealing with the health issues of others, but it may also increase their risk of exposure to infection and contamination. For example, the opening paragraph on the Doctors Without Borders website states "From organizing a mass vaccination initiative for measles or triaging an influx of displaced people fleeing conflict, nurses save lives in a variety of conflict zones". The organisation is acutely aware of the inherent risks involved and makes them explicit to potential expatriates. Therefore, in addition to the generic risk assessment that takes into account geographic and industry differences in risks faced by expatriates, MNEs should also consider preparing individual risk profiles for different occupations in danger zones. Below we discuss four occupations to illustrate how occupational differences should be taken into account in expatriate risk management.

Nurses

Figure 6.4 illustrates a pro forma hypothetical risk profile for nurses, which shows the increased risks for nurses, such as the risks of infection, assault and theft, and psychological trauma. Thus, the risk management practices for nurses should be tailored to match the severity and frequency of the risks that they face (Fee & McGrath-Champ, 2017; Posthuma et al., 2017). For example, expatriate nurses will be exposed to contact with locals and need to be carefully trained on protocols to minimise that risk. In addition, nurses are more often female than male.

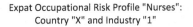

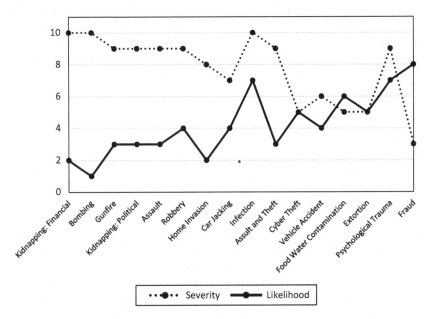

Figure 6.4 Sample Expat Risk Profile for Nurses: Listing Risks and the Likelihood and Severity of Each.

In many developing countries the risk of sexual violence is greater than in developed countries. Therefore, nurses will need to be trained in recognising and avoiding dangerous situations.

Expatriates employed as nurses tend to be interested in working and communicating with people so that they can provide help and service to them. From the perspective of expatriate risk management this tendency can be used as an advantage. Nurses may be in a much better position to gather information from locals about risks to expatriates and how to avoid them. They may be more adept at building social networks with locals because of their benevolent contacts with them. Therefore, nurses should be trained and encouraged to build relationships with locals in order to manage the risks that they face.

In addition, because of the work they perform, nurses are more likely than other occupations to be exposed to biological hazards such as infectious diseases. For that reason, subject matter experts should identify the specific risks that they will face and prepare location specific protocols including protective measures, treatment and medical evacuation plans if necessary. However, one of the strengths that nurses have is their knowledge of medicine and hygienic procedures. Therefore, they should be consulted and actively involved in identifying and managing these risks for themselves and others. Following two separate attacks in the Democratic Republic of Congo (category 2) on the Doctors Without Borders, Ebola Treatment Centers (ETC) in 2019, the organisation suspended its medical activities. Unidentified assailants set fire to their facilities and several vehicles at the ETC in the city of Butembo. Due to risk management training, they were able to contain the blazes and no staff or patients were harmed, but the teams were forced to immediately cease patient care.

Foreign Correspondents

Foreign correspondents are likely to be motivated by interesting, headline grabbing stories. This may induce them, more than others, to go towards danger – rather than away from it. For example, Ricchiardi (2001) notes how correspondents were attracted to Afghanistan shortly after the war on terror began. Employers wanted these reporters to come back with great stories, yet they needed to adapt security and safety protocols to prevent reporters from taking unnecessary risks. For correspondents this is likely to go beyond simple training in the risks they face. Rather, performance on safety-related matters will need to be more closely imposed because of their natural tendency to ignore safety in order to chase a story. Moreover, the very nature of their work may make them targets by those who oppose what they report (Barton, 2009). The kidnapping of Alan Johnston, a British journalist for the BBC, by the Palestinian Army of Islam in Gaza City for 114 days is a chilling reminder of the danger involved with covering hostile environments.

However, correspondents may also have an advantage over other occupations because they tend to develop relationships with locals in order to gain access to information. This closeness can also be used to enable correspondents to develop more finely tuned intuition about the dangers they may face, and how to manage or avoid them. For example, Murrell (2010) explained how locally hired 'fixers' are often relied upon by reporters in danger zones.

The use of fixers and other local people may be particularly important in countries where there is an elevated risk and greater degree of corruption. In those environments, it is less likely that correspondents could rely on formal authorities to provide a safe environment. Thus, from a risk management perspective, correspondents may need to be encouraged to develop relationships with locals, a form of cultural capital, that can enhance their job performance and make them safer.

Biologists

In contrast, scientists such as biologists tend to have very different interests and, therefore, face a different set of risks. Their primary interest is investigation. This narrow focus on discovery may lead them to ignore environmental risks in the foreign locale of their work. This can include exposure to infectious microorganisms that they would not face in their home country.

Although biologists are typically well trained in microbiological and laboratory safety protocols to ensure that they are not harmed from exposure to hazards that arise from their work, while working as an expatriate, they are unlikely to have the same degree of control that they would have in a safety-protocol-driven laboratory. The typical environment of their home country could include personal protective equipment such as goggles, masks, rubber gloves, hand washing stations and carefully designed techniques for the disposal of hazardous materials. Yet, in an expatriate environment, safety procedures may be more flexible and safety equipment may not be as readily available (Phillips, 1961). Researchers in foreign environments may be accustomed to fewer safety restrictions, and safety norms may be more lax (Adler, 2000). Biologists are driven by the desire to conduct research to discover a new and interesting phenomenon. This may lead expatriate biologists to cut corners on safety protocols and engage in riskier behaviours.

To counter this, the employers of expatriate biologists and other scientists should use subject matter experts to identify the risks that their expatriates face while in foreign environments and assess the likelihood and severity of the harm that could occur. Following that, training and safety protocols, vaccination programmes, etc. specifically adapted to the foreign environment should be adopted and enforced (Phillips, 1961).

Civil Engineers

Civil engineers can be thought of as realistic problem solvers. However, unlike nurses, they may tend to have a lower interest in building social relationships. Rather, they will seek to investigate situations and identify and implement realistic solutions. Thus, risk management for expatriate civil engineers will be very different from positions that inherently engender contacts with locals such as foreign correspondents. They may be less adept at building social relationships that will enable them to gather information about risks and how to avoid them. However, civil engineers have other strengths.

Expat civil engineers may be particularly skilful in gathering information from subject matter experts about the likelihood and severity of risks that they themselves, and other expatriates, face. Thus, data and information could be gathered from those with greater interest or skills in establishing social connections with locals. Then civil engineers can use their skills to compile the information into a logical risk assessment, analysis and risk management plan that could be used by their employers. For example, civil engineers could be used to help identify the best travel routes to and from expatriate residences and places of work, making recommendations for structural risk management methods such as access controls, lighting, walls and so forth. In this way, risk management for civil engineers can be tailored to improve outcomes for those expatriates and for others in their organisation.

Occupational Adaption of Expatriates Risk Management

Our discussion has illustrated how different occupations can influence the type of risk management practice that is appropriate for expatriates. It is important to illustrate this because employers feel institutional pressure to adopt a global or standardised set of risk management practices in order to keep their expatriate employees safe. Nevertheless, research has shown that MNEs often face the dilemma of choosing between global standardisation, that can bring efficiency, and local adaptation, that can enhance local effectiveness. Adopting globally standardised risk management practices may subject expatriates to practices that they see as excessive or unnecessary. When this occurs, expatriates may be less likely to comply with employers' risk management practices. They may feel a sense of frustration and lower job satisfaction, which could result in more risk, lower commitment to their jobs and ultimately higher turnover.

Therefore, it is recommended that employers of expatriates recognise the need for a balanced risk management approach that will avoid overly zealous and generic safety practices that can be costly and irrelevant to particular situations. Instead, employers should tailor customised practices to obtain better fit with circumstances. These circumstances should include risks faced not only in different countries, but also in different occupations. When organisations adapt their expatriate risk management practices this way, they will reduce negative reactions and increase willingness to use recommended practices. This should enhance the safety and security of expatriates, ensuring they return home safely having completed important work.

Recommendations for Future Research

This chapter has highlighted the need for a better understanding of the risks that expatriates face while working abroad. However, past research has tended to focus primarily on the psychological adjustment of expatriates and their families, with very little attention towards expatriate risk management. We suggest that much more research examines the risks expatriates face and how the context in which they work affects those risks. Moreover, not only are there differences in risks by country and within countries, but also depending on the type of work that is done. There is almost no research that examines the occupation-specific risks faced by expatriates. Furthermore, there is almost no research on the appropriateness and success of different risk management practices for different expatriate occupations. Future research should focus on these important differences.

Future research should also identify how expatriate risk management practices can be tailored to specific occupations in order to enhance user acceptance and successful implementation, avoiding a one-size-fits-all approach. In this way, organisations can more strategically deploy their risk management programmes at lower costs, while simultaneously enhancing the safety and security of employees working overseas.

Conclusion

Earlier we mentioned the motion picture industry's view of expatriates and Hollywood's fascination with people working internationally. The many movies that deal with expatriates can help us to understand the differences in the appropriate risk management techniques that should be adopted for different occupations. For example, the film *Whiskey, Tango, Foxtrot* illustrates how a correspondent subjects herself to dangers in order to get a headline story. However, that film also illustrates how she was closely dependent on locals with knowledge of the people and situations in which she was working. The film *Medicine Man* illustrates how the biology researcher learned about the cures to diseases from locals. The film *No Escape* illustrates how the father of a family uses his analytical problem-solving skills to extract his family from a dangerous situation. Finally, the film *Florence Nightingale* illustrates how the altruistic motivations of nurses can induce them to be exposed to unsanitary conditions that they can nevertheless overcome. Hopefully, readers will take the time to view one or more of these films in order to enhance their understanding of the different risks that expatriates face and how those risks can be managed effectively through the adaptation of risk management plans to specific occupations and circumstances.

This is important because expatriates continue to be some of the most crucial employees in MNEs. In this chapter we illustrated how organisations can better identify the risks that expatriates face. This can be done through a careful analysis of the likelihood and severity of the dangers in different locations. However, analyses must also take into account the differences in risks that are faced by different occupations. Employers can significantly enhance the effectiveness and efficiency of their risk management programmes for expatriates if they consider these important factors.

Appendix

Countries Ranked by Travel Warning Levels and Alphabetically, Showing
Corresponding Corruption Perception Index Measures

Country	Travel warning level	Corruptions perceptions index
Algeria	2	33
Azerbaijan	2	31
Bahamas	2	65
Bangladesh	2	28
Belgium	2	75
Bosnia and Herzegovina	2	38
Brazil	2	37
Cameroon	2	25
China	2	41
Colombia	2	37
Comoros	2	27
Cote d'Ivoire	2	36
Cuba	2	47
Denmark	2	88
Dominican Republic	2	29
Egypt	2	32
Eritrea	2	20
Ethiopia	2	35
France	2	70
Germany	2	81
Guatemala	2	28
Guinea	2	27
Guyana	2	38
India	2	40
Indonesia	2	37
Israel	2	62
Italy	2	50
Jamaica	2	44
Jordan	2	48
Kenya	2	28
Kosovo	2	39
Madagascar	2	24
Maldives	2	33
Mexico	2	29
Nepal	2	31
Netherlands	2	82
Papua New Guinea	2	29
Philippines	2	34
Republic of the Congo	2	21
Russia	2	29
Saudi Arabia	2	49
Sierra Leone	2	30
South Africa	2	43
Spain	2	57
Tajikistan	2	21
Tanzania	2	36
Togo	2	32

Country	Travel warning level	Corruptions perceptions index
Trinidad and Tobago	2	41
Tunisia	2	42
Uganda	2	26
Ukraine	2	30
United Kingdom	2	82
Zimbabwe	2	22
Burkina Faso	3	42
Burundi	3	22
Chad	3	20
Democratic Republic of Congo	3	21
El Salvador	3	33
Haiti	3	22
Honduras	3	29
Lebanon	3	28
Mauritania	3	28
Nicaragua	3	26
Niger	3	33
Nigeria	3	27
Pakistan	3	32
Sudan	3	16
Turkey	3	40
Venezuela	3	18
Afghanistan	4	15
Central African Republic	4	23
Iran	4	30
Iraq	4	18
Libya	4	17
Mali	4	31
North Korea	4	17
Somalia	4	9
South Sudan	4	12
Syria	4	14
Yemen	4	16

References

Adler, J. H. (2000). More sorry than safe: Assessing the precautionary principle and the proposed international biosafety protocol. *Texas International Law Journal*, 35, 173–206.

Bader, B. (2015). The power of support in high-risk countries: Compensation and social support as antecedents of expatriate work attitudes. *International Journal of Human Resource Management*, 26(13), 1712–1736.

Barton, V. (2009). *Killed in the line of duty: Who is killing foreign correspondents and why?* Doctoral dissertation, Auckland University of Technology.

Bhaskar-Shrinivas, P., Harrison, D. A., Shaffer, M. A. & Luk, D. M. (2005). Input-based and time-based models of international adjustment: Meta-analytic evidence and theoretical extensions. *Academy of Management Journal*, 48(2), 257–281.

Brookfield Global Relocation Services. (2015). *Global mobility trends survey*, Report 20. Lisbon: Brookfield Global.

Fee, A. & McGrath-Champ, S. (2017). The role of human resources in protecting expatriates: Insights from the international aid and development sector. *International Journal of Human Resource Management*, 28(14), 1960–1985.

Fee, A., McGrath-Champ, S. & Berti, M. (2017). Protecting expatriates in hostile environments: Institutional forces influencing the safety and security practices of internationally active organizations. *International Journal of Human Resource Management*. doi: 10.1080/09585192.2017.1322121

Gannon, J. & Paraskevas, A. (2017). In the line of fire, managing expatriates in hostile environments. *International Journal of Human Resources Management*. doi: 10.1080/09585192.2017.1322122

Haslberger, A., Brewster, C. & Hippler, T. (2014). *Managing performance abroad: A new model for understanding expatriate adjustment*. London: Routledge.

Hathaway, C. (2013). Using film, television, and other media to teach management and leadership concepts. *Nurse Educator*, 38(6), 239–240.

Hechanova, R., Beehr, T. A. & Christiansen, N. D. (2003). Antecedents and consequences of employees' adjustment to overseas assignment: A meta-analytic review. *Applied Psychology*, 52(2), 213–236.

Holland, J. L. (1985). Vocational choices: A theory of vocational personality and work environment. *Personalities and Work Environment*, 2nd ed, Englewood Cliffs, NJ: Prentice-Hall.

Kraimer, M., Bolino, M. & Mead, B. (2016). Themes in expatriate and repatriate research over four decades: What do we know and what do we still need to learn? *Annual Review of Organizational Psychology and Organizational Behavior*, 3, 83–109.

Leet, D. & Houser, S. (2003). Economics goes to Hollywood: Using classic films and documentaries to create an undergraduate economics course. *Journal of Economic Education*, 34(4), 326–332.

Murrell, C. (2010). Baghdad bureaux: An exploration of the interconnected world of fixers and correspondents at the BBC and CNN. *Media, War & Conflict*, 3(2), 125–137.

Peterson, N. G., Mumford, M. D., Borman, W. C., Jeanneret, P. R., Fleishman, E. A., Levin, K. Y., ... & Gowing, M. K. (2001). Understanding work using the occupational information network (O* NET): Implications for practice and research. *Personnel Psychology*, 54(2), 451–492.

Phillips, G. B. (1961). *Microbiological safety in U.S. and foreign laboratories*. Arlington, VA: Defense Technical Information Agency.

Posthuma, R. A., Ramsey, J. R., Flores, G. L., Maertz, C. & Ahmed, R. O. (2017). A risk management model for research on expatriates in hostile work environments. *International Journal of Human Resource Management*. doi: 10.1080/09585192.2017.1376222

Ricchiardi, S. (2001). Assignment: Afghanistan; Journalists reporting from the front lines in one of the world's harshest landscapes encounter no shortage of obstacles and dangers. *American Journalism Review*, 23(9), 18–23.

Suder, G., Reade, C., Riviere, M., Birnik, A. & Nielsen, N. (2017). Mind the gap: The role of HRM in creating, capturing and leveraging rare knowledge in hostile environments. *International Journal of Human Resource Management*. doi: 10.1080/09585192.2017.1351462

7 Emergency Workers
Working with Violence

Hannah Meacham, Patricia Pariona Cabrera,
Jillian Cavanagh and Timothy Bartram

Introduction

Workplace violence is becoming a major public health concern, with increased media coverage of violence against healthcare workers in recent years (Kowalenko et al., 2012; Safe Work Australia, 2017). Workplace violence can be defined as a situation in which an individual is verbally threatened or physically attacked on work premises or whilst carrying out their work duties (Pourshaikhian, Gorji, Aryankhesal, Khorasani-Zavareh, & Barati, 2016). Physical violence includes but is not limited to punching, kicking, slapping. Verbal violence includes but is not limited to shouting, emotional abuse, aggressive voice tone (Copeland & Henry, 2017). Employee advocacy groups, healthcare services and the broader community are concerned for the safety of those tasked with providing medical care to the infirm and saving lives (Biçkes, Çizmeci, Göver, & Pomak, 2017). Violent behaviour against staff across the healthcare industry is reportedly so widespread (Fujita et al., 2012; Speroni, Fitch, Dawson, Dugan, & Atherton, 2014) that it is, for example, in Australia, becoming 'part of the job' and in some ways accepted and even tolerated (Boyle, Koritsas, Coles, & Stanley, 2007; Pich, Hazelton, Sundin, & Kable, 2010). In the USA, Gates (2004) demonstrated that only 27% of nurses studied in their research perceived violence as an issue in their workplace, suggesting that only when extreme critical incidences occur, such as a homicide, does this perception change. In Australia studies of occupational homicides report that 24% of violence in the workplace that leads to the death of a worker occur in the medical services sector (Boyle et al., 2007; Pich et al., 2010).

Workplace violence can have implications for the worker, the workplace and wider society (Arnetz, Hamblin, Essenmacher et al., 2015; Blando, Ridenour, Hartley, & Casteel, 2015). Violence itself along with anxiety due to the fear of violence can negatively affect employee well-being, individual and ultimately organisational performance (Pourshaikhian et al., 2016). Whilst research has recommended procedures to deal with violent acts, such as employee training and workplace protocols, there is a dearth of systematic research on how to reduce the number of violent attacks on healthcare workers (Duncan et al., 2016; Linsley, 2016). This chapter discusses violence against healthcare workers, focusing on emergency department workers and paramedics. The reporting of incidents, training of staff to more effectively manage violence and the impact on staff and organisations will be considered before considering best practice strategies in contemporary healthcare services.

Emergency Department Workers

Emergency department workers include nurses, doctors, porters and administrative staff. Research has shown that emergency department workers are at high risk from verbal and physical violence from patients, patient family members and visitors (Arnetz, Hamblin, Essenmacher et al., 2015; Phillips, 2016). Emergency department workers often report never feeling safe at work (Catlette, 2005; Speroni et al., 2014) due to unpredictable patient behaviour and a lack of management support. In the UK, statistics have shown that police were called to emergency departments 521 times during the 2017/2018 reporting period, that's at least once a day (BBC News, 2018b). Administrative staff, such as reception workers who are the departments' front line, report feeling less safe compared to nurses and doctors (Stene, Larson, Levy, & Dohlman, 2015) due to overcrowding and long wait times for patients and visitors. Moreover, they are also usually the first to greet patients and administrate financial issues, which may cause tension for patients and patient families (Copeland & Henry, 2017). For example, in the USA, administration occupations, such as receptionists, have an injury rate of 20.4 per 10,000 workers due to assaults, whereas practitioners, such as nurses and doctors, have a rate of 6.1 per 10,000 (Bureau of Labor Statistics, 2018). Violence against emergency nurses from colleagues or other emergency workers has also been on the increase, mainly due to long work hours, increased stress and workplace demands. In the USA, one case of a nurse being violently arrested for 'doing her job' and not handing over a blood sample to a police detective rocked the headlines (Amatulli, 2017).

Reporting Incidents

Research has indicated a low reporting rate for patient violent behaviour (Arnetz et al., 2015; Stene et al., 2015). Physical assaults are more likely to be reported due to visible injuries, with emotional abuse less likely to be reported due to its invisibility and such abuse is often accepted as part of the job (Crilly, Chaboyer, & Creedy, 2004; Findorff, McGovern, Wall, & Gerberich, 2005). Despite the low reporting rates overall, Gates, Ross, and McQueen (2006) found 67% of nurses had reported at least one assault against them in a six-month period. Emergency department nurses are four times more likely to report they had been assaulted compared with nurses from other departments (Gerberich et al., 2005; Lanctôt & Guay, 2014). Due to many patients presenting with dementia or mental health issues, healthcare workers often excuse the behaviour as part of a patient's condition (ALBashtawy, 2016; Hogarth, Beattie, & Morphet, 2016). This may explain low reporting rates of violent behaviour, as behaviour attributed to a patient's condition may be perceived as just another symptom requiring treatment (Arnetz, Hamblin, Ager et al., 2015; Crilly et al., 2004; Pich, Kable, & Hazelton, 2017). For example, Gerberich et al. (2005) found that 44% of nurses did not report incidents of assault due to the attribution of this behaviour being 'part of the job'. Reporting of visitor assaults is often higher (Pompeii et al., 2015) as abusive visitor behaviour is more likely to be regarded as unacceptable (Hogarth et al., 2016). This could be due to high workload expectations with nurses not having the time to fill in incident reports, especially if the incident did not result in an injury or was not witnessed by another member of staff (Catlette, 2005). Currently in the USA, there is no obligation to report violent incidents to authorities, meaning research on causes is limited (Almendrala, 2017). This lack of reporting is a worrying issue that needs to be addressed by health service management through ways such as identifying and documenting risk, outlining and communicating reporting procedures, and planning interventions that reduce risks of workplace violence (Arnetz, Hamblin, Ager et al., 2015).

Training

Workplace violence prevention training is often designed to protect staff, patients and visitors from violent behaviour (Gacki-Smith et al., 2009). Training often includes classroom-style methods on specific hospital safety policies and procedures; predicting aggression and violence; characteristics of violent patients; verbal and physical methods for diffusing a violent patient; self-defence techniques and the resources available to a victim of violent behaviour (Peek-Asa et al., 2007). The use of violence prevention training is less widespread than expected, with some studies reporting just 38% of participants having violence prevention training (Gerberich et al., 2005). This is even more alarming when emergency department nurses and doctors report only 8% have been trained in violence prevention (Gillespie, Gates, Kowalenko, Bresler, & Succop, 2014). This lack of training can be put down to budget restrictions and the reliance on security staff, who may take time to respond to violent attacks dependent on where they are in the hospital (Gates, Gillespie, Smith et al., 2011; McPhaul & Lipscomb, 2004). Moreover, violence prevention training may not be adequate, taking a classroom-based approach, where in reality employees often encounter many different violent situations (Blando et al., 2015; Catlette, 2005). Therefore, role-play and simulation-based teaching methods have been suggested as better suited to all emergency department staff including administrative staff, managers, nurses, doctors and security personnel (Behnam, Tillotson, Davis, & Hobbs, 2011). Such training approaches can increase employee knowledge and confidence in recognising signs of violent behaviour, thus preventing any violence before an incident may occur (Peek-Asa et al., 2007; Speroni et al., 2014). A pilot study for simulation-based violence training conducted in the USA indicated that undergraduate students felt more confident and knowledgeable in dealing with violent patients (Martinez, 2017).

Drivers of Violence in Emergency Departments

Patient assaults are commonly attributed to alcohol and drug use, psychiatric conditions or stress induced by a crisis situation (Fujita et al., 2012; Pich et al., 2017; Speroni et al., 2014). Care for such patients can be complex and involve a number of emergency department workers treating the patient simultaneously, all increasing patient stress levels and possibly triggering a violent outburst (Duncan et al., 2016; Wei, Chiou, Chien, & Huang, 2016). When patients and visitors use emergency departments it is often at a time when they are injured and feeling vulnerable, instantly heightening any anxiety, frustration and perceptions of losing control (Carter, Pouch, & Larson, 2014; Weigl, Müller, Holland, Wedel, & Woloshynowych, 2015). However, there are increasing numbers of unprovoked attacks on emergency department workers. In 2017, a leading Australian heart surgeon was punched and killed outside the hospital he worked for after asking a visitor not to smoke in a non-smoking area. The attacker was later jailed for manslaughter (Cooper, 2018b).

Increased drug use, and the spread of the drug crystal methamphetamine or 'ice' has been a focus of many media reports as a main contributing factor to increased violence in emergency departments (Chalmers, Lancaster, & Hughes, 2016; Cleary et al., 2017). The 'ice' users tend to become neurotic, paranoid and unaware of their surroundings, making them prone to unpredictable violent behaviour (Tomlinson, Brown, & Hoaken, 2016). The use of drugs such as 'ice' may have also contributed to the increased level of social violence that is then brought into hospital emergency departments (Gordon & de Jong, 2018; Ross, Adams, & Beovich, 2017). Given that few individuals with drug dependency issues seek treatment for the drug use, aggressive behaviour linked to drug use presents an ongoing concern (Hoaken et al., 2012). For example, an estimated 8.3 tonnes of ice were consumed in Australia in 2017 (The Australian Criminal Intelligence Commission, 2018). Prevalence levels for annual use of ice in Australia at 2.3% are higher than those in the USA (0.3%) and Europe (0.5%) (Alcohol and Drug Foundation, 2017).

An increasing number of dementia patients may also have contributed to the surge in violence: sudden changes in behaviour and patients 'lashing out' can often occur (Fujita et al., 2012; Gates, 2004). Research suggests that patients suffering with dementia can demonstrate impaired moral judgement, low interpersonal conduct and anti-social behaviour (Defrancesco, Kemmler, Huber, & Deisenhammer, 2014; Doenyas, 2017). Violent behaviour may occur in such patients when they misinterpret environmental surroundings, or become frustrated when helped by a clinician to do a perceived simple task (Cipriani, Lucetti, Danti, Carlesi, & Nuti, 2016). Although it may be impossible to avoid all violence against emergency department workers, dealing with these high-risk patients through early identification and actions to minimise violence episodes is an important starting point to reduce the potential for violence.

Paramedics

Paramedics are often the first responders to medical incidents (Boyle et al., 2007; Maguire, O'Meara, O'Neill, & Brightwell, 2018). They work in a unique setting where incidents could involve critical and dangerous situations in which they have to react safely and treat the emergency needs of patients (Bigham et al., 2014; Roberts, Sim, Black, & Smith, 2015). Due to the public environment in which they work there is a high possibility of violent interactions with patients or bystanders (Pourshaikhian et al., 2016) with 90% of paramedics reporting at least one incident of violence against them in their career (Bigham et al., 2014; Maguire et al., 2018).

In Australia, it has been found that 87.5% of paramedics have been exposed to violence in the workplace with verbal abuse being the most common and physical violence second (Boyle et al., 2007; Wongtongkam, 2017). Internationally, verbal abuse was again the most common. In Sweden, 80% of paramedics reported verbal abuse (Suserud, Blomquist, & Johansson, 2002), whilst in the USA, 61% of paramedics had reported physical abuse in the workplace at the rate of one experience every three months (Maguire & Smith, 2013). Types of physical assault against paramedics can also vary across nations. American studies have reported that physical assault with a weapon occurred most frequently (Mock, Wrenn, Wright, Eustis, & Slovis, 1999). Types of assault on paramedics are similar to those on emergency department workers. Verbal assault is often perpetrated by patients and patient family members, including offensive language and threats of physical violence (Baydin & Erenler, 2014; Maguire et al., 2018). Bingham et al. (2014) noted that, intimidation was not only common from patients, but work colleagues and other emergency services. Intimidating behaviour can include verbal threats, violent behaviour (not against the person) and gestures

(Gormley, Crowe, Bentley, & Levine, 2016). Physical assault by a patient, including punching and kicking is more likely to occur in the back of the ambulance, when only one paramedic is with the patient (Bigham et al., 2014). Sexual harassment and sexual assault, including obscene gestures, propositions and groping, specifically against female paramedics, is also common once in transit to hospital where one paramedic is on their own with the patient (Boyle & Wallis, 2016). One example in Australia, where a paramedic was attacked by members of the public, leaving him unable to work, shows just how unfair the system can be (Cooper, 2018a). His attackers' jail sentences were quashed on appeal, meaning they walked free from court. This weak response has angered paramedics, who have protested to increase the penalties for such occurrences (Cooper, 2018a). Another example, at the Christchurch's Hilmorton Hospital in New Zealand, a nurse was stabbed in the leg with surgical scissors by a patient. In the same hospital, a nurse suffered serious burns because a patient threw a cup of boiling water over her, leaving her with second degree burns and future scarring (Lewis & Clarkson, 2018).

Violence is considered by paramedics to be the number one cause of stress, often leading to work disengagement, burnout and turnover (Regehr & Millar, 2007). Research has led to implementation of some safe workplace strategies for emergency department workers; however, such strategies have not been as impactful on workplace violence against paramedics (Bigham & Welsford, 2015). This could be due to differing work environments and the unpredictable nature of paramedic work (Bigham et al., 2014; Boyle et al., 2007). By being exposed to workplace violence, healthcare professionals experience negative emotions such as feelings of emotional exhaustion and lack of personal accomplishment (Wongtongkam, 2017), which may lead to a lost interest in the field work (Canton et al., 2009), and finally may lead to leave their career (Heponiemi, Kouvonen, Virtanen, Vänskä, & Elovainio, 2014).

Reporting incidents of workplace violence is also an issue for paramedics (Bernaldo-De-Quirós, Piccini, Gómez, & Cerdeira, 2015). Similar to emergency department staff, types of assault less likely to be reported include verbal assault and patient intimidation due to a lack of visible injury as evidence and perceiving this patient behaviour as a condition symptom (Koritsas, Boyle, & Coles, 2009; Rahmani, Hassankhani, Mills, & Dadashzadeh, 2012). Other factors leading to a low reporting rate include how incidents are reported. Poor administrative systems, reporting forms and lack of procedural training all contribute (Boyle et al., 2007). A lack of management support once incidents have been reported is also likely to cause low reporting levels (Bigham et al., 2014; Koritsas et al., 2009). However, when managers promote non-acceptance of workplace violence by a consistent use of their language and behaviour (Kennedy, 2005), provide support to staff reporting with a 'no blame focus' (Copeland & Henry, 2017) and establish a follow-up after an incident of violence (Stene et al., 2015), it may promote a culture of reporting workplace violence by healthcare professionals.

Impacts of Violence on Staff

Employees can suffer short-term physical injury such as broken bones and lacerations and long-term physical injury such as chronic pain and even disability (Gates, Gillespie, & Succop, 2011). These consequences of violence are common and found to be more prevalent with emotional or psychological violence than physical violence (Biçkes et al., 2017; Gerberich et al., 2005; Speroni et al., 2014). In addition to this, employees can face short-term and long-term psychological issues such as nightmares, depression, anxiety and frustration (Biçkes et al., 2017; Lanctôt & Guay, 2014), with consequences from emotional violence also found to be greater than physical violence consequences (Gerberich et al., 2005; Wei et al., 2016).

Emergency workers are more likely than others to suffer job stress, burnout and occupational dissatisfaction even before they are subjected to violent behaviour (Duncan et al., 2016; Gates et al., 2006; Lanctôt & Guay, 2014). Outcomes of violence against emergency healthcare staff are progressively associated with decreased job satisfaction, increased occupational strain, and poor patient care outcomes (Gates, 2004; Laeeque, Bilal, Babar, Khan, & Ul Rahman, 2018). Researchers have also found that emergency medical workers can often suffer symptoms of post-traumatic stress disorder (PTSD) (Caldwell, 1992; Catlette, 2005). As such, the after effects of workplace violence can occur years after, affecting the long-term well-being of clinicians (Lanctôt & Guay, 2014). The reluctance to care for patients is due to a decrease in staff confidence in the organisation, depersonalisation of patients and lower job satisfaction (Chapman, Perry, Styles, & Combs, 2008). For example, a New Zealand nurse mentioned

> I shouldn't have to go to work fearing the people I'm there to help. It's a near daily occurrence for someone to complain to me, to lose the plot, to yell, to say rude things, to attempt to physically hit, swing or spit at me.
>
> (Gerrets, 2018)

Impact on Individual and Organisational Performance

Emergency medical staff intention to leave may be affected by patient violence (Arnetz, Arnetz, & Söderman, 1998; Choi & Lee, 2017; Li, Chao, & Shih, 2018). As previously mentioned, not only are the consequences for employees dire, for employers costs can also be high

(Fujita et al., 2012; Wei et al., 2016). In the USA, McGovern et al. (2000) found that violence cost hospitals per registered nurse an estimated US\$31,000. Such costs can include lost wages, medical fees and legal fees, along with sick leave, low retention rates and workers compensation. Violence against staff can affect turnover, workers' compensation, and medical and psychological care of staff, and cause absenteeism (Gerberich et al., 2005; Speroni et al., 2014). Studies have shown that the perception of safety can be related to job satisfaction (Catlette, 2005; Duncan et al., 2016). The more unsafe an employee feels at work, the less reported job satisfaction which can lead to high turnover rates (Li et al., 2018; Wei et al., 2016). In America, turnover rates for emergency medical staff stand at 17.5% for 2017/2018 (Bureau of Labor Statistics, 2018).

Productivity can also be affected, along with the quality of patient care due to employees' reluctance to treat and care for patients if there is a threat of further violence (Gates, Gillespie, & Succop, 2011). As noted, job satisfaction is another critical factor that can be affected, which it is linked to key organisational outcomes such as quality of patient care (Johansen, 2014; Leggat, Bartram, Casimir, & Stanton, 2010). Exposure to patient-related violence impacts negatively on the way emergency medical staff interact with patients (Hogarth et al., 2016). Violence in the workplace may lead to a disruption of nursing care and patients could be at risk (Merecz, Rymaszewska, Mościcka, Kiejna, & Jarosz-Nowak, 2006). Emergency staff may experience a lack of concentration at work, inappropriate communication, and a lack of empathy affect their skills and efficiency in their work, which may lead to higher possibility for medical errors (Hassankhani, Parizad, Gacki-Smith, Rahmani, & Mohammadi, 2018). For example, a wrong medication or a late administration of medications may occur resulting in an increase in the number of medications errors which may compromise the quality of patient care (Chapman et al., 2008; Najafi, Fallahi-Khoshknab, Ahmadi, Dalvandi, & Rahgozar, 2018). Hence, it is imperative to take measures to mitigate and manage violence in the workplace among emergency workers (Hassankhani et al., 2018; Kowalenko et al., 2012).

Conclusion

Violence in the healthcare sector may never be eliminated due to the volatile and complex nature of patient care (Copeland & Henry, 2017; Wongtongkam, 2017). To manage and minimise workplace violence, employers need to create supportive workplaces that acknowledge the trauma associated with violence, offer programmes that support the well-being of employees after a violent incident and produce practices that minimise patient violence from the outset (Blando et al., 2015). Employees themselves need to feel comfortable in the workplace setting to report incidents of violence and should be encouraged to do so to measure the success of prevention practices in place (Arnetz, Hamblin, Ager et al., 2015; Duncan et al., 2016). Studies highlight the need for further research to examine workplace violence explicit in emergency medical workers such as emergency nurses and paramedics (ALBashtawy, 2016; Speroni et al., 2014). In the New Zealand healthcare system, a nurse outlined

> we need to design our workplaces in a way that helps mitigate escalation of aggression and violence. Some emergency department workers were supported to wear personal alarms, but this has not been rolled out nationwide. We might all need personal alarms. We need our employers to stand up for us and say this isn't going to be tolerated.
>
> (Gerrets, 2018)

Recently, the Welsh parliament passed legislation that doubles the jail time for perpetrators of violence against nursing staff and paramedics, it is hoped that the rest of the UK will follow suit (BBC News, 2018a). The use of body cameras for paramedics and nurses has also become commonplace throughout the UK to deter possible offenders and to record violent attacks to ensure perpetrators are convicted. In counties where this is already in place, paramedics especially are noticing the difference with one union member noting that it is an 'extra safety mechanism' (BBC News, 2018a).

Violent episodes by colleagues, managers and the public would not be tolerated in other industries (Gates, 2004). Violence in the healthcare industry, and especially in emergency departments, should be dealt with similarly to other industries, where employees would be dismissed for gross misconduct and the public asked to leave (Arnetz et al., 1998; Blando et al., 2015). In dealing with this violence, healthcare workplaces will become safer for employees, the industry and occupations will become more desirable and the shortage of emergency medical workers will be addressed. Patient violence prevention can be reliant on management, administration and security personnel intervention (Gacki-Smith et al., 2009; Jackson, Clare, & Mannix, 2002). Therefore, it is imperative that a multi-faceted solution is utilised for patients, thus decreasing stress and possible violent/frustrated behaviour and increasing communication between administrative staff and patients to reduce uncertainty (Condon, Burford, Ghosal, Denning, & Rees, 2018; Leggat et al., 2016). For paramedics, a redesign could include how they respond to jobs or the utilisation of other emergency response workers (Boyle et al., 2007;

Wongtongkam, 2017). Table 7.1 presents possible recommendations, which may contribute to the management and mitigation of workplace violence in emergency departments.

Table 7.1 Recommendations

Areas	Recommendations
Emergency department leadership	Emergency department leadership need to drive cultural change at the executive and organisational level to develop and implement interventions to address high-risk situations, recognise, manage and mitigate workplace violence
Responsiveness of management	Positive support from management is needed to establish a culture of safety, to control resources to exert cultural transformations and implement effective practices
Policies and procedures	Clear policies and procedures need to be established by management for encouraging formal reporting
	Development of workplace violence and procedures need to engage emergency staff to have more control over their work environment
Formal reporting	A user-friendly, simpler, and less time-consuming process of incident reporting may be implemented by management
Feedback	Emergency staff need to have a feedback of formal reports to track the progress of their report and able to learn from the outcome and to see the value of reporting
Training and development	Emergency staff need to receive training to raise awareness of verbal abuse as a form of violence and emphasise the benefits of reporting
	Emergency managers and emergency staff need to receive training in cue recognition to identify high-risk patients and volatile situations
Safety measures	Permanent emergency department security guard and increased security presence are needed to increase feelings of safety among emergency staff
Redesign	Transforming physical design of emergency departments to reduce length to stay, to increase communication between staff and patients

References

Alcohol and Drug Foundation (Producer). (2017). Inquiry into crystal metham-phetamine. Retrieved from https://adf.org.au/drug-facts/

ALBashtawy, M. (2016). Emergency nurses' perspective of workplace violence in Jordanian hospitals: A national survey. *International Emergency Nursing*, 24, 61–65.

Almendrala, A. (Producer). (2017). Violence against nurses is a serious problem, but hospitals are basically policing themselves. Retrieved from https://www.huffingtonpost.com.au/entry/violence-nurses-hospital-responsibility_us_59bad5a3e4b02da0e1404e47

Amatulli, J. (Producer). (2017). Nurse sobs 'help me' while getting arrested for simply doing her job. Retrieved from https://www.huffingtonpost.com.au/entry/nurse-sobs-help-me-while-getting-arrested-for-simply-doing-her-job_us_59a98902e4b0b5e530fe51d2

Arnetz, J. E., Arnetz, B. B., & Söderman, E. (1998). Violence toward health care workers: Prevalence and incidence at a large, regional hospital in Sweden. *AAOHN Journal*, 46(3), 107–114.

Arnetz, J. E., Hamblin, L., Ager, J., Luborsky, M., Upfal, M. J., Russell, J., & Essenmacher, L. (2015). Underreporting of workplace violence: Comparison of self-report and actual documentation of hospital incidents. *Workplace Health & Safety*, 63(5), 200–210.

Arnetz, J. E., Hamblin, L., Essenmacher, L., Upfal, M. J., Ager, J., & Luborsky, M. (2015). Understanding patient-to-worker violence in hospitals: A qualitative analysis of documented incident reports. *Journal of Advanced Nursing*, 71(2), 338–348.

Baydin, A., & Erenler, A. K. (2014). Workplace violence in emergency department and its effects on emergency staff. *International Journal of Emergency Mental Health*, 16(2), 288–290.

BBC News (Producer). (2018a). Body cams for paramedics in Wales after attack spike. Retrieved from https://www.bbc.com/news/uk-wales-44502834

BBC News (Producer). (2018b). Police called everyday to violence against NHS staff. Retrieved from https://www.bbc.com/news/uk-wales-44630481

Behnam, M., Tillotson, R. D., Davis, S. M., & Hobbs, G. R. (2011). Violence in the emergency department: A national survey of emergency medicine residents and attending physicians. *The Journal of Emergency Medicine*, 40(5), 565–579.

Bernaldo-De-Quirós, M., Piccini, A. T., Gómez, M. M., & Cerdeira, J. C. (2015). Psychological consequences of aggression in pre-hospital emergency care: Cross sectional survey. *International Journal of Nursing Studies*, 52(1), 260–270.

Biçkes, D. M., Çizmeci, B., Göver, H., & Pomak, I. (2017). Investigation of health care workers' stress, depression and anxiety levels in terms of work-related violence. *Journal of Human Sciences*, 14(3), 2628–2642.

Bigham, B., Jensen, J., Tavares, W., Drennan, I., Saleem, H., Dainty, K., & Munro, G. (2014). Paramedic self-reported exposure to violence in the emergency medical services (EMS) workplace: A mixed-methods cross-sectional survey. *Prehospital Emergency Care*, 18(4), 489–494.

Bigham, B., & Welsford, M. (2015). Applying hospital evidence to paramedicine: Issues of indirectness, validity and knowledge translation. *Canadian Journal of Emergency Medicine, 17*(3), 281–285.

Blando, J., Ridenour, M., Hartley, D., & Casteel, C. (2015). Barriers to effective implementation of programs for the prevention of workplace violence in hospitals. *Online Journal of Issues in Nursing, 20*(1), 1861–1868.

Boyle, M., Koritsas, S., Coles, J., & Stanley, J. (2007). A pilot study of workplace violence towards paramedics. *Emergency Medicine Journal, 24*(11), 760–763.

Boyle, M., & Wallis, J. (2016). Working towards a definition for workplace violence actions in the health sector. *Safety in Health, 2*(1), 4.

Bureau of Labor Statistics. (2018). *EMTs and Paramedics*. US Department of Labor, Washington.

Caldwell, M. F. (1992). Incidence of PTSD among staff victims of patient violence. *Psychiatric Services, 43*(8), 838–839.

Canton, A. N., Sherman, M. F., Magda, L. A., Westra, L. J., Pearson, J. M., Raveis, V. H., & Gershon, R. R. (2009). Violence, job satisfaction, and employment intentions among home healthcare registered nurses. *Home Healthcare Now, 27*(6), 364–373.

Carter, E. J., Pouch, S. M., & Larson, E. L. (2014). The relationship between emergency department crowding and patient outcomes: A systematic review. *Journal of Nursing Scholarship, 46*(2), 106–115.

Catlette, M. (2005). A descriptive study of the perceptions of workplace violence and safety strategies of nurses working in level I trauma centers. *Journal of Emergency Nursing, 31*(6), 519–525.

Chalmers, J., Lancaster, K., & Hughes, C. (2016). The stigmatisation of 'ice' and under-reporting of meth/amphetamine use in general population surveys: A case study from Australia. *International Journal of Drug Policy, 36*, 15–24.

Chapman, R., Perry, L., Styles, I., & Combs, S. (2008). Consequences of workplace violence directed at nurses. *British Journal of Nursing, 17*(20), 1256–1261.

Choi, S. H., & Lee, H. (2017). Workplace violence against nurses in Korea and its impact on professional quality of life and turnover intention. *Journal of Nursing Management, 25*(7), 508–518.

Cipriani, G., Lucetti, C., Danti, S., Carlesi, C., & Nuti, A. (2016). Violent and criminal manifestations in dementia patients. *Geriatrics & Gerontology International, 16*(5), 541–549.

Cleary, M., Jackson, D., Woods, C., Kornhaber, R., Sayers, J., & Usher, K. (2017). Experiences of health professionals caring for people presenting to the emergency department after taking crystal methamphetamine ("ICE"). *Issues in Mental Health Nursing, 38*(1), 33–41.

Condon, L., Burford, S., Ghosal, R., Denning, B., & Rees, G. (2018). Prudent healthcare in emergency departments: A case study in Wales. *Emergency Nurse: The Journal of the RCN Accident and Emergency Nursing Association, 25*(10), 20–23.

Cooper, A. (Producer). (2018a). 'Justice hasn't been done', says bashed ambo after women avoid jail. Retrieved from https://www.theage.com.au/national/victoria/freedom-for-ambo-bashing-pair-who-judge-says-turned-their-lives-around-20180515-p4zff7.html

Cooper, A. (Producer). (2018b). Punch to doctor over smoke warning so hard it 'caused hospital tile to crack'. Retrieved from https://www.theage.com.au/national/victoria/punch-to-doctor-over-smoke-warning-so-hard-it-caused-hospital-tile-to-crack-20180212-p4z01n.html

Copeland, D., & Henry, M. (2017). Workplace violence and perceptions of safety among emergency department staff members: Experiences, expectations, tolerance, reporting, and recommendations. *Journal of Trauma Nursing, 24*(2), 65–77.

Crilly, J., Chaboyer, W., & Creedy, D. (2004). Violence towards emergency department nurses by patients. *Accident and Emergency Nursing, 12*(2), 67–73.

Defrancesco, M., Kemmler, G., Huber, R., & Deisenhammer, E. (2014). Correlation of mental activity with cognitive functions in mild cognitive impairment and early stage dementia. *Der Nervenarzt, 85*(3), 350–355.

Doenyas, C. (2017). Self versus other oriented social motivation, not lack of empathic or moral ability, explains behavioral outcomes in children with high theory of mind abilities. *Motivation and Emotion, 41*(6), 683–697.

Duncan, S. M., Hyndamn, K., Estabrooks, C. A., Hesketh, K., Humphrey, C. K., Wong, J. S., ... Giovannetti, P. (2016). Nurses' experience of violence in Alberta and British Columbia hospitals. *Canadian Journal of Nursing Research Archive, 32*(4), 57–78.

Findorff, M. J., McGovern, P. M., Wall, M. M., & Gerberich, S. G. (2005). Reporting violence to a health care employer: A cross-sectional study. *AAOHN Journal, 53*(9), 399–406.

Fujita, S., Ito, S., Seto, K., Kitazawa, T., Matsumoto, K., & Hasegawa, T. (2012). Risk factors of workplace violence at hospitals in Japan. *Journal of Hospital Medicine, 7*(2), 79–84.

Gacki-Smith, J., Juarez, A. M., Boyett, L., Homeyer, C., Robinson, L., & MacLean, S. L. (2009). Violence against nurses working in US emergency departments. *Journal of Nursing Administration, 39*(7/8), 340–349.

Gates, D. (2004). The epidemic of violence against healthcare workers. BMJ Publishing Group Ltd.

Gates, D., Gillespie, G., Smith, C., Rode, J., Kowalenko, T., & Smith, B. (2011). Using action research to plan a violence prevention program for emergency departments. *Journal of Emergency Nursing, 37*(1), 32–39.

Gates, D., Gillespie, G., & Succop, P. (2011). Violence against nurses and its impact on stress and productivity. *Nursing Economics, 29*(2), 59–66.

Gates, D., Ross, C., & McQueen, L. (2006). Violence against emergency department workers. *The Journal of Emergency Medicine, 31*(3), 331–337.

Gerberich, S. G., Church, T. R., McGovern, P. M., Hansen, H., Nachreiner, N. M., Geisser, M. S., ... Jurek, A. (2005). Risk factors for work-related assaults on nurses. *Epidemiology, 1*, 704–709.

Gerrets, S. (2018). 'I shouldn't have to fear the people I'm there to help': The violent reality of working in healthcare. https://thespinoff.co.nz/society/04-12-2018/i-shouldnt-have-to-fear-my-patients-the-violent-reality-of-working-in-healthcare/

Gillespie, G. L., Gates, D. M., Kowalenko, T., Bresler, S., & Succop, P. (2014). Implementation of a comprehensive intervention to reduce physical assaults and threats in the emergency department. *Journal of Emergency Nursing, 40*(6), 586–591.

Gordon, D. G., & de Jong, G. (2018). Gaps in the ice: Methamphetamine in Australia; its history, treatment, and ramifications for users and their families. *International Journal of Mental Health Nursing, 6*, 1861–1868.

Gormley, M. A., Crowe, R. P., Bentley, M. A., & Levine, R. (2016). A national description of violence toward emergency medical services personnel. *Prehospital Emergency Care, 20*(4), 439–447.

Hassankhani, H., Parizad, N., Gacki-Smith, J., Rahmani, A., & Mohammadi, E. (2018). The consequences of violence against nurses working in the emergency department: A qualitative study. *International Emergency Nursing, 39*, 20–25.

Heponiemi, T., Kouvonen, A., Virtanen, M., Vänskä, J., & Elovainio, M. (2014). The prospective effects of workplace violence on physicians' job satisfaction and turnover intentions: The buffering effect of job control. *BMC Health Services Research, 14*(1), 19.

Hogarth, K. M., Beattie, J., & Morphet, J. (2016). Nurses' attitudes towards the reporting of violence in the emergency department. *Australasian Emergency Nursing Journal, 19*(2), 75–81.

Jackson, D., Clare, J., & Mannix, J. (2002). Who would want to be a nurse? Violence in the workplace—A factor in recruitment and retention. *Journal of Nursing Management, 10*(1), 13–20.

Johansen, M. L. (2014). Conflicting priorities: Emergency nurses perceived disconnect between patient satisfaction and the delivery of quality patient care. *Journal of Emergency Nursing, 40*(1), 13–19.

Kennedy, M. P. (2005). Violence in emergency departments: Under-reported, unconstrained, and unconscionable. *The Medical Journal of Australia, 183*(7), 362–365.

Koritsas, S., Boyle, M., & Coles, J. (2009). Factors associated with workplace violence in paramedics. *Prehospital and Disaster Medicine, 24*(5), 417–421.

Kowalenko, T., Cunningham, R., Sachs, C. J., Gore, R., Barata, I. A., Gates, D., ... Kerr, H. D. (2012). Workplace violence in emergency medicine: Current knowledge and future directions. *The Journal of Emergency Medicine, 43*(3), 523–531.

Laeeque, S. H., Bilal, A., Babar, S., Khan, Z., & Ul Rahman, S. (2018). How patient-perpetrated workplace violence leads to turnover intention among nurses: The mediating mechanism of occupational stress and burnout. *Journal of Aggression, Maltreatment & Trauma, 27*(1), 96–118.

Lanctôt, N., & Guay, S. (2014). The aftermath of workplace violence among healthcare workers: A systematic literature review of the consequences. *Aggression and Violent Behavior, 19*(5), 492–501.

Leggat, S. G., Bartram, T., Casimir, G., & Stanton, P. (2010). Nurse perceptions of the quality of patient care: Confirming the importance of empowerment and job satisfaction. *Health Care Management Review, 35*(4), 355–364.

Leggat, S. G., Gough, R., Bartram, T., Stanton, P., Bamber, G. J., Ballardie, R., & Sohal, A. (2016). Process redesign for time-based emergency admission targets. *Journal of Health Organization and Management, 30*(6), 939–949.

Lewis, O., & Clarkson, D. (Producer). (2018). Nurse assaults sparks urgent WorkSafe meeting request. Retrieved from https://www.stuff.co.nz/national/health/109045338/patient-who-stabbed-nurse-at-christchurch-hospital-trying-to-harm-himself-police-say

Li, Y.-F., Chao, M., & Shih, C.-T. (2018). Nurses' intention to resign and avoidance of emergency department violence: A moderated mediation model. *International Emergency Nursing, 39*, 55–61.

Linsley, P. (2016). *Violence and Aggression in the Workplace: A Practical Guide for all Healthcare Staff.* CRC Press, Oxford.

Maguire, B. J., O'meara, P., O'neill, B. J., & Brightwell, R. (2018). Violence against emergency medical services personnel: A systematic review of the literature. *American Journal of Industrial Medicine, 61*(2), 167–180.

Maguire, B. J., & Smith, S. (2013). Injuries and fatalities among emergency medical technicians and paramedics in the United States. *Prehospital and Disaster Medicine, 28*(4), 376–382.

Martinez, A. J. S. (2017). Implementing a workplace violence simulation for undergraduate nursing students: A pilot study. *Journal of Psychosocial Nursing and Mental Health Services, 55*(10), 39–44.

McGovern, P., Kochevar, L., Lohman, W., Zaidman, B., Gerberich, S. G., Nyman, J., & Findorff-Dennis, M. (2000). The cost of work-related physical assaults in Minnesota. *Health Services Research, 35*(3), 663.

McPhaul, K. M., & Lipscomb, J. A. (2004). Workplace violence in health care: Recognized but not regulated. *Online Journal of Issues in Nursing, 9*(3), 7.

Merecz, D., Rymaszewska, J., Mościcka, A., Kiejna, A., & Jarosz-Nowak, J. (2006). Violence at the workplace—A questionnaire survey of nurses. *European Psychiatry, 21*(7), 442–450.

Mock, E. F., Wrenn, K. D., Wright, S. W., Eustis, T. C., & Slovis, C. M. (1999). Anxiety levels in EMS providers: Effects of violence and shift schedules. *The American Journal of Emergency Medicine, 17*(6), 509–511.

Najafi, F., Fallahi-Khoshknab, M., Ahmadi, F., Dalvandi, A., & Rahgozar, M. (2018). Antecedents and consequences of workplace violence against nurses: A qualitative study. *Journal of Clinical Nursing, 27*(1–2), e116–e128.

Peek-Asa, C., Casteel, C., Allareddy, V., Nocera, M., Goldmacher, S., OHagan, E., ... Harrison, R. (2007). Workplace violence prevention programs in hospital emergency departments. *Journal of Occupational and Environmental Medicine, 49*(7), 756–763.

Phillips, J. P. (2016). Workplace violence against health care workers in the United States. *New England Journal of Medicine, 374*(17), 1661–1669.

Pich, J., Hazelton, M., Sundin, D., & Kable, A. (2010). Patient-related violence against emergency department nurses. *Nursing & Health Sciences, 12*(2), 268–274.

Pich, J., Kable, A., & Hazelton, M. (2017). Antecedents and precipitants of patient-related violence in the emergency department: Results from the Australian VENT Study (Violence in Emergency Nursing and Triage). *Australasian Emergency Nursing Journal, 20*(3), 107–113.

Pompeii, L. A., Schoenfisch, A. L., Lipscomb, H. J., Dement, J. M., Smith, C. D., & Upadhyaya, M. (2015). Physical assault, physical threat, and verbal abuse perpetrated against hospital workers by patients or visitors in six US hospitals. *American Journal of Industrial Medicine, 58*(11), 1194–1204.

Pourshaikhian, M., Gorji, H. A., Aryankhesal, A., Khorasani-Zavareh, D., & Barati, A. (2016). A systematic literature review: Workplace violence against emergency medical services personnel. *Archives of Trauma Research, 5*(1).

Rahmani, A., Hassankhani, H., Mills, J., & Dadashzadeh, A. (2012). Exposure of Iranian emergency medical technicians to workplace violence: A cross-sectional analysis. *Emergency Medicine Australasia, 24*(1), 105–110.

Regehr, C., & Millar, D. (2007). Situation critical: High demand, low control, and low support in paramedic organizations. *Traumatology, 13*(1), 49–58.

Roberts, M. H., Sim, M. R., Black, O., & Smith, P. (2015). Occupational injury risk among ambulance officers and paramedics compared with other healthcare workers in Victoria, Australia: Analysis of workers' compensation claims from 2003 to 2012. *Occupational and Environmental Medicine*, oemed-2014-102574.

Ross, L., Adams, T., & Beovich, B. (2017). Methamphetamine use and emergency services in Australia: A scoping review. *Journal of Paramedic Practice, 9*(6), 244–257.

Safe Work Australia. (2017). Workplace Violence. Retrieved from https://www.safeworkaustralia.gov.au/workplace-violence

Speroni, K. G., Fitch, T., Dawson, E., Dugan, L., & Atherton, M. (2014). Incidence and cost of nurse workplace violence perpetrated by hospital patients or patient visitors. *Journal of Emergency Nursing, 40*(3), 218–228.

Stene, J., Larson, E., Levy, M., & Dohlman, M. (2015). Workplace violence in the emergency department: Giving staff the tools and support to report. *The Permanente Journal, 19*(2), e113.

Suserud, B. O., Blomquist, M., & Johansson, I. (2002). Experiences of threats and violence in the Swedish ambulance service. *Accident and Emergency Nursing, 10*(3), 127–135. doi: 10.1054/aaen.2002.0361

The Australian Criminal Intelligence Commission. (2018). National Wastewater Drug Monitoring Program. Retrieved from https://www.acic.gov.au/sites/g/files/net3726/f/nwdmp4.pdf?v=1522809564

Tomlinson, M. F., Brown, M., & Hoaken, P. N. (2016). Recreational drug use and human aggressive behavior: A comprehensive review since 2003. *Aggression and Violent Behavior, 27*, 9–29.

Wei, C.-Y., Chiou, S.-T., Chien, L.-Y., & Huang, N. (2016). Workplace violence against nurses–Prevalence and association with hospital organizational characteristics and health-promotion efforts: Cross-sectional study. *International Journal of Nursing Studies, 56*, 63–70.

Weigl, M., Müller, A., Holland, S., Wedel, S., & Woloshynowych, M. (2015). Work conditions, mental workload and patient care quality: A multisource study in the emergency department. *BMJ Quality Safety*, bmjqs-2014-003744.

Wongtongkam, N. (2017). An exploration of violence against paramedics, burnout and post-traumatic symptoms in two Australian ambulance services. *International Journal of Emergency Services, 6*(2), 134–146.

8   Changing Places of Work

Daniel Wheatley

Introduction

This chapter explores work performed outside of the traditional workplace. The pace of change in patterns of paid work, including the digitisation and globalisation of paid work and the recently observed relative decline in the share of employment in full-time permanent roles in a number of developed economies (e.g. Trade Union Congress, 2014), is resulting in changes to workplaces and spaces which have important consequences for workers, organisations and society. There has been a growth in forms of paid work which involve tasks that differ in their organisation and methods of completion when compared to more traditional forms of work organisation. Non-standard or atypical forms of work refer to paid work that does not involve a standard contractual arrangement and/or working patterns. Also often referred to as contingent, or in some cases precarious (Kalleberg, 2009), these forms of work include reduced hours, zero hours, fixed-period, short-term contracts, temporary jobs and certain forms of self-employment including gig working, e-lancing and e-entrepreneurship (Carré & Heintz, 2013, 62; Green, 2017).

While it must be acknowledged that the majority of paid work continues to be undertaken by employees in standard workplace locations in urban centres (Zhu, 2013, 2441), the growth in non-standard work is creating greater diversity in workplace location. Many non-standard forms of work are characterised by taking place in locations outside of the regular office, factory or other workplace. In addition, the digitisation of paid work has increased both opportunities, and demand, for employees in more traditionally organised employment to work more flexibly, including in their workplace location. These changes are reflected in a rise in the incidence of work being performed in non-standard workplace locations including virtual workplaces, shared working spaces, on the move, at client sites, public spaces and working at home (Green, 2017; Hislop & Axtell, 2009; Wheatley, 2017; Wheatley & Bickerton, 2016). Workplace, therefore, is an increasingly fluid concept with important consequences for the future of work.

Following this introduction the chapter begins by contextualising workplace with respect to historical developments in workplace and space. The chapter then considers the workplaces of contemporary developed societies, including the impacts of recent trends in work which have created greater scope for flexibility and diversity in workplace. The chapter also considers the closely tied relationship between work-related travel and our places of work, including working during travel and incidence of long-distance commuting. Finally, the chapter ends with a discussion of the potential implications for workers, organisations and society that recent and future changes in the structures and routines of paid work will have on the places and spaces in which we work.

Workplace in Historical Context

Historically the home acted as a key location of work, for example, in occupations associated with agriculture, crafts and artisan skilled trades, e.g. baker, blacksmith. The development of employment and population centres began to centralise economic activity; however, it was the Industrial Revolution, in the 18th and 19th centuries, which resulted in a large-scale separation of home and work. This period witnessed significant labour movements from rural areas and small towns to cities to work in fixed spatial settings in cotton textile mills and factories (Bienefeld, 1972; Horrell & Humphries, 1995). Facilitated by the development and expansion of the rail network during this period, these developments enabled the large-scale movement of goods – and the labour force. Centralising workplace location was considered greatly beneficial to employers, allowing them to enact control and monitoring of work (Marglin, 1974). By the mid-19th century around half of the population in Britain, for example, lived in urban areas (Williamson, 2000). From the mid-19th century there was also a considerable growth in skilled service work, for example, clerks, who worked in offices in urban centres. Further centralisation and growth in economic activity was driven by large-scale manufacturing in the late 19th and early 20th centuries, epitomised by the concepts of Taylorism (Taylor, 1967) and Fordism. Taylorism and Fordism extended the division of labour, and displaced skilled craft-based workers for mass production by low-skilled employees working on an assembly line (Figart, 2001). The institutional arrangements present in industry during the 20th century aided the spatial fixity of economic activity and the division of labour between home and work (Figart & Golden, 1998, 412).

There was, however, a significant shift towards flexible specialisation in manufacturing in the latter half of the 20th century, as industrialised countries found it increasingly difficult to compete with newly industrialising countries in the mass production of highly standardised goods (see Chapter 10). During this period, there was large-scale deindustrialisation in developed societies and a significant shift towards services, with the

latter increasing in its share of employment from around half of all workers in the mid-20th century to three-quarters by the end of the century
(O'Mahoney, 1999). The growth in the service sector had important implications for the nature and location of workplace. The latter half of the
20th century witnessed significant growth in offices in urban and suburban locations, while there was further automation in industry and movements of workplaces outside of urban centres to industrial parks. Office
environments themselves have continued to undergo significant change
including the move to open plan offices and the establishment of the so-
called factories of the service sector, call centres (Jenkins et al., 2010).

The digital age has led to further changes in the structures of paid
work characterised by greater flexibility and diversity in workplace location. The workplace has extended beyond traditional office-style settings, to the home, business incubators, co-working spaces, and a range
of public spaces. For employers, locating workers in one place nevertheless continues to offer certain advantages, providing agglomeration
benefits, including labour market pooling and knowledge spill-overs,
and enabling employers to benefit from economies of scale (Zhu, 2013,
2441). However, there is increasing acknowledgment of the benefits of
flexibility and diversity in workplace location, both from the employer
perspective, e.g. cost reduction (Wheatley, 2012a), and from that of the
worker, e.g. job satisfaction, greater flexibility (Vartiainen & Hyrkkänen, 2010; Wheatley, 2017).

Contemporary Workplaces in Developed Societies

As noted, structural changes in the economies of developed societies,
including the dominant share of services, have driven a growing polarisation in the labour market. Rising demand for workers at opposite
ends of the labour market has been, in part, driven by the growth in
'creative' highly skilled occupations, which, in turn, increases demand
for non-creative workers in support roles (Shutters et al., 2016) as well
as demand for lower skilled services, e.g. cleaning, gardening, caring.
The net result is a reduction in intermediate-skill level jobs referred to
in discourse as a 'hollowing out of the middle' (Wilson et al., 2016).
Concurrent with these labour market developments, a raft of work-life
balance and family-friendly policies targeting greater flexibility in paid
work have driven a rise in non-standard employment contracts and
flexible working (Lewis & Plomien, 2009). Meanwhile, the digital age
has created new ways of working and resulted in changes to existing
work practices (Green, 2017; Hislop & Axtell, 2009). There has been a
growth in homeworking, mobile working and teleworking. Teleworking,
or telecommuting, is often conflated with homeworking, but is broader
in definition, referring to remote paid work, usually involving the use of
information and communications technologies (ICTs) which takes place
outside of the normal or main workplace, and is alternatively referred

to as distributed work (Pyöriä, 2011; Sullivan, 2003, 159). Common among growth areas of work outside of the traditional place of work is the use of ICTs, including cloud computing, wireless technologies and smartphones which offer 24/7 connectivity and both virtual and location-independent working.

These changes in many developed economies have driven a growth in non-standard forms of work. Table 8.1 summarises this growth in the UK context, drawing on data from the UK Labour Force Survey. It shows growth in a range of forms of non-standard 'precarious' or 'contingent' work (Kalleberg, 2009, 2), including, in particular, growth in part-time self-employment which to some degree captures the growth in the gig economy. The gig economy or gig work refers to on-demand labour or 'piecework' (Friedman, 2014; Lehdonvirta, 2018) which is provided by workers classed as independent contractors or consultants and is usually facilitated by online and smartphone platforms (NESTA, 2014; Srnicek, 2017). It includes work in transportation, cleaning and some forms of clerical work and work in ICTs (De Stefano, 2016, 471). Estimates suggest that somewhere between 10% and 18% of workers in the Netherlands, Sweden, UK and US report working in the gig economy (Friedman, 2014; Huws & Joyce, 2016a, 2016b, 2016c, cited in Howcroft & Bergvall-Kåreborn, 2018). Estimates are difficult, however, given that workers can be registered with a number of different companies in the same month, week or even day (De Stefano, 2016, 472). Table 8.1 also shows significant growth in zero hours contracts. Zero hours contracts are a form of employment that involves non-guaranteed hours; i.e. they provide no guarantee of work or pay from week to week. These contracts are controversial as they also provide fewer rights to employees, including over sickness and holiday pay (Mandl, 2015).

Table 8.1 Non-standard and Contingent Workers in the UK

Type of employment	2008 (%)	2013 (%)	2017 (%)	Change 2008–2017
Part-time employee	21.8	22.6	21.8	0.0
Self-employed full-time	9.9	10.2	10.6	+0.7
Self-employed part-time	3.1	4.0	4.4	+1.3
Zero hours	0.5	1.9	2.8	+2.3
Temporary (all, also includes 'other' category)	4.5	5.3	4.9	+0.4
Fixed-period	2.0	2.3	2.0	0.0
Agency	0.8	1.0	0.9	+0.1
Casual	1.0	1.1	1.0	0.0
Seasonal	0.3	0.3	0.3	0.0

Source: UK Labour Force Survey 2008, 2013 and 2017.

Notes: Figures are percentages of total workforce. Figures are four-quarter averages, derived from author's own calculations.

The growth in self-employment, in particular, has been the focus of a significant amount of interest from policymakers and academics. In itself it is evidence of the polarisation present in the labour market, with expansion recorded among highly skilled and those in lower skilled occupations (Wheatley, 2018; Wilson et al., 2016). From the employer perspective the use of contingent workers reflects a lower risk than taking on employees, enabling the workforce to be increased and reduced in size with relative ease with changes in demand, something that has been particularly attractive to businesses since the 2007–2009 global economic crisis (Davies, 2012). The conditions of work present in these new forms of 'employment' vary significantly with some workers, more often the highly skilled, benefiting from the high levels of flexibility offered (Osnowitz & Henson, 2016, 348). Gig work in particular has been argued as offering workers the opportunity to combine work with the rest of their lives with a greater degree of choice, including over workplace location, with associated benefits in the form of higher levels of productivity and work-life balance (Lehdonvirta, 2018, 13). However, this may be a privilege enjoyed by some workers while others encounter high degrees of uncertainty and precarity in work (Green, 2011). Employers, meanwhile, benefit from reductions in transaction/ fixed costs (Aloisi, 2016, 654). Employers may also benefit from a more diverse talent base that may have been difficult to access if more standard workplace requirements were in place, e.g. due to workers preferences, caring responsibilities or a disability.

Despite the changes highlighted, the spaces and places in which we work continue to be dominated by the more general patterns observed in paid work. The majority of work remains performed by employees for employers, and, in turn, the majority of this work is performed in more standard workplace locations. UK estimates from the *Understanding Society* survey suggest around 85% of the workforce can be classed as employees, and that four-fifths of these employees work in offices, factories, retail outlets and other more standard and relatively static workplace locations (Wheatley, 2018). This, notwithstanding the greater fluidity present in paid work, results in greater diversity in the spaces and places we work, as well as an increasing blurring of the temporal and spatial boundaries between work and non-work (Bulger et al., 2007). The boundaryless nature of work, which enables many to work at all times and in any location, creates significant opportunities to tailor working routines to worker preferences and/or business need (Glavin & Schieman, 2012; Ituma & Simpson, 2010). However, it also heightens difficulties in creating a separation between work and the rest of our lives (Wheatley, 2017). Highly flexible forms of work may also create significant peaks and troughs of work with intense schedules and work involving multiple clients, employers (or intermediaries in the case of gig work) or distinct jobs which occur simultaneously and may involve multiple workplaces. Although diverse by their nature, some highly flexible forms of work create significant demands on workers who are required to move between job locations or indeed move as part of a task in the case of jobs involving, for example, the delivery of goods. This can render workplace location highly uncertain and, in some cases, 'sticky' in the short term (Bergman & Gustafson, 2008, 192; Graham & Woodcock, 2018). Health and safety concerns are also present, associated with both the potential for over-work among those classed as independent contractors, mental health and depression among those working alone (King, 2017), and physical dangers of working on the move and making frequent movements for work.

Working at Home

Changes in the labour market in recent decades have driven an increase in the incidence of homeworking, in particular in the form of home-based teleworking, i.e. working at home with the use of mobile technologies. Homeworking takes two main forms: (1) industrial homeworking, and (2) home-based teleworking. Industrial homeworking, for example, craft workers whose shop is also their residence, is a form of work which has been present for millennia. Home-based teleworking is a more recent phenomenon. A sub-category of teleworking, it captures homeworking facilitated by ICTs among salaried, contract and self-employed workers, and also includes *ad hoc* homework among workers whose main workplace is in a standard employer premise, e.g. office in an urban location (Mokhtarian et al., 2004). While many homeworkers may not use advanced ICTs (Sullivan, 2003, 160), use of ICTs is now common among homeworkers in the majority of occupations (Green, 2017). Patterns reflect both homeworking among employees, but also perhaps more significantly the growth in e-lancing and gig work. Recent homeworking statistics indicate incidence among employees as remaining relatively low at around 2–3%; however, a much greater proportion of the self-employed, around one-third, report their home as their primary workplace (Wheatley, 2018). It should also be noted that growth in this form of work is found among those whose main workplace is relatively static and report working at home flexibly for one or two days per week or on an *ad hoc* or occasional basis, than it is among those working at home on a full-time basis. UK statistics suggest around 7.4% of employees whose main workplace is an employer premises report working at home on an occasional or *ad hoc* basis (Wheatley, 2017, 116).

Studies of homeworkers suggest a number of benefits including higher levels of reported satisfaction with work and life overall (Morganson et al., 2010; Wheatley, 2012b, 2017), although experiences of homeworking differ between highly skilled employees who generally report good job quality, and part-time and self-employed homeworkers, more often women, some of whom report lower quality jobs (Wheatley, 2018). Homeworking can result in a lengthening of the working day and associated higher levels of unpaid overtime and reduced leisure time, as it blurs the boundaries between work and non-work (Nätti et al., 2011). It may be the product of cost reduction exercises among employers, rather than evidencing an attempt to improve the job quality and work-life balance of workers. Employers may also engage in high levels of monitoring of homeworkers as they have concerns over the misuse of company time (Wight & Raley, 2009), which can act as a driver of the aforementioned long working hours and result in increased work-related stress and invasion of privacy, countering potential work-life balance benefits (Russell et al., 2009, 89). Absence from the workplace can also have negative career implications (e.g. reduced access to training) due to lack of face-to-face contact, and result in the loss of professional and social networks, potentially resulting in isolation (Tietze et al., 2009).

Working on the Move and in Multiple Locations

Mobile working, which is alternatively termed multi-location working or mobile teleworking (Hislop & Axtell, 2009, 74), takes a number of forms from work performed on the move, to working at client sites, and working in a wide range of remote locations such as coffee shops, airports and other public spaces. By its nature this form of work often involves workers having no main workplace, although many workers do still report into a base at an employer premises (although with differing levels of frequency). Mobile working is the main form of paid work for a growing minority of workers. It is, perhaps, more often an increasingly common activity among many workers who work at an employer/ business premises the majority of the time, and undertake mobile work on a less regular, and in some cases more informal, basis. Working in multiple locations provides benefits to workers in the form of greater flexibility and discretion over work, and job satisfaction derived from completing tasks in secondary workplaces, e.g. client offices, and interacting with different colleagues/ clients (Vartiainen & Hyrkkänen, 2010, 133). More mobile and satellite forms of work also enable organisations to reduce costs, for example, through reducing the need for capital investment in workspaces and allowing the use of hot-desking/ agile working and similar schemes (Wheatley, 2012a).

While mobility in paid work has increased considerably, including incidence of business travel, it is also argued that this has driven a growth in the intensity of paid work (Gustafsen, 2014, 73). A large proportion of workers, estimated in one study as between 50 and 60% (Holley, 2008), report working during business travel, in part as a method of managing workload. Mobile workers engage in a wide range of tasks when on the move, from reading, writing reports and communicating via email and phone (Koroma et al., 2014, 149). Many of these tasks involve the use of ICTs. Recent research, further, emphasises that the nature of work tasks heavily impacts on the ability of an individual to work productively on the move or remotely. Certain tasks provide a better fit than others, while it has been suggested that differences both at the individual level and between workplace teams may have a considerable influence over the ability to perform certain tasks (Boell et al., 2016, 125–126). Further potential drawbacks faced by mobile workers include a lack of consistent social contact (especially among those in the most mobile roles), workers having to continually adapt to different workplace environments, technology failures impacting the short-term ability to work, and the potential for data and property loss/ theft when working in remote and public spaces (Hislop & Axtell, 2009, 73; Vartiainen & Hyrkkänen, 2010, 133).

Finally, work which by its nature involves travel has also undergone notable change in recent years. Much of this work is not new in its core function, for example, taxi driving and delivery of goods. However, the nature of this work has been altered dramatically by the development of online and smartphone platforms (Srnicek, 2017). This is especially the case in urban areas, where new forms of app-driven taxi and delivery services have developed and witnessed significant growth in demand. Consistent with other forms of gig working these forms of work provide a number of benefits to workers including flexibility over the timing of work (Howcroft & Bergvall-Kåreborn, 2018; Osnowitz & Henson, 2016, 348). They also present a range of challenges for workers, however, including potentially long, intense and unsociable working hours, (short-term) uncertainty over patterns of work, (relatively) low pay, work-related stress, and health and safety concerns (Di Stefano, 2016; Scholtz, 2016; Srnicek, 2017).

Co-Working Spaces

The growth in entrepreneurial and self-managed work has created demand for shared or co-working spaces. Co-working spaces provide small firms, start-ups and freelancers with a location to centre their business activity for a pay-for-use fee which is more flexible than a traditional rental agreement for an office space (Spinuzzi, 2012). They provide a space which is neither a business premise in the traditional sense or a home office. Co-working spaces are designed to encourage collaboration, creativity, idea sharing, networking, socialising and the generation of business opportunities (Fuzi, 2015, 462). Considerable growth has been recorded in these workplaces. In 2013 it was estimated around half a million individuals made use of around 2,000 co-working spaces worldwide (Johns & Gratton, 2013). By 2017, estimates for the USA alone suggested, in the region of half a million individuals make use of around 4,000 co-working spaces (Emergent Research, 2018, cited by Small Business Labs, 2018). Currently co-working spaces are more common in creative service clusters in urban areas, with many located outside of the city centre in order to avoid high accommodation costs (Mariotti et al., 2017), but examples have also been recorded in more sparsely populated and rural areas (Fuzi, 2015).

Co-working spaces offer the potential to revitalise urban areas through the creation of innovative services, e.g. events, and the wider economic impact of the local working community (Mariotti et al., 2017, 60). Smaller co-working spaces may offer fairly simple office-style accommodation. Larger co-working spaces, however, often provide a wider range of facilities including spaces to meet, socialise and relax, e.g. gardens, cafes/ restaurants and conference spaces (Mariotti et al., 2017, 58). Co-working spaces can generate agglomeration and networking benefits among micro-entrepreneurs and freelance workers (Bouncken & Reuschl, 2018; Fuzi, 2015), as well as avoiding some of the problems, including isolation, associated with a number of other contemporary flexible modes of work including home-based teleworking (Fuzi, 2015, 467; King, 2017). Aside from the fee paid for use, some barriers and concerns have been identified with co-working spaces including self-exploitation among entrepreneurs, loss of privacy, knowledge leakage, competition between micro-entrepreneurs/freelancers acting as a barrier to some of the benefits of co-working spaces and the potential negative impacts of opportunistic behaviour, e.g. the misuse of knowledge or contacts, and the theft of both physical and intellectual property (Bouncken & Reuschl, 2018, 331).

Makers-Spaces

Makers-spaces are an alternative type of shared working space specifically associated with the manufacture of goods by makers, i.e. artisan craft makers, tinkerers and digital-era inventors (Dougherty, 2012). Fabrication laboratories (Fab Labs) and hackerspaces are common forms with the prior involving the use of flexible computer-controlled tools, while the latter usually involves individuals sharing their interest in programming and/ or tinkering with technology in a community-funded and -managed collective space (Rosa et al., 2017). These workspaces share a number of benefits and problems common with co-working spaces. They offer particular benefits to makers, through providing the necessary infrastructure to design, innovate and manufacture goods, without the cost, conservatism and constraining bureaucracy which is often present in a large-scale manufacturing business (Dougherty, 2012). In many cases the capital investment may be relatively low-cost in itself, e.g. basic 3D printing equipment, reflecting that many makers may not display preferences towards large-scale commercial gain from their endeavour. Benefits can nevertheless be realised in the local economy as makers disseminate innovations in design and production knowledge. Makers-spaces are argued as offering a number of wider economic benefits through adding to the entrepreneurial stock, strengthening the supply chain and aiding the development of emergent industries (Doussard et al., 2018).

Impacts of Working Outside of the Workplace

Working in non-standard locations does present a number of difficulties for workers. They can suffer from isolation resulting from working alone (King, 2017; Tietze, 2009; Vartiainen & Hyrkkänen, 2010, 133). Interactions with clients and less frequent interaction with colleagues (including using virtual methods) can, though, act to mediate these negative impacts (Hislop & Axtell, 2011, 48). Mobile workers and those using co-working spaces also have to be highly adaptable to the different workplace environments in which they find themselves (Fuzi, 2015; Hislop & Axtell, 2009, 73). Lack of centralisation of workplace and physical proximity between workers, and with their employer, can reduce coherency and results in some difficulties in effectively communicating and monitoring job activity. There are a range of digital methods for conducting these activities. However, they suffer from a number of limitations. For example, employers may use methods of technical control, e.g. software used to monitor and evaluate workers by automatically recording and producing data on productivity and task completion (Callaghan & Thompson, 2001). These systems, which can be applied to workers in most non-standard workplaces, emphasise target and task completion and promote discretionary effort from the worker. However, these systems can result in micro-management of workers generating high intensity and stressful working conditions. These systems can also be exploited, for example, a worker could simply ask others to log in to monitoring systems, or may engage in occasionally logging activity when actually not working. These potential issues may limit buy-in from some employers, due to concerns of misuse of company time (Wight & Raley, 2009), but also result in greater efforts to employ Taylorist 'low discretion' work organisation focusing on monitoring and surveillance mechanisms, and potentially limiting the flexibility of workplace (Choi et al., 2008). However, this perpetuates higher levels of work intensity being encountered by workers.

The Spatial Separation of Home and Work

Alongside changes in the structures of paid work, developments in transportation networks during the 20th century and the growing preferences of households to locate outside of employment centres in suburbs and rural hinterlands acted as a further driver of the large-scale separation witnessed between home and work and the development of regular movements for work, i.e. the commute (Pooley et al., 2005). Spatial divisions between home and work expanded as a result of two major technological shifts in transport, led by significant improvements in both public and private transport networks and infrastructure. These began, in the 19th century, with the development of rail and bus services to serve those with sufficient income (Pooley & Turnbull, 2000; Pooley et al., 2005). By the 1930s the previous trend of walking to work had been largely replaced by the use of buses and the bicycle. For example, in the UK while in the 1890s 59% of all journeys to work were undertaken on foot, this had decreased to just 8% by the 1990s (Pooley et al., 2005). Train use during this period remained relatively constant, and aided easier commuting as distances between work and home increased (Lindsay, 2003, 141). Then in the 1960s the use of the private motor car became the most prominent method of transport to work. More than 40% of individuals were using this method of travel by the 1970s (Pooley & Turnbull, 1999, 287). The 20th century witnessed a major shift towards use of the car, which has since dominated as the primary form of transport for commuting and leisure purposes (Eriksson et al., 2013). By the end of the 20th century not only was car ownership and use the norm, but there had been a significant growth in the number of households with two or more cars, which increased, for example, in the UK from 7% in 1970 to 28% by 2000 (Lindsay, 2003, 141).

Household decision-making has also played a significant role in these trends. Historically, decisions over residential location were driven by the primary earner, often male, and the remaining members of the household would simply follow (Green, 2004). However, as growth in dual earning and dual career households has changed the structure of the labour market, it has also led to revisions in the relationship between workplace and residential location. In many cases workers trade-off the commute with migration, at least during certain stages of their careers. Workers may consider their current employment as a more temporary position or may simply wish to avoid the costs and other challenges involved in engaging in residential movements. Residential location is determined not only by the working routines of partners within a household, but also by a range of other factors including the housing market (and wider cost of living), proximity to family and friends, and local schools (Hardill & Green, 2003, 220). The growth in households where both partners pursue careers creates additional pressures as workplace locations may be geographically dispersed, especially where partners pursue more specialised occupations which may

Dual earner household is a term that captures households in which both partners engage in paid employment. Dual career households are a sub-set of dual earner households where both partners are employed in managerial, professional or associate professional occupations (Hughes, 2013; Wheatley, 2012a).

necessarily mean more distant opportunities and more frequent job moves (Lindsay, 2003, 141). Partners may choose to compromise and locate around transport nodes somewhere between each other's workplace locations; however, this can result in lengthier commutes for both partners (Pooley & Turnbull, 2000, 22). In some cases where migration is not possible or preferred, workers may engage in long-distance commutes, including those occurring on a weekly or other basis, which can themselves involve dual location living arrangements (Sandow, 2014; Sandow & Westin, 2010). Despite the diversity present in the nature of contemporary movements for work, it should be noted that for a majority of workers the commute remains a frequent, usually daily, activity over a relatively short time-distance (Wheatley, 2012a). And while a range of virtual methods of conducting economic activity can be used to circumvent physical movements, the global nature of many businesses also renders domestic and international mobility for business travel an increasing feature of many worker's lives (Hislop & Axtell, 2009; Jeong et al., 2013). This creates demand for international travel, including air travel, and results in its own set of benefits and difficulties for workers engaged in these activities (see Bergström-Casinowsky, 2013; Wheatley & Bickerton, 2016).

The digitisation of paid work has influenced patterns of residential location, as it has been widely evidenced that those engaging in teleworking and other more mobile forms of work tend to report lengthier distances between their home and main workplace (Mokhtarian et al., 2004). At the same time the growth in service employment and ICT developments have expanded the potential for homeworking (Moos & Skaburskis, 2007), which intrinsically allows workers to avoid the regular commute entirely (Wheatley, 2012a). It nevertheless has been suggested that urban (and suburban within short commuting time-distance) residential locations remain preferred by some mobile and gig workers, as these locations provide a larger number of employment and networking opportunities (Fenwick, 2006). Low incomes and job insecurity, however, could act as primary drivers for habitation in less prosperous urban areas among some of these workers (Moos & Skaburskis, 2007, 1782), as can the geographical stickiness of some gig working jobs, e.g. delivery driving (Graham & Woodcock, 2018). Homeworking in most cases by its nature is less dependent on proximity to specific locations, and so homeworkers are more likely to reside in rural and suburban locations as they are able to benefit from the quality of life benefits available in these locations (Shields & Wheatley Price, 2005, 533). However, some highly skilled homeworkers may locate in urban areas where housing and other living costs are higher, due to both potential client bases and the attraction offered by more abundant leisure amenities (Moos & Skaburskis, 2007). Urban centres retain a strong pull with respect to both employment and broader socio-economic opportunities.

The Future of Workplaces and Spaces

Despite all of the changes in paid work since the latter part of the 20th century, as already noted the majority of workers remain located in (relatively) fixed workplaces and spaces in urban economic centres. A number of high-profile contributions from so-called futurists had suggested an end to the traditional city resulting from progress in ICTs eliminating demand for face-to-face communication (see Zhu, 2013, 2441); however, this has not been realised. It is likely that we will witness a continued growth in more flexible forms of work, associated with developments in ICTs, and an associated growth in flexibility in workplace location. Both the effects of technological developments and the demands of workers and employers have increased, and are likely to continue to increase, the contractual, temporal and spatial flexibility of paid work. For many workers this may continue to involve completing work at home, on the move and in remote workplaces, while still retaining a work hub in some form from which they base their activities, whether it be an employer/ business premises or co-working space, even if this is visited relatively less frequently. There remains demand from employers, clients and workers for employment centres and face-to-face interaction at work (Aguilera, 2008). While certain occupations and industries may lend themselves to full-time remote working, it is highly unlikely that there will be any large-scale shift in overall work patterns in developed societies towards full-time remote forms of working, at least in the near future. There have been a number of high-profile examples among large employers of movements away from expansive use of teleworking, remote working and working in other non-standard locations. For example, in recent years, both Google and Facebook have created large workplaces with a focus on agglomeration through pooling and sharing ideas including the benefits derived from informal corridor and watercooler discussions (Waber et al., 2014). These new workspaces provide high levels of flexibility in the timing and ways in which work is conducted, but importantly with a spatially fixed workplace location.

The growth in online and platform-based businesses may strengthen the polarisation present in the labour market, while also having a dual impact on the geography of paid work. On the one hand it creates greater scope for mobile working and working in non-standard locations. For example, e-lancers completing contract work at home or at client locations. On the other hand, equally the growth in online shopping, for example, creates demand for large warehousing facilities which centre employment activity in specific locations while increasing demand for occupations associated with the movement and delivery of goods. In turn, the growth of online businesses, alongside high rental costs, is undoubtedly impacting the high street within many towns and cities, and extending to out-of-town retail shopping centres and malls, which are witnessing reductions in the number of business units used for retail purposes (Millington & Ntounis, 2017). This has a knock-on effect for certain groups of workers, as there is a reduction in demand for workers in retail and other occupations in urban retail locations, and a concurrent increase in demand in industrial parks. For the growing portion of workers engaged in gig work and other highly flexible forms of work, workplace is likely to remain highly fluid. For many of these workers workplace is a constantly changing variable, or one that at least undergoes periods of change and uncertainty. The fast-moving nature of self-employment, and recent trends of growth in forms of micro-entrepreneurship and free/ e-lancing, is likely to increase the demand for, and use of, shared working spaces (Bouncken & Reuschl, 2018). Demand is likely to be felt in urban centres and also in rural locations where agglomeration benefits may be particularly pronounced (Fuzi, 2015).

There will also remain demand for services which are difficult to automate/digitise and which render non-standard or virtual workplaces impractical. For example, the growing polarisation of the labour market and growth of households in which both partners work full-time in jobs often involving long working hours and time spent in work-related travel has resulted in a growth in demand for marketised household services, e.g. cleaning, gardening and caring (Wheatley & Wu, 2014). Changing demographics are also responsible for some of this demand, e.g. ageing populations creating demand for care services. These marketised services take place in residential areas and often within the household, in the majority of cases involving workers travelling to multiple locations on a daily basis to complete these tasks for multiple clients, but in a smaller proportion of cases involves live-in staff who work within the home. This service employment is often low paid, and the mobility required in these roles can result in intense schedules and work-life conflict.

The relationship between workplace and residential location is likely to remain relatively consistent with current observations, in part as a result of the slow-changing nature of the housing market (and stock). Patterns of commuting remain under scrutiny from government and international bodies. The commute has a number of negative economic, environmental and well-being impacts which are well documented and evidenced (Pooley et al., 2005; Sweet, 2014; Wheatley, 2012a). Governments have focused on attempts to reduce the reliance on the car as a method of transport to work. However, the capacity (and image) of public transport networks limits their ability to reduce the reliance on the car. In addition, commutes often form part of multi-activity journeys involving other activities, e.g. the school-run, which make it particularly challenging to reduce car use (Pooley et al., 2005, 136; Wheatley, 2013, 2014). Growth in work performed outside of traditional workplaces, and use of virtual methods of contact, may facilitate reductions in car use. In the latter case changes are likely to continue to be limited, however, by preferences of both employers and workers for face-to-face contact (Aguilera, 2008). Investment in faster and more reliable methods of public transport, including high-speed rail, could reduce reliance on the car and effectively open up larger labour market areas to workers, although cost and availability may limit the number of workers who benefit from these developments.

The workplace is an increasingly fluid and diverse concept with respect to the lived experiences of many workers, and one which reflects a range of opportunities as well as challenges. The locations in which we work are changing, with growth observed in homeworking, mobile working, shared spaces and households reporting ever more complex and diverse relationships between workplace and residential location. However, it remains the case for a majority of workers that workplace follows a relatively traditional form, involving work being performed at an employer/ business premises which is commuted to on a regular basis, at least for the majority of the time.

References

Aguiléra, A. (2008). Business travel and mobile workers. *Transportation Research Part A: Policy and Practice*, 42(8), 1109–1116.

Aloisi, A. (2016). Commoditized workers: Case study research on labor law issues arising from a set of on-demand/gig economy platforms. *Comparative Labor Law and Policy Journal*, 37(3), 653–690.

Bergström-Casinowsky, G. (2013). Working life on the move, domestic life at standstill? Work-related travel and responsibility for home and family. *Gender, Work and Organisation*, 20(3), 311–326.

Bienefeld, M. A. (1972). *Working hours in British Industry*. London: Weidenfeld and Nicolson.

Boell, S., Cecez-Kecmanovic, D. and Campbell, J. (2016). Telework paradoxes and practices: The importance of the nature of work. *New Technology, Work and Employment*, 31(2), 114–131.

Bouncken, R. and Reuschl, A. (2018). Co-working-spaces: How a phenomenon of the sharing economy builds a novel trend for the workplace and for entrepreneurship. *Review of Managerial Science*, 12(1), 317–334.

Bulger, C., Matthews, R. and Hoffman, M. (2007). Work and personal life boundary management: Boundary strength, work/personal life balance, and the segmentation-integration continuum. *Journal of Occupational Health Psychology*, 12(4), 365–375.

Carré, F. and Heintz, J. (2013). Employment change and economic vulnerability in the US. In, Parker, S. (ed.), *The squeezed middle: The pressure on ordinary workers in America and Britain*. Bristol: Policy Press, 61–72.

Choi, S., Leiter, J. and Tomaskovic-Devey, D. (2008). Contingent autonomy technology, bureaucracy, and relative power in the labor process. *Work and Occupations*, 35(4), 422–455.

Davies, G. (2012). Unemployment drops to 2.51m, the lowest level for a year. *Chartered Institute of Personnel and Development (CIPD)*. Available at: http://www.cipd.co.uk/pm/peoplemanagement/b/weblog/archive/2012/11/14/unemployment-drops-to-2-51m-the-lowest-level-for-a-year-2012-11.aspx.

De Stefano, V. (2016). The rise of the just-in-time workforce: On-demand work, crowdwork, and labor protection in the gig-economy. *Comparative Labor Law & Policy*, 37, 471–504.

Dougherty, D. (2012). The maker movement. *Innovations*, 7(3), 11–14.

Doussard, M., Schrock, G., Wolf-Powers, L., Eisenburger, M. and Marotta, S. (2018). Manufacturing without the firm: Challenges for the maker movement in three U.S. cities. *Environment and Planning A*, 50(3), 651–670.

Eriksson, L., Friman, M. and Gärling, T. (2013). Perceived attributes of bus and car mediating satisfaction with the work commute. *Transportation Research Part A: Policy and Practice*, 47, 87–96.

Fenwick, T. (2006). Contradictions in portfolio careers: Work design and client relations. *Career Development International*, 11(1), 66–79.

Figart, D. (2001). Wage-setting under Fordism: The rise of job evaluation and the ideology of equal pay. *Review of Political Economy*, 13(4), 405–425.

Friedman, G. (2014). Workers without employers: Shadow corporations and the rise of the gig economy. *Review of Keynesian Economics*, 4(1), 171–188.

Fuzi, A. (2015). Co-working spaces for promoting entrepreneurship in sparse regions: The case of South Wales. *Regional Studies, Regional Science*, 2(1), 462–463.

Glavin, P. and Schieman, S. (2012). Work–family role blurring and work–family conflict: The moderating influence of job resources and job demands. *Work and Occupations*, 39(1), 71–98.

Graham, M. and Woodcock, J. (2018). Towards a fairer platform economy: Introducing the fairwork foundation. *Alternate Routes*, 29, 242–253.

Green, A. (2004). Is relocation redundant? Observations on the changing nature and impacts of employment-related geographical mobility in the UK. *Regional Studies*, 38(6), 629–641.

Green, A. (2017). Implications of technological change and austerity for employability in urban labour markets. *Urban Studies*, 54(7), 1638–1654.

Green, F. (2011). Unpacking the misery multiplier: How employability modifies the impacts of unemployment and job insecurity on life satisfaction and mental health. *Journal of Health Economics*, 30(2), 265–276.

Gustafson, P. (2014). Business travel from the traveller's perspective: Stress, stimulation and normalization. *Mobilities*, 9(1), 63–83.

Hislop, D. and Axtell, C. (2009). To infinity and beyond? Workspace and the multi-location worker. *New Technology, Work and Employment*, 24(1), 60–75.

Hislop, D. and Axtell, C. (2011). Mobile phones during work and non-work time: A case study of mobile, non-managerial workers. *Information and Organisation*, 21(1), 41–56.

Holley, D., Jain, J. and Lyons, G. (2008). Understanding business travel time and its place in the working day. *Time & Society*, 17(1), 27–46.

Horrell, S. and Humphries, J. (1995). Women's labour force participation and the transition to the male breadwinner family, 1790–1865. *Economic History Review*, 48(1), 89–117.

Howcroft, D. and Bergvall-Kåreborn, B. (2018). A typology of crowdwork platforms. *Work, Employment and Society*, 33(1), 21–38.

Hughes, J. L. (2013). Persisting problems with operationalizing dual-career couples: A proposal to use the term dual-income couples. *Marriage and Family Review*, 49(8), 694–716.

Huws, U. and Joyce, S. (2016a). Crowd working survey: New estimate of the size of Dutch 'Gig Economy'. *FEPS*. Available at: http://www.feps-europe.eu/assets/778d57d9-4e48-45f0-b8f8-189da359dc2b/crowd-working-survey-netherlands-finalpdf.pdf.

Huws, U. and Joyce, S. (2016b). Crowd working survey: Size of Sweden's 'Gig Economy' revealed for the first time. *FEPS*. Available at: http://www.feps-europe.eu/assets/3f853cec-1358-4fb4-9552-274b55e05ecf/crowd-working-survey-swedenpdf.pdf.

Huws, U. and Joyce, S. (2016c). Crowd working survey: Size of the UK's 'Gig Economy' revealed for the first time. *FEPS*. Available at: http://www.feps-europe.eu/assets/a82bcd12-fb97-43a6-9346-24242695a183/crowd-working-surveypdf.pdf.

Ituma, A. and Simpson, R. (2009). The boundaryless' career and career boundaries: Applying an institutionalist perspective to ICT workers in the context of Nigeria. *Human Relations*, 62(5), 727–761.

Jenkins, S., Delbridge, R. and Roberts, A. (2010). Emotional management in a mass customised call centre: Examining skill and knowledgeability in interactive service work. *Work, Employment and Society*, 24(3), 546–564.

Jeong, Y.-J., Zvonkovic, A., Sano, Y. and Acock, A. (2013). The occurrence and frequency of overnight job travel in the USA. *Work, Employment and Society*, 27(1), 138–152.

Johns, T. and Gratton, L. (2013). The third wave of virtual work. *Harvard Business Review*, 91(1), 66–73.

Kalleberg, A. (2009). Precarious work, insecure workers: Employment relations in transition. *American Sociological Review*, 74(1), 1–22.

King, S. (2017). Co-working is not about workspace — It's about feeling less lonely. *Harvard Business Review*. Available at: https://hbr.org/2017/12/coworking-is-not-about-workspace-its-about-feeling-less-lonely.

Koroma, J., Hyrkkänen, U. and Vartiainen, M. (2014). Looking for people, places and connections: Hindrances when working in multiple locations: A review. *New Technology, Work and Employment*, 29(2), 139–159.

Lehdonvirta, V. (2018). Flexibility in the gig economy: Managing time on three online piecework platforms. *New Technology, Work and Employment*, 33(1), 13–29.

Lewis, J. and Plomien, A. (2009). 'Flexicurity' as a policy strategy: The implications for gender equality. *Economy and Society*, 38(3), 433–459.

Lindsay, C. (2003). A century of labour market change: 1900 to 2000. *Labour Market Trends*, 133–144.

Mandl, I., Curtarelli, M., Riso, S., Vargas, O. and Gerogiannis, E. (2015). *New Forms of Employment in Europe*. Dublin: Eurofound.

Marglin, S. (1974). What do bosses do? The origins and functions of hierarchy in capitalist production. *Review of Radical Political Economics*, 6(2), 60–112.

Mariotti, I., Pacchi, C. and Di Vita, S. (2017). Co-working spaces in Milan: Location patterns and urban effects. *Journal of Urban Technology*, 24(3), 47–66.

Millington, S. and Ntounis, N. (2017). Repositioning the high street: Evidence and reflection from the UK. *Journal of Place Management and Development*, 10(4), 364–379.

Mokhtarian, P., Collantes, G. and Gertz, C. (2004). Telecommuting, residential location, and commute-distance traveled: Evidence from State of California employees. *Environment and Planning A*, 36(10), 1877–1897.

Moos, A. and Skaburskis, M. (2007). The characteristics and location of home workers in Montreal, Toronto and Vancouver. *Urban Studies*, 44(9), 1781–1808.

Morganson, V. J., Major, D. A., Oborn, K. L., Verive, J. M. and Heelan, M. P. (2010). Comparing telework locations and traditional work arrangements. *Journal of Managerial Psychology*, 25(6), 578–595.

Nätti, J., Tammelin, M., Anttila, T. and Ojala, S. (2011). Work at home and time use in Finland. *New Technology, Work and Employment*, 26(1), 68–77.

NESTA (2014). *Making Sense of the UK Collaborative Economy* [online]. Available at: http://www.nesta.org.uk/sites/default/files/making_sense_of_the_uk_collaborative_economy_14.pdf.

O'Mahoney, M. (1999). *Britain's Productivity Performance, 1950–1996: An International Perspective*. London, National Institute of Economic and Social Research.

Osnowitz, D. and Henson, K. (2016). Leveraging limits for contract professionals: Boundary work and control of working time. *Work and Occupations*, 43(3), 326–360.

Pooley, C. G. and Turnbull, J. (1999). The journey to work: A century of change. *Area*, 31(3), 281–292.

Pooley, C. G. and Turnbull, J. (2000). Modal choice and modal change: The journey to work in Britain since 1890. *Journal of Transport Geography*, 8(1), 11–24.

Pooley, C. G., Turnbull, J. and Adams, M. (2005). *A Mobile Century? Changes in Everyday Mobility in Britain in the Twentieth Century*. Hampshire: Ashgate Publishing.

Pyöriä, P. (2011). Managing telework: Risks, fears and rules. *Management Research Review*, 34(4), 386–399.

Rosa, P., Ferreti, F., Guimarães Pereira, Â., Panella, F. and Wanner, M. (2017). *Overview of the Maker Movement in the European Union*. EUR 28686 EN, Publications Office of the European Union, Luxembourg.

Russell, H., O'Connell, P. and McGinnity, F. (2009). The impact of flexible working arrangements on work–life conflict and work pressure in Ireland. *Gender, Work and Organisation*, 16(1), 73–97.

Sandow, E. and Westin, K. (2010). The persevering commuter – duration of long-distance commuting. *Transportation Research Part A: Policy and Practice*, 44(6), 433–445.

Sandow, E. (2014). Til work do us part: The social fallacy of long-distance commuting. *Urban Studies*, 51(3), 526–543.

Shields, M. and Wheatley Price, S. (2005). Exploring the economic and social determinants of psychological wellbeing and perceived social support in

England. *Journal of the Royal Statistical Society: Series A (Statistics in Society)*, 168(3), 513–537.

Scholz, T. (2016). *Uberworked and Underpaid*. Cambridge: Polity.

Shutters, S., Muneepeerakul, R. and Lobo, S., (2016). Constrained pathways to a creative urban economy. *Urban Studies*, 53(16), 3439–3454.

Small Business Labs (2018). U.S. Co-working forecast: 2018 to 2022 [online]. Available at: http://www.smallbizlabs.com/2018/01/us-co-working-forecast-2018-to-2022.html.

Spinuzzi, C. (2012). Working alone together co-working as emergent collaborative activity. *Journal of Business and Technical Communication*, 26(4), 399–411.

Srnicek, N. (2017). *Platform Capitalism*. London: Polity.

Sullivan, C. (2003). What's in a name? Definitions and conceptualisations of teleworking and homeworking. *New Technology, Work and Employment*, 18(3), 158–165.

Sweet, M. (2014). Traffic congestion's economic impacts: Evidence from US metropolitan regions. *Urban Studies*, 51(10), 2088–2110.

Taylor, F. (1967). *The Principles of Scientific Management*. London: Norton.

Tietze, S., Musson, G. and Scurry, T. (2009). Homebased work: A review of research into themes, directions and implications. *Personnel Review*, 38(6), 585–604.

Trade Union Congress (2014). *Only One in Every Forty Net Jobs Since the Recession is for a Full-Time Employee, Says TUC* [online]. Available at: https://www.tuc.org.uk/economic-issues/labour-market-and-economic-reports/only-one-every-forty-net-jobs-recession-full-time.

Vartiainen, M. and Hyrkkänen, U. (2010). Changing requirements and mental workload factors in mobile multi-location working. *New Technology, Work and Employment*, 25(2), 117–135.

Waber, B., Magnolfi, J. and Lindsay, G. (2014). Workspaces that move people. *Harvard Business Review*, 92(10), 68–77.

Wheatley, D. (2012a). Work-life balance, travel-to-work, and the dual career household. *Personnel Review*, 41(6), 813–831.

Wheatley, D. (2012b). Good to be home? Time-use and satisfaction levels among home-based teleworkers. *New Technology, Work and Employment*, 27(3), 224–241.

Wheatley, D. (2013). Location, vocation, location? Spatial entrapment among women in dual career households. *Gender, Work and Organisation*, 20(6), 720–736.

Wheatley, D. (2014). Travel-to-work and subjective well-being: A study of UK dual career households. *Journal of Transport Geography*, 39, 187–196.

Wheatley, D. (2017). Employee satisfaction and patterns in availability and use of flexible working arrangements. *Work, Employment and Society*, 31(4), 567–585.

Wheatley, D. (2018). *Workplace Location and the Quality of Work*. Paper presented at the Association for Heterodox Economics 20th Annual Conference.

Wheatley, D. and Bickerton, C. (2016). Time-use and well-being impacts of travel-to-work and travel-for-work. *New Technology, Work and Employment*, 31(3), 238–254.

Wight, V. and Raley, S. (2009). When home becomes work: Work and family time among workers at home. *Social Indicators Research*, 93(1), 197–202.

Wilson, R., Sofroniou, N., Beaven, R., May-Gillings, M., Perkins, S., Lee, M., Glover, P., Limmer, H. and Leach, A., on behalf of the UK Commission for Employment and Skills (2016). *Working Futures 2014–2020, Evidence Report 100.* London: UKCES.

Zhu, P. (2013). Telecommuting, household commute and location choice. *Urban Studies*, 50(12), 2441–2459.

9   Total Surveillance

Electronic Monitoring and Surveillance in the 21st Century

Peter Holland and Tse Leng Tham

Introduction

Monitoring and surveillance has been a fundamental aspect of the employee relationship for centuries. As work has evolved there have been ever more sophisticated ways developed to monitor and observe the workforce. From Jeremy Bentham and his panopticon through to F.W. Taylor's conception of scientific management and Henry Ford's architecture of mass production underpinned by time and motion studies, such strategies have been a part of the process and contested terrain of managing and controlling employment relationships for centuries. However, the advance of information technology and communication (ICT), as well as the migration of work into the cyberspace, has created a profound shift in the first two decades of the 21st century, not just the way we work, but also the way we are watched (Allen, Coopman, Hart, & Walker, 2007; Barnes, Holland, & Balnave, 2018; Lane, 2003). What this paradigm shift has also provided is a new and intense level of electronic monitoring and surveillance (EMS) of the work and the workforce both inside and outside the workplace. Such ability to monitor and observe has never been so pervasive or wide-ranging, to the extent that Gilliom and Monahan (2012) argue, managerial control has gone from supervision to 'Super Vision'. The nature and rise of EMS of employees (both inside and outside work) has emerged at such a rapid rate that it has left the law, ethics and the management of the employment relationship trailing in its wake in terms of understanding how such changes are impacting on our day-to-day working lives and how they should be managed (Ball, 2010; Barnes et al., 2018; Holland, Cooper, & Hecker, 2015). With D'Urso (2006), we argue that the significant and extreme level of EMS in the workplace requires exploration and investigation. This chapter therefore looks at the level, intensity, impact and effects of electronic monitoring and surveillance on work, the worker and the workplace and how, in a vacuum of legislation, we can manage these changes in the employment relationship.

Electronic Monitoring and Surveillance at Work: A New Frontier

A useful metaphor in understanding the supervisory role in the workplace is Foucault's (1977) adoption of Benthem's panopticon prison design, in which a central tower could view all cells. The key to the supervision or control was to get the prisoners to 'manage' themselves. As Danaher, Schirato and Webb (2000) note, Foucault argued that the effect of the panopticon was to self-discipline and manage those under surveillance who would perceive they were under constant observation and thus behave accordingly (Bauman & Lyon, 2013). However, whilst the metaphor of the panopticon has been used extensively in the discussion around monitoring and surveillance, we would argue that the depth and extent to which these electronic practices pervade the 21st-century workplace make such techniques and strategies effectively part a continuous approach to the supervision and surveillance of the workforce (Holland et al., 2015). This is because monitoring and surveillance through electronic means is now at a point where workers can be observed 24 hours a day, seven days a week, both inside or outside the workplace, be it on the internet, or through electronic cards or smart devices they carry and now microchip implants. From computer keystoke speed to your private internet conversations, all is within the grasp of your employer – if they choose to pursue it. These last sentences are as contentious as the issues of whether an employer would or should invade an employee's *privacy* or *trust*. Instead, we argue and emphasise that there is a need for (ethical) boundaries to be established around EMS to guide management. Whether, when or if the law in this area catches up, such issues are central to the contemporary employment relationship.

Electronic Monitoring and Surveillance and Trust

In interviews and conversations we have had with managers discussing and researching workplace EMS, we have asked why they do it: the most common response is – "because we can"! Implicit in this perspective is a pervading lack of trust within the employment relationship (Barnes et al., 2018; Holland et al., 2015; Zureik, 2003). However, with the rise of EMS, the level of intrusion has exponentially increased in its range and unrelenting intensity (Adler, 2001). The irony and paradox of this decision to increase monitoring and surveillance is in the fact that there has been an equally strong focus, particularly within the field of human resource management (HRM), on engaging and improving commitment of employees to the goals of the organisation (Boxall & Purcell, 2016). A key argument of the HRM literature is that trust in the employment relationship is a critical element that organisations need to foster in the workplace (Innocenti, Pilati, & Peluso,

2011; Nichols, Danford, & Tasiran, 2009). This is because trust is seen as the basis for quality relationships, cooperation and stability in the workplace (Gould-Williams, 2003; Holland, Cooper, & Sheehan, 2017; Searle et al., 2011). Therefore, in the workplace context, trust is a key element in understanding the quality of the employment relationship (Holland, Cooper, Pyman, & Teicher, 2012; Tzafrir, Harel, Baruch, & Dolan, 2004). The employment relationship is seen as a series of ongoing exchange relationships and in particular, unspecified obligations. Over time, such perceived obligations in the exchange relationship establish the structure of employment interaction. Trust allows and enables such interaction (and obligations) to develop and allows the employment relationship to function effectively (Blau, 1964; Boxall & Purcell, 2016).

From an HRM perspective, this helps us to understand interdependence and reciprocity in the employment relationship. It is also important in explaining how and why employees reciprocate the treatment they receive from management as the relationship unfolds, develops and is maintained (Farndale, Hope-Hailey, & Kelliher, 2011; Tyler, 2003). As Boxall and Purcell (2016) argue, managing the employment relationship means considering the underlying processes in which trust is a key dynamic. Trust (or lack thereof) is also being identified in the employee voice literature, illustrated by the growing amount of research on employee silence (Bryson, 2004; Donaghey, Cullinane, Dundon, & Wilkinson, 2014; Holland, Teicher, & Donghey, 2019), and what is termed 'deaf-ear', where the employer deliberately or subtly manages out employee voice (Pinder & Harlos, 2001). This lack of managerial response is a key issue at the level of trust and therefore of the (effectiveness of the) employment relationship (Holland et al., 2012, 2015).

Trust, in essence, is about the confidence that one party to the exchange relationship has that they will not have their vulnerabilities exploited by the other party (Korczynski, 2000). This explanation is appropriate when considering the levels of EMS available to management today. Research by Holland, Cooper and Hecker (2016) and Martin, Wellen and Grimmer (2016) found that as the level and intensity of EMS increased, the level of trust in the employment relationship by employees declined and incidences of counterproductive behaviours increased. Studies by the International Labour Organisation - World of Work (ILO) also indicate that high levels of monitoring and surveillance can have negative occupational health and safety consequences as they have been linked to stress-related illnesses and increased quit rates (ILO, 2007). What such research highlights is that such strategies can create deadly combinations of HRM policies and practices (Becker, Huselid, Pickus, & Spratt, 1997) where practices like EMS could undermine or actively work against other HRM policies developed to increase employee satisfaction, engagement, commitment and trust.

Electronic Monitoring and Surveillance and Employee Privacy

It is clear that the paradigm shift of work and surveillance into cyber-space has generated considerable debate over the concept of privacy for the employee (Determann & Sprague, 2011). In the midst of this paradigm shift, which is increasingly seen as part of the fourth indus-trial revolution (Friedman, 2016; Schwab, 2016), it is worth exploring the seminal work on contemporary privacy as a foundation for under-standing its position in the new workplace. The two main contempo-rary theories of privacy were developed by Westin (1967) and Altman (1975). As Margulis (2003) notes, their theories on privacy are both insightful and have stood the test of time. Westin (1967) identified the fact that privacy operates through individual, group, organisational and institutional levels and took the approach that the individual proactively manages their privacy, and that tensions arise from intrusions into previ-ously balanced relations between the public and private self, which were not anticipated. The key intrusion force he identified as technology. Al-though written over 50 years ago, this argument is probably more rele-vant today than ever before. In this imbalanced state, Westin argues that people are less protected than before against these pressures. Not least in Westin's framework of privacy was that the individual could limit and protect their information and communications by setting boundaries for sharing information with trusted others (Margulis, 2003; Westin, 1967). However, this concept has effectively been shattered by the inter-net and other advanced ICT. The later works of Altman (1975) built on these integrated aspects of privacy but crucially focused on the dynamic and changing nature of the environment within which privacy operates, i.e. the context (Altman, 1975, 1990; Marguis, 2003). Whilst Altman's approach (as with that of Westin's) identified the perceived control the individual had over their privacy, he also noted that privacy was bi-directional, involving input from others to create this privacy. This final point provides the opportunity to reflect on how much privacy we can and should expect and how much we have in the 21st century. This can be put in context by the following vignette:

> **Welcome to a world where your privacy is being sold for billions**
> Before she's even awake, Susan is under surveillance.
> She has another wrestles night, through her sleep tracker this in-formation is recorded in a database, indicating she maybe stressed.
> Reading the news over breakfast (on her smart devise), exploit-ing this knowledge of her sleep patterns an advertiser sends her an ad for a meditation app. Susan downloads the app. When she uses the app both the time and her location are recorded in another database.

Susan visits a car dealership. Even though she hasn't searched online, she is served with multiple adverts from other car dealerships for a week. And three different banks offer her a personal loan through more online advertising.

Susan is fictional, of course, but every technique described in that scenario is real.

Data can and is extracted from almost everything we do that is online. Apps can track your location, who you communicate with, what you photograph and when and how you sleep. That data is swapped and traded, melded with even more data, and used to create even more data to make inferences and assumptions about you in ways that are only beginning to be explored.

It has been assessed that Facebook collects some $53 billion a year by parlaying personal data into advertising revenue. This is only the most visible player in a vast global ecosystem of data collectors, data brokers, advertising platforms and others who form the so-called "surveillance economy".

Adapted from Prying Eyes is a new Crikey series, edited by technology writer Stilgherrian. Crikey July 3, 2018

The question that emerges from this scenario is why would the workplace be any different? It could be argued that in the context of good HRM policies to build trust in the workplace, ethical considerations would increasingly be seen as providing checks and balances within a system of increasing intrusion in the privacy of employees.

The Ethics of Electronic Monitoring and Surveillance

Even looking at EMS from an ethical perspective, it remains difficult to assess the positive aspects of the extent and level of such blanket policies and practices in the workplace. Consequential theories judge the morality of an issue based on the consequences it generates, arguing that an action is morally right if all decision makers in a given situation freely decide to pursue either their short-term desires or long-term interests (Crane & Matten, 2016). Applying this theory to EMS, we would argue that the stress and pressures these techniques put individuals under, combined with the negative impact on the employment relationship including counterproductive work behaviours (Holland et al., 2016; Martin et al., 2016), would see little gained from such practices in the long term. This point, we would argue is reinforced by the Utilitarianism position of bringing about the greatest good for the greatest number of people affected by the action (Crane & Matten, 2016). Adopting a utilitarian perspective, it is difficult to see how engaging in EMS is the morally preferable action, as it generates negative outcomes for both the individual and the organisation, through primarily undermining trust and privacy. The potential outcomes of such action being to damage the employment relationship (see Holland et al., 2016; Martin et al., 2016). Such outcomes are the antitheses of contemporary HRM objectives (Boxall & Purcell, 2016).

The deontological approach would also consider such practices to not be in the interest of the individual or organisations. We assess this based on the three basic principles of the deontological approach. Based on the first principle, of 'universality', the question is already answered by the fact that management do not place themselves under the same level of scrutiny. Based on the second principle, of 'human dignity', the question to ask is if employees are able to freely and autonomously make decisions, would they agree and allow EMS? Employees often have little choice in the matter, as these practices are usually required as part of their employment terms and conditions. Hence, such practices are morally questionable by the measure of the second principle. Based on the third principle, of 'practical test', the question to ask is if every other rational being, including your family, friends and strangers, would condone the action, and apply the same rule. It seems doubtful that all other rational human beings would accept EMS as a general principle to follow. As such, it is increasingly difficult to see the positives of intensive and mass EMS, based upon on the simple principle noted earlier – "we do it because we can"!

However, we need to be realistic and accept that these potential forms of scrutiny will only increase. A key feature therefore, is how we manage them and the decision to electronically watch or not to watch. The next section of this chapter explores the nature and extent of leading issues in EMS and the reader can reflect on the issues of privacy, trust and ethics as each aspect of this new frontier is examined.

Biometric Testing and the Workplace

Approximately two decades ago, in the film *Minority Report* facial recognition technology was used to identify people as they travelled within a city – it blew science fiction fans away. Fast forward to today, such biometric recognition technology is not only well-advanced, but is increasingly becoming a common feature in many workplaces – with iris, facial or fingerprint scanners fast replacing the conventional text-based passwords and pins (Carpenter, Maasberg, Hicks, & Chen, 2016). Biometrics typically refers to technologies that measure and analyse unique physical and/or behavioural characteristics in order to either identify an individual or verify the identity of an individual (Jackson, 2009; Norris-Jones, 2012). These characteristics include what you are (physiological, e.g. blood type, scent, fingerprints, hand geometry) and what you do (behavioural, e.g. gait or the way someone walks or voice patterns) which are generally considered innate, immutable and distinctive to the individual (Du, Yang, & Zhou, 2011; Magnet, 2011; Moradoff, 2010).

The 9/11 terrorist attacks in the USA have been seen as the catalyst for such advances with the implementation of biometric authentication systems initially introduced as a means of greater immigration security controls (Moradoff, 2010). However, such is the nature of technological functional creep that it has since been applied in other sectors including hospitals for access to patients' electronic health records, consumer electronics where products such as the iPhone X features include the use of facial recognition to unlock phones and financial institutions using fingerprints as a means of identity authentication. The use of biometric technology has also grown substantially in the workplace, particularly as a means of identity verification. It is seen as more accurate, convenient and safer as iris patterns, facial geometry and vascular patterns are unique to that individual and is not easily replicable (Jackson, 2009; Nanavati, Thieme, & Nanavati, 2002).

At the workplace, biometrics are used largely to ensure workplace security, access control, theft prevention and attendance record-keeping (Ball, 2010; Rao, 2018; Zielinski, 2018). For example, the use of iris scans instead of swipe cards when entering a secure facility may be more effective in preventing unauthorised access: swipe cards can be easily stolen or swapped; irises not so easily. The use of biometrics as a means of log-on authentication could also help improve productivity and reduce costs. For example, an IT department servicing over 1,000 municipal employees in California used to be distracted from its core work with over 50 calls per day requesting assistance with passwords. This represented significant costs of IT staff's productive time, and unproductive time of employees waiting for renewed access to the system. The replacement of the conventional username/password authentication method with a fingerprint single sign-on system significantly reduced this issue (Aponovich, 2001). Imagine no longer having to remember complicated passwords with symbols, numbers and uppercase letters that must be reset every few months! Biometric recording of employee time and attendance has also been purported to be a more reliable and accurate in ascertaining an employee's hours worked (Rao, 2018; Zielinski, 2018), and more effective in preventing 'buddy punching', where employees clock in and out for friends who may not have been physically present for work (Hussain, 2015).

Despite such apparent benefits of the use of biometric technology at the workplace, its introduction has spurred considerable debate and even resistance in its adoption (Carpenter et al., 2016; Rao, 2018). Carpenter et al.'s (2016) review of the literature suggests some of these key concerns include: (1) the creation of a pervasive and omnipresent regime of surveillance technology where perceived bodily privacy is being infringed, especially where the scope of monitoring is not clearly defined (Ball, 2010; Bolle, Connell, Pankanti, Ratha, & Senior, 2004), (2) the extent to which such biometric data will be used for its intended purposes only and (3) the security of data storage (Rao, 2018). The first two issues run together. Biometrics information is highly personal and has capabilities of revealing private details of an individual, details that even the individual may not have knowledge of. By extension, this may risk providing additional information without the overt consent of the employees (Ball, 2010). For instance, fingerprint data can reveal, with up to 80%–90% accuracy, an individual's gender and could potentially detect genetic disorders such as Down's syndrome (Dantcheva, Elia, & Ross, 2015; Zhai & Qui, 2010). This opens up potential fears of, and possibilities for, systematic discrimination should such information be intentionally or unintentionally taken into account to make decisions related to recruitment, promotions and conditions of employment (Currah & Mulqueen, 2011). Additionally, this also puts into question whether certain personal boundaries are being crossed without the knowledge of the employee. With the collection of biometric data such as facial geometry and gait, it is theoretically possible to re-identify an anonymous individual even in publicly accessible areas – this essentially creates the possibility of omnipresent surveillance (Schumann & Monari, 2014). Indeed, as Barbeler (2018) points out, the ethical question then arises as to how reasonable it is for employers to require employees to provide biometric data. Moreover, studies have indicated that when such organisational monitoring or surveillance extend beyond the realm of work-related performance, employees often see such monitoring to be an invasion of privacy (Alder & Ambrose, 2005) and signs of mistrust (Holland et al., 2016). Employees are more likely to adopt defensive measures as a response, including unionisation (York & Carty, 2006) or renegotiation of labour contracts (Kelly & Herbert, 2004).

The third key concern suggested by Carpenter et al.'s (2016) review of the collection and use of biometric data in the workplace revolves around data security and safety (Rao, 2018). The issue of privacy and safety of this unique data in an era of highly sophisticated 'hacking' raises an obvious concern. Essentially, biometric data such as fingerprint patterns are scanned and recorded in digital form. Much like how we are all concerned that our Facebook accounts can be hacked, digital data and digital biometric data is no different and can just as easily be 'stolen' (Roberg-Perez, 2017). Furthermore, fingerprints can be 'lifted' from coffee cups or keyboards – so the notion of the increased level of security from such bio-data needs to be considered in the context of how it can be compromised and how, from an HRM perspective, it can compromise the employment relationship.

Microchip Implants – or, You Will Probably Get Microchipped for Work One Day!

IT technology continues to extend the boundaries of workplace issues, to challenge the relationship between work and workplaces (see Chapter 8) and between work and employment (see Chapter 2) and with it the implications of monitoring and surveillance at work. Concerns which are now starting to emerge may have seemed fanciful only a decade ago. For example, if you have a smartphone or a tablet you can be tracked, the use of Radio-Frequency Identification or RFID and GPS devices, which were initially seen as way to track freight, can just as easily be used for tracking people. Now with the ability to microchip employees (little pets or cattle), implants are the new frontier we are breaking through.

Like many of these things, they start as quirky ideas as we see people get microchip implants (the size of a grain of rice) implanted under their skin (usually in the hand). With a simple wave they can scan on public transport, walk into club, open their car or, most importantly, start their coffee machine in the morning! However, like with most of these electronic breakthroughs it isn't long before they emerge in the workplace as the new advance in the way we 'manage' work. In several high-profile case study companies such as Three Square Market in the USA and Epicenter in Sweden staff have voluntarily got 'chipped'. This has allowed these employees to access through security doors, log into computers and office equipment and pay at the work canteen for food and drink. You may think 'well I can do all this now without having a microchip inserted under my skin'. However, the key, as with all technology, as Weiss (2018) notes, is the (technological) tipping point of these devices: when they become so useful or so convenient that they are hard to refuse. Now just put that smartphone next to you on silent (or even turn it off) and consider a time when (if ever, if you are a millennial) that you did not need to be connected 24/7 to the world? There are more books on the shelves of (airport) bookshops about how I lived without a smart device for a weekend than how I live with it. So, when will this tipping point come? Maybe it will come when people appreciate the ability to store large amounts of personal data such as health records on these chips, which can simply be downloaded in a clinic or hospital. Or maybe it will come when these devices can constantly monitor your vital signs and keep you healthy. In this context, concerns arise about the long-term effects of everyone in the workplace receiving and sending non-stop radio waves. Other issues raised include the fact that like all technology the information can be hacked. There are also health issues associated with chips interfering with the use of MRI machines or defibrillators. At the extreme, there have been cases of people having a hand severed, so that those who did it can breach security systems with the embedded microchip (Weiss, 2018).

From our work perspective, the clear concern is of unlimited monitoring and surveillance by those in power. Weiss (2018) notes that a key aspect of controlling the use of implant technology is legislation. However, this is easier said than done, as technology moves at a much faster rate than legislation. In the UK, trade unions have already raised concerns about the potential for staff to be microchipped on the grounds of security, a concern also endorsed by the UK employer group, the CBI. The union group particularly raise the issues of control, coercion and privacy (Kollewe, 2018). These points return us to the underpinning framework of this chapter, the cost and benefits of the introduction on the grounds of trust, privacy and ethics of such advanced electronic technology. From an HRM perspective, how do you divorce the private person from the employee with the potential information and surveillance such technologies provide? You can't assume the information system will not be hacked – in such cases the keypad number for the photocopier can be changed; but the personal information included in health records cannot (Wright, 2017). As one IT expert noted, the microchipping of employees is an absolutely horrible idea. The technology is similar to that used in the proximity cards that are used to enter hotel bedrooms and technologically speaking it is easy to duplicate the information (Mc-New in Wright, 2017). As such the considerations are whether such intrusive EMS, and the concerns and issues that go with them, outweighs the (potential) impact on trust, privacy and ethical boundaries of the employment relationship.

In concluding this section, we have referred to the technology tipping point as crucial in the mass acceptance of certain technologies in everyday (work) life with the 'smart' devices being the key tool of the current age. However, as we have noted elsewhere in this book, technology is changing the nature of how, where and when we work more than at any other time in living memory. So as we hear the predictions of how change will become more rapid and disruptive (Friedman, 2016; Schwab, 2016) where jobs now being replaced by AI will themselves be replaced by AI (Brewster & Holland, 2019), consider this interesting proposition by the UK-based research centre, the Work Foundation – Would you have a microchip implanted in your brain if it would significantly help your career? The idea being that if competition for jobs is increasing rapidly between humans and technology, implants could enhance human capabilities. A poll after the debate found the audience evenly divided on the prospects (Harris, 2013). The concept of the cyborg, a word apparently first coined by Manfred Clynes and Nathan S Kline in 1960 to denote a part-organic, part-technological being, and first portrayed in the sci-fi series '$6 million man' in the 1970s, like the smartphones in the first series of Star Trek less than 50 years ago, and the mass use of implant technology in *Minority Report*, may not be too far into the (workplace) future.

The Fluid Boundaries of EMS at Work

The continued advances in ICT, have allowed employers to monitor workers' time at work and outside work, taking managerial control from the panopticon of perceived constant surveillance to what Gilliom and Monahan (2012) call 'Super Vision'. As the law struggles to keep up with the changing nature of what has also been called liquid surveillance, as it seeps into every aspect of your life (Zygmunt & Lyon, 2012), there has been increasing interest and debate around the management of these new and fluid frontiers of EMS. The first boundary debate is: what is the appropriate level and intensity of these new forms of monitoring and surveillance? As we have noted, the combination of functional creep and the technological tipping point means that this is a fluid boundary. Second, where are the personal and private boundaries? And third, to what extent does the employer have the right to encroach into these areas, particularly the non-work sphere? Should, for example, an employer have the right to read an employee's email or social media knowing, as Barnes et al. (2018) and Oliver (2002) point out, that this threatens employee privacy and is likely to result in the employer obtaining personal information about the employee. All these issues have the potential to breach ethical boundaries and the key elements of the employment relationship – trust and privacy. This is an important point, as growing evidence indicates that workplace EMS has a negative impact on employees' attitudes towards their work (Martin et al., 2016). This, in turn, leads to a host of negative cognitive and behavioural implications at work, including diminished levels of trust and empowerment in the employment relationship (Holland et al., 2016) and poorer workplace interactions (Allen et al., 2007). Research has also found that higher levels of perceived surveillance were associated with lower task performance (Douthitt & Aiello, 2001), higher counterproductive work behaviours (Martin et al., 2016) and less organisational citizenship behaviour (Jensen & Raver, 2012). Ironically, these employee behaviour and attitudes are the opposite of the central tenets of HRM policies on engagement and commitment.

These fluid boundaries therefore require management – often through HRM – to make proactive decision about the relationship management wants with their workforce. We argue that a good starting point is setting boundaries around trust, privacy and the ethics of EMS. This provides a framework of decision-making to guide the extent or level of intrusiveness of EMS and goes back to our original point in this chapter that EMS is not a given – it is a managerial decision. This involves reflections on the extent to which trust, respect and ethics are key considerations at work. This is important as we have seen that advances in technology mean that EMS can be used as a tool to reinforce the employer's power by promoting the enforcement of worker obedience (Sewell & Barker, 2006). It is this imposition of technology by an employer which can be seen to contribute to the erosion of worker' rights and increased perceived powerlessness in the employment relationship (Sewell, Barker, & Nyberg, 2012). And, in an increasingly complex and competitive environment (Barnes et al., 2018; Sempill, 2001; Stanton & Stam, 2003), it may not produce the outcomes that the employer expects.

Conclusions

This chapter illustrates the rapid rise of EMS, which has created and is creating new problems and complexities surrounding the development of work and work relationships as it moves apace in the 21st century. It is clear that the intensity and depth of EMS continues ahead of legal guidelines across the world and across state boundaries. Appropriate levels of EMS are a vexed question. At what point does the prerogative of the employer's right to protect, manage and run their organisations conflict or infringe upon worker' rights to privacy? It is clear from this overview that detailed assessments of both the tangible and intangible costs and benefits can be made in relation to EMS in the workplace. In dealing with issues of managerial prerogative and employee privacy rights we argue that building a framework to guide organisations is the key to maintaining trust and commitment within the employment relationship. This we argue cannot be underestimated. In other words, the fundamental question in this context is *why* organisations have decided to implement EMS? Without consideration of these issues, a breakdown of the working relationship can occur. Understanding the views of all stakeholders is required to ensure all available options are considered, all available information is consulted and the practicalities of EMS are fully understood, before the employer chooses to watch or not watch.

References

Adler, G. (2001). Employee reactions to electronic performance monitoring: A consequence of organizational culture. *Journal of High Technology Management Research, 12*, 323–342.

Alder, S. & Ambrose, M. (2005). Toward understanding fairness judgements associated with computer performance monitoring: An integration of the feedback, justice, and monitoring research. *Human Resource Management Review, 15*, 43–67.

Allen, M., Coopman, S., Hart, J. & Walker, K. (2007). Workplace surveillance and managing privacy boundaries. *Management Communication Quarterly, 21*, 172–200.

Altman, I. (1975). *The environment and social behavior: Privacy, personal space, territory, crowding.* Monterey, CA: Brooks/Cole.

Altman, I. (1990). Toward a transactional perspective: a personal journey. In I. Altman and K. Christensen (eds.), *Environment and behavior studies: Emergence of intellectual traditions.* Plenum, New York, pp. 335–355.

Aponovich, D. (2001). *Biometrics eases city's network access security woes,* Datamation, available at: http://itmanagement.earthweb.com/secu/article.

php/863861/Case-Study-Biometrics-Eases-Citys-Network-Access-Security-Woes.htm (Accessed 19 December 2018).

Ball, K. (2010). Workplace surveillance: An overview. *Labor History*, 51(1), 87–106.

Barbeler, D. (2018). Turn on, tune in, drop out. *HR Monthly*, June, pp. 12–17.

Bauman, Z. & Lyon, D. (2013). *Liquid surveillance*. Cambridge: Polity Press.

Barnes, A., Holland, P. & Balnave, N. (2018). "Utterly disgraceful": Social media and the workplace. *Australian Journal of Public Administration*, 77(3), 492–499.

Becker, B., Huselid, M., Pickus, P. & Spratt, M. (1997). HR as a source of shareholder value: Research and recommendations. *Human Resource Management*, 36(1), 39–47.

Blau, P. M. (1964). *Exchange and power in social life*. New York: Wiley.

Bolle, R., Connell, J., Pankanti, S., Ratha, N. & Senior, A. (2004). *Guide to biometrics*. New York: Springer.

Boxall, P. & Purcell, J. (2016). *Strategy and human resource management* (4th ed.). Basingstoke: Palgrave Macmillan.

Brewster, C. & Holland, P. (2020). Work or employment in the 21st century: It impact on the employment relationship. In A. Wilkinson and M. Barry (eds.), *The research agenda for the future of work*. Cheltenham: Edward Elgar (forthcoming).

Bryson, A. (2004). Managerial responsiveness to union and non-union worker voice in Britain. *Industrial Relations*, 43(1), 213–241.

Carpenter, D., Maasberg, M., Hicks, C. & Chen, X. (2016). A multicultural study of biometric privacy concerns in a fire ground accountability crisis response system. *International Journal of Information Management*, 36(5), 735–747.

Carpenter, D., McLeod, A., Hicks, C. & Maasberg, M. (2016). Privacy and biometrics: An empirical examination of employee concerns. *Information Systems Frontiers*, 20(1), 91–110.

Crane, A. & Matten, D. (2016). *Business ethics: Managing corporate citizenship and sustainability in the age of globalization*. Oxford: Oxford University Press.

Currah, P. & Mulqueen, T. (2011). Securitizing gender: Identity, biometrics and transgender bodies at the airport. *Social Research*, 78(2), 557–582.

D'Urso, S. (2006). Who's watching us at work? *Communication Theory*, 16, 281–303.

Danaher, G., Schirato, T. & Webb, J. (2000). *Understanding Foucault*. Sydney: Allen and Unwin.

Dantcheva, A., Elia, P. & Ross, A. (2015). What else does your biometric data reveal? A survey on soft biometrics. *IEEE Transactions on Information Forensics and Security*, I(3), 441–467.

Determann, L. & Sprague, R. (2011). Intrusive monitoring: Employee privacy expectations are reasonable in Europe, destroyed in the United States. *Berkeley Technology Law*, 26, 979–1036.

Donaghey, J., Cullinane, N., Dundon, T. & Wilkinson, A. (2011). Reconceptualising employee silence: Problems and prognosis. *Work, Employment & Society*, 25(10): 51–67.

Douthitt, E. A. & Aiello, J. R. (2001). The role of participation and control in the effects of computer monitoring on fairness perceptions, task satisfaction, and performance. *Journal of Applied Psychology, 86*(5), 867.

Du, E. Y., Yang, K. & Zhou, Z. (2011). Key incorporation scheme for cancelable biometrics. *Journal of Information Security, 2*(4), 185.

Farndale, E., Hope-Hailey, V. & Kelliher, C. (2011). High commitment performance management: The role of justice and trust. *Personnel Review, 10*(1), 5–23.

Friedman, T. L. (2016). *Thanks for being late: An optimist's guide to thriving in the age of acceleration.* New York: Allen Lane.

Foucault, M. (1977). *Discipline and punish: The birth of the prison.* Harmondsworth: Penguin.

Gilliom, J. & Monahan, T. (2012). *SuperVision.* Chicago, IL: University of Chicago Press.

Gould-Williams, J. (2003). The importance of HR practices and workplace trust in achieving superior performance: A study of public-sector organizations. *International Journal of Human Resource Management, 14*(1), 28–54.

Harris, S. (2013). Would you have a microchip implanted in your brain? *Engineer Online,* opinion piece.

Holland, P., Cooper, B. & Hecker, R. (2015). Electronic monitoring and surveillance in the workplace: The effects on trust in management, and the moderating role of occupational type. *Personnel Review, 44*(1), 1–27.

Holland, P., Cooper, B. & Hecker, R. (2016). Social media: The new employee voice? *International Journal of Human Resource Management, 27*(21), 2621–2634.

Holland, P., Cooper, B., Pyman, A. & Teicher, J. (2012). Trust in management: The role of employee voice arrangements and perceived managerial opposition to unions. *Human Resource Management Journal, 22*(4), 377–391.

Holland, P., Cooper, B. & Sheehan, C. (2017). Employee voice, supervisor support and engagement: The mediating role of trust. *Human Resource Management, 50*(6), 915–929.

Holland, P. J., Teicher, J. & Donaghey, J. (eds.). (2019). *Employee voice at work.* Springer.

Hussain, A. (2015). *Using biometric identification technology to combat time theft in workforce management.* Available: http://blog.m2sys.com/workforce-management/using-biometric-identification-technology-combat-time-theft-workforce-management/. Last accessed 19 December 2018.

Innocenti, L., Pilati, M. & Peluso, A. M. (2011). Trust as moderator in the relationship between HRM practices and employee attitudes. *Human Resource Management Journal, 21*(3), 303–317.

Jackson, L. A. (2009). Biometric technology: The future of identity assurance and authentication in the lodging industry. *International Journal of Contemporary Hospitality Management, 21*(7), 892–905.

Jensen, J. M., & Raver, J. L. (2012). When self-management and surveillance collide: Consequences for employees' organizational citizenship and counterproductive work behaviors. *Group & Organization Management, 37*(3), 308–346.

Kelly Jr., D. & Herbert, W. A. (2004). *When James Bond enters the workplace: Use and abuses of technology – A guide for in-house counsel and litigators.* Retrieved from http://www.bna.com/bnabooks/ababna/annual/2004/kelly.doc

Kollewe, J. (2018). Alarm over talks to implant UK employees with microchips. *The Guardian*, November 12.

Korczynski, M. (2000). The political economy of trust. *Journal of Management Studies*, 37(1), 1–23.

Lane, F. S. (2003). *The naked employee: How technology is compromising workplace privacy*. New York: Amacom.

Magnet, S. (2011). *When biometrics fail: Gender, race, and the technology of identity*. Duke University Press.

Margulis, S. (2003). On the status and contribution of Westin's and Altman's theories of privacy. *Social Issues*, 59(2), 411–429.

Martin, A., Wellen, J. & Grimmer, M. (2016). An eye on your work: How empowerment affects the relationship between electronic surveillance and counterproductive work behaviours. *International Journal of Human Resource Management*, 27(21), 2635–2651.

Moradoff, N. (2010). Biometrics: Proliferation and constraints to emerging and new technologies. *Security Journal*, 23(4), 276–298.

Nanavati, S., Thieme, M. & Nanavati, R. (2002). *Biometrics: Identity verification in a Networked World*, New York: John Wiley & Sons, Inc.

Nichols, T., Danford, A. & Tasiran, A. (2009). Trust, employer exposure and the employment relations. *Economic and Industrial Democracy*, 30(2), 241–265.

Norris-Jones, L. (2012). Biometric access control in the workplace: benefit or bind?. *International Journal of Information Technology and Management*, 11(1/2), 61–71.

Oliver, H. (2002). Email and internet monitoring in the workplace: Information privacy and contracting-out. *Industrial Law Journal*, 31(4), 321–352.

Pinder, C. & Harlos, K. (2001). Employee silence: Quiescence and acquiescence as responses to perceived injustice. *Research in Personnel and Human Resource Management*, 20, 331–369.

Rao, U. (2018). Biometric bodies, or how to make electronic fingerprinting work in India. *Body & Society*, 24(3), 68–94.

Roberg-Perez, S. (2017). The future is now: Biometric information and data privacy. *Antitrust*, 31(3), 60–65.

Schumann, A. & Monari, E. (2014). A soft-biometrics dataset for person tracking and re-identification. *11th IEEE International Conference on Advanced Video and Signal Based Surveillance* (AVSS), Seoul, South Korea.

Schwab, K. (2016). *The fourth industrial revolution*. Cologny: World Economic Forum.

Searle, R., Den Hartog, D. N., Weibel, A., Gillespie, N., Six, F., Hatzakis, T. & Skinner, D. (2011). Trust in the employer: The role of high-involvement work practices and procedural justice in European organizations. *International Journal of Human Resource Management*, 22(5), 1069–1092.

Sempill, J. (2001). Under the lens: Electronic workplace surveillance. *Australian Journal of Labour Law*, 14, 111–144.

Sewell, G. & Barker, J. R. (2006). Coercion versus care: Using irony to make sense of organizational surveillance. *Academy of Management Review*, 31(4), 934–961.

Sewell, G., Barker, J. R. & Nyberg, D. (2012). Working under intense surveillance. *Human Relations*, 65(1), pp. 189–215.

Stanton, J. M., & Stam, K. R. (2003). Information technology, privacy and power within organizations: A view from boundary theory and social exchange perspectives. *Surveillance & Society*, *1*(2), 152–190.

Stilgherrian, I. (2018). Prying eyes. *Crikey*, July 3.

Tyler, T. (2003). Trust within organisations. *Personnel Review*, *32*(5), 556–568.

Tzafrir, S., Harel, G., Baruch, Y. & Dolan, S. (2004). The consequences of emerging HRM practices for employees' trust in their managers. *Personnel Review*, *33*(6), 628–647.

Weiss, H. (2018). Why you're probably getting a microchip implant someday. *The Atlantic*. https://www.theatlantic.com/technology/archive/2018/09/...i...microchip/570946/

Westin, A. F. (1967). *Privacy and freedom*. New York: Atheneum Press.

World of Work (2007). *RFID and surveillance in the workplace* (Vol. 59, April pp. 16–19). Geneva: ILO.

Wright, A. (2017). *Microchipping employees: Do the pros outweigh the cons?* Alexandria, Virginia: SHRM.

York, A. & Carty, L. (2006). *Privacy: Biometric technology and privacy in the workplace*. Retrieved from http://www.blakes.com/english/publications/businesswithcanada/bwc/html/article.asp?article=413

Zhai, X. & Qui, R. (2010). The status quo and ethical governance in biometrics in mainland China. In A. Kumar & D. Zhang (eds.), *Ethics and policy of biometrics* (pp. 127–137). Berlin/Heidelberg: Springer.

Zielinski, D. (2018). Use of Biometric Data Grows, Though Not Without Legal Risks. *HRNews*, Aug 23, 2018.

Zureik, E. (2003). Theorizing surveillance: The case of the workplace. In D. Lyon (ed.), *Surveillance as social sorting* (pp. 31–56). Oxon: Routledge.

Zygmunt, B., & Lyon, D. (2012). *Liquid surveillance: A conversation*. Cambridge: Polity

10 Working in 'Sweatshops'

Outsourcing to Developing Nations

Julian Teicher and Sardana Islam Khan

Introduction

Although the precise origins of the term 'sweatshop' are unclear, the term emerged in the context of British industrialisation and the horrific working conditions experienced by workers and their families. The earliest recorded usage was in 1877 and thereafter it has been used with increasing frequency (see Figure 10.1).

In contemporary parlance the term sweatshop has been narrowed and tends to denote businesses such as clothing manufacture in developing countries like Bangladesh and also to cover child labour. According to Oxfam a sweatshop is:

> a manufacturing facility where workers endure poor working conditions, long hours, low wages and other violations of labour rights. Unfortunately, places known as sweatshops are particularly common in developing countries where labour laws are often not enforced.[1]

By implication, then sweatshops in the 21st century are associated with similar evils to those experienced by factory workers in Western nations during the Industrial Revolution, except that today they form part of a global process commonly described as offshoring.

The existence and extent of exploitative and dangerous work in developing nations is mostly invisible to people in advanced economies. The working conditions and lives of workers in sweatshops only become visible when there is some kind of disaster such as a factory fire or building collapse leading to multiple injuries and deaths (Chowdhury, 2017; Hoskins, 2015). A recent exception to the norm of invisibility is strikes and protests by Bangladesh garment workers; though it is most likely that world attention was captured by the drama of police using water cannons, rubber bullets and tear gas to disperse protesters (Anner, 2015; *The Guardian*, 2019). This drama highlights the plight of sweatshop workers with the challenge of achieving acceptable wages and working conditions being intensified by a deficit of democratic rights.

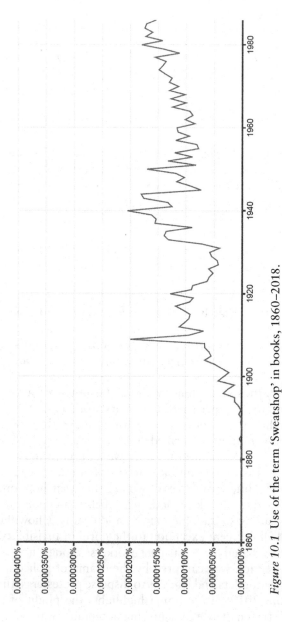

Figure 10.1 Use of the term 'Sweatshop' in books, 1860–2018.

Source: https://books.google.com/ngrams/graph?content=sweatshops&year_start=1860&year_end=2008&corpus=15&smoothing=0&share=&direct_url=t1%3B%2Csweatshops%3B%2Cc0#t1%3B%2Csweatshops%3B%2Cc0

Recurrent tragedies in garment and textile factories across Asia have prompted efforts by the 'big fashion brands' and retailers to shore up their image in the face of adverse publicity and potential consumer boycotts (Hoskins, 2015; Khan, Bartram, Cavanagh, Hossain, & Akter, 2019). In the case of Bangladesh, the collapse of the Rana Plaza factory complex in 2013 led to a unique initiative, the creation of two transnational governance mechanisms designed to implement effective regulation of working conditions in the face of widespread governance failures (Khan et al., 2019).

In this chapter we argue that overseas sweatshops are fostered by strategies of advanced nation retailers focused almost entirely on reducing costs and then are sustained by socio-cultural, economic, legal and political conditions in the host economies that thwart efforts to ameliorate exploitative employment practices and working conditions. In the first part of this chapter we outline the major disciplinary discourses regarding offshoring as they underpin the contemporary debates on the appropriate regulatory and other responses to the proliferation of overseas sweatshops. The second part highlights the nature of the Global Competitiveness Agenda which has fostered offshoring albeit with some novel features associated with the unfolding of what is often labelled the Fourth Industrial Revolution, that is, high-technology sweatshops. This is followed by an examination of the case study of the Bangladesh readymade garment (RMG) sector and the largely ineffective attempts that have been made to regulate it. This lays the groundwork for the fourth section which reviews sweatshops through an example of a wicked problem. Finally, we reflect on efforts both regulatory and otherwise to manage the wicked problem of sweatshops and briefly consider the possible trajectory of this persistent problem.

Controversies over Offshore Outsourcing

The term outsourcing refers to one business contracting part or all of its production process to another business. When this process extends beyond national boundaries in today's global economy, it is also offshoring (Kedia & Lahiri, 2007; Sartor & Beamish, 2014). Offshoring also includes investment by a company in production facilities in another country. In this study we confine our attention to offshore outsourcing. From a business and economics standpoint offshore outsourcing is considered to be a cost minimising strategy; concerns over labour exploitation tend to be confined to the fields of employment relations and ethics.

Business and Economics

The international business literature assesses global outsourcing strategies favourably or unfavourably depending on management intention and on the outcomes. Cost cutting through utilisation of lower cost labour and resources remains the major motivation behind the recourse to offshoring, although in reality cost savings are not an inevitable outcome. For example, a study of 200 Dutch manufacturing firms (Mol, Van Tulder, & Beije, 2005) found that the decision to take production offshore is a balance between lower overseas production costs compared with lower transaction costs in the home economy with no particular impact on firm performance. Interestingly another study of Dutch enterprises, 156 of them this time, by Ok (2011) categorised the decision to offshore as motivated by the desire to 'access cheaper resources' in the face of increasing competition, 'access scarce and distinctive resources' and 'reduce other production costs'. Additional motivations for offshoring include strengthening supply chains through access to alternative sources of raw materials, labour, production technology and innovation independently of short run cost reductions (Jabbour & Zuniga, 2016; Ok, 2011). In this context, it may be access to particularly skilled labour, as in the case of IT specialists in India, rather than low-cost labour that drives the move (Oshri, Kotlarsky, & Willcocks, 2015).

In the international business literature offshoring is also presented as a sustainable human resource development strategy for both multinational enterprises and emerging economies in which they locate. Anderson (2015) argues that offshoring extends the scope for knowledge sharing, inter-country training and the development of cultural intelligence and global leadership for MNEs. The stock of human capital in developing economies is also claimed to benefit from increasing knowledge and skills, creation of networks and access to superior technology and 'knowhow'.

In summary while economics and international business discourses focus on cost reduction in the home country, a variety of other considerations are also relevant to the offshoring decision. These disciplines tend to report rather positively on the concept of offshoring.

Ethics and Employment Relations

In other disciplines, however the business case for offshoring is increasingly challenged as an unethical business practice reliant on exploiting workers in host nations. The ethics and employment relation discourses posit that offshoring by companies in advanced economies creates opportunities to profit from sweatshop operations in the more flexible and less regulated labour markets of developing nations (Preiss, 2014; Zwolinski, 2007). Central to this critique is the choice of organisational and managerial arrangements that can be used in order to distance home country producers and retailers from oppressive employment regimes further down the supply chain, for example, by operating a wholly owned subsidiary with local management or contracting out production to an unrelated entity. Therefore, from the perspective of employment relations and business ethics the intentions and outcomes of offshoring may be viewed as unethical, ill-intended, unsustainable and exploitative (Coakley & Kates, 2013; Maitland, Beauchamp, & Bowie, 1997; Preiss, 2014). Similarly, the ILO's Decent Work programme which also forms part of the UN's 2030 Sustainable Development Goals (SDGs) advocates for both employment generation and decent work conditions by calling for a social safety, employee voice and choice of work on top of a living wage and workplace safety (ILO, 2016).

Notwithstanding, some employment relations scholars (e.g. Maitland et al., 1997; Powell & Skarbek, 2006) have questioned the utility of applying the sweatshop tag, arguing that overseas factories can provide better wages and working conditions than many companies producing solely for domestic markets in host nations. Similarly, evidence from once emerging economies such as Indonesia and South Korea is sometimes used to argue that as an economy grows and develops around the export sector, rising expectations will lead to widespread improvements in wages and working conditions (see Maitland et al., 1997; Powell, 2018; Powell & Skarbek, 2006). In effect this is a version of 'trickle down' economics and says little about the timing and extent of these wage effects in specific settings.

Those opposing targeted sweatshop regulation argue against third-party (government regulations or consumer boycotts) interventions while supporting workers' rights to choose employment under what is characterised as sweatshop conditions (Faraci, 2019). These authors encourage regulators to increase alternatives to sweatshops to provide more choice to the workers rather than resort to increasing regulation (Flanigan, 2018). This argument also speaks to a debate over whether a short-term detriment should be tolerated for the sake of the long-term gain in economic welfare and to a market-oriented discourse that higher wages for some comes at the expense of jobs for other workers.

The Global Competitiveness Agenda

Factory production in the developing nations is longstanding. In colonial era India it was integral to the supply chain of the British textile industry first by providing raw materials and later by producing cotton and other fabrics more cheaply than could be achieved domestically (Tripathi, 1996). In other words, with employment regulation in developed economies in its infancy in the 19th century, sweatshops enabled production to be located where labour and materials could be secured more cheaply, typically under more dangerous conditions and more brutal supervision. Similarly, in the era of mass production which lasted until at least the 1970s, it was common to turn to low-cost suppliers often offshore again with scant regard to the conditions under which products were produced. Indeed, this was the purpose served by Japan from the aftermath of the Second World War until the 1960s. Subsequently, rising labour costs and other factors saw a shift from low-cost production to more sophisticated manufacturing under the label of 'mass customisation' including the adoption of robotics and outsourcing to other nations that now had lower labour costs.

As the model of global production developed during the late 20th century and the first decades of the 21st century, there emerged a Global Competitiveness Agenda (Horlings & Marsden, 2014; Knight, 2010); this was not directly the result of globalisation but was articulated first by the US government with the support of the UK and then fostered by national governments and transnational bodies such as the International Monetary Fund and the World Bank. As Stiglitz (2002, p. 13) observed:

> The most dramatic change in these institutions occurred in the 1980s, the era when Ronald Reagan and Margaret Thatcher prescribed free market ideology ... The IMF and the World Bank became the new missionary institutions through which these ideas were pushed on the reluctant poor countries that often badly needed their loans and grants.

The Global Competitiveness Agenda was also associated with efforts by many advanced nation governments along with major international corporations and employer groups. Collectively they worked to secure a range of economic 'reforms' including deregulation of labour and product markets, fiscal policy discipline, tax reform particularly the introduction of broad-based taxes, reduced tariff and non-tariff barriers to trade, floating exchange rates and reduced government production of goods and services (privatisation).

In developed countries the Global Competitiveness Agenda was manifested in the continuing threat of production being relocated offshore or replaced by imported products. And the corollary for employers in the developed countries was a considerable incentive to bypass costly regulation at home by outsourcing both internally and externally. Internal outsourcing consists of contracting elements of production to other providers in the home country who typically pay labour piece rates in a 'shadow economy' intended to bypass health and safety and wages and conditions regulations. External outsourcing differs principally in that it occurs outside the home economy, typically in developing nations where, as we have observed, protective labour legislation tends to be underdeveloped and its enforcement is largely ineffectual with profits being maximised at the expense of workers' health and well-being (Barrientos, Mayer, Pickles, & Posthuma, 2011).

While traditionally outsourcing to offshore sweatshops largely involved low skilled labour, this is changing in the era of flexible specialisation with the associated uptake of information technology and robotics in the manufacture of high-technology products. This development has at least partly been enabled by increased literacy and more generally, rising education levels in developing countries (Horgos, 2011). Perhaps the best-known example of this is the manufacture of smart phones for companies such as Apple with the iPhone being assembled at plants across China by more than one million skilled workers. At the Longhua plant of Foxconn near Shenzhen in 2010 there were 18 reported suicide attempts and 10 confirmed deaths:

> Suicide notes and survivors told of immense stress, long workdays and harsh managers who were prone to humiliate workers for mistakes, of unfair fines and unkept promises of benefits.
>
> (Marchant, 2017)

Perhaps Foxconn is an extreme case but it is illustrative of the trend towards 'electronic sweatshops' producing consumer goods largely destined for advanced market economies (Chan, Pun, & Selden, 2016; Pun et al., 2016). Other companies that have been cited as utilising high-technology sweatshops include Dell, HP and Sony (Chamberlain, 2011; Moore, 2011). Also concerning is that home-grown Chinese high-technology companies such as Huawei, Xiaomi and Oppo that have benefited from the technology transfer associated with outsourcing may also undermine internationally accepted employment standards without attracting the media or consumer backlash that was faced by Apple and other outsourcing companies.

The Ready-Made Garment (RMG) Sector, the Global Economy and Regulation

Bangladesh has achieved rapid progress in its transition from an agrarian to an industrial economy, and the RMG sector is central to that process. Economic growth has been rapid in the last 25 years, though corruption remains endemic, income inequality is persistently high (the Gini coefficient was 32.4 in 2016) and the rate of poverty reduction has slowed.[2] Bangladesh is now the second largest clothing producer in the world after China and the sector is the country's largest exporter, accounting for 85% of all exports (Emran, Kyriacou, & Rogan, 2019; Rahman, Habibullah, & Abdullah-Al-Masum, 2017). The RMG sector directly employs more than four million workers, and the minimum wage for the various grades of labour is lower than its major competitors, Cambodia, China, India and Vietnam. For every clothing item sold by Australian retailers, for example, only 2% of the final price is received by the factory workers as wages and for employers overall the industry remains highly profitable (Rahman, Habibullah, & Abdullah-Al-Masum,

2017) About 80% of RMG workers in Bangladesh are women most of whom came out of rural poverty; they are typically uneducated and in a deeply conservative patriarchal society their experience is one of being denied basic human rights (Jinnah, 2013). The paradox which this presents is that some women enjoy a measure of economic independence but continue to experience deprivation of basic human rights.

Economically the sustainability of the RMG sector is linked to the growth and survival of other sectors including cotton cultivation, spinning of yarn, weaving of cloth, dyeing, professional services, real estate and housing services, construction, banking and insurance and other telecom based financial services, storage, machinery, maintenance and security services. Because Bangladesh is now the second largest international supplier of apparel to the global market, the sustainability of the RMG sector has become a global concern (Emran et al., 2019).

The RMG sector has been widely criticised by international human rights organisations, trade unions, Western media and consumer associations. It has frequently been accused of maintaining sweatshop conditions in terms of wage theft, job insecurity, verbal, physical and sexual abuse, and the inability of workers to organise (Emran et al., 2019). Attention has also been drawn to persistent labour unrest and a shocking death toll from fire and building collapses. A complex set of socio-economic and political dynamics in Bangladesh has contributed to turning this once widely ignored problem of labour exploitation and injustice into a 'wicked problem' for policy makers, employers, international clothing brands and retailers along with other international actors (Carlson & Bitsch, 2018). A wicked problem is one that is resistant to a solution because of one or more conditions including incomplete or conflicting information, the number of contesting opinions and the interconnectedness of this and other problems. As a wicked problem the persistence and growth of sweatshops is seemingly resistant to conventional policy measures and continues to mutate.

Major interventions to address the sweatshop issues in the RMG sector have typically emerged as a reaction to catastrophic accidents or industrial unrest. In regard to industrial unrest, the Government of Bangladesh has been instrumental in forging tripartite agreements with trade unions and employers' associations principally aimed at resolving minimum wage and overtime-related issues. Though these tripartite agreements usually set a higher minimum wage for the RMG workers compared to that prescribed for other employers, the negotiation process and implementation phase has always been tainted by workers' mistrust of the role played by government officials, union representatives and employers (Khanna, 2011; TIB, 2018). The agreements reached are widely regarded as tainted by politicisation and personal influence, which is a manifestation of the socio-political culture of Bangladesh and the nature of unions in post-independence era. Specifically, the representatives of the various actors are widely viewed as corrupt and open to taking bribes while the major union federations are directly affiliated with the major political parties. Moreover, these unions represent workers in less than 10% of factories (*New Age Business*, 2018) and have a history of pursuing partisan political agendas ahead of workers' rights. As a result, breaches of the agreements are frequent and enforcement of them almost non-existent.

Concerns about union legitimacy are demonstrated by reference to major labour unrest among RMG workers in 2006, which resulted in the historic signing of a Tripartite Memorandum of Understanding between employers, workers and the government's Labour and Employment ministries. This provided for ten major reforms including creating a Wage Board and replacing the *Factory Act, 1965* with a modernised *Bangladesh Labour Act, 2006*. Optimism quickly turned into disappointment when the Wage Board fixed the minimum wage for unskilled workers at approximately 50% of the level demanded by the workers and by the Government declaring a state of emergency and banning of all forms of workers' association in 2007. In response, workers in the Export Processing Zones formed workers associations to protect their rights at work and these later turned into 'Workers Welfare Societies' through Association and *Industry Relations (Amendment) Bill 2009* (Khanna, 2011).

The implementation of the *Bangladesh Labour Act, 2006* has been tainted by the lack of credibility of the legal systems and the governing bodies essentially due to the political affiliation of the trade unions, professional associations, business associations and newspapers (Chowdhury & Mahmood, 2012: 5). This reflects the underlying socio-political culture of a weak and unreliable set of formal societal institutions which contest with a much powerful set of informal institutions that have made Bangladesh more complex and unpredictable than most other Asian nations (Khan, 2013: 34). Widespread corruption, patrimonial politics, and lack of an ethical culture in the ruling administrative machinery have been identified as the informal societal institutions in Bangladesh that counteract and undermine the benefits of reasonably standardised and well-written laws according to Khan (2013). Therefore, the outcome of any negotiations between employers, unions and government is not trusted by either the workforce, human rights activists or other international bodies (http://www.industriall-union.org/over-11600-bangladesh-garment-workers-lose-jobs-and-face-repression). It is little wonder that continuing unrest has been characteristic of the RMG sector.

Health and safety issues and worker's rights of association have traditionally been advocated by international agencies and human rights activists (https://www.ilo.org/dhaka/Areasofwork/workers-and-employers-organizations/lang--en/index.htm). However, a recent study (Khan et al., 2019) suggests that the RMG workers' focus is on wage and financial benefits rather than safety issues with the workers tending to rely on the foreign buyers, international bodies and human rights activists to ensure their rights to a safe working environment (Khan et al., 2019). In this regard the 'Accord' on Fire and Building Safety in Bangladesh' was created in the Netherlands in 2013 primarily in response to the Western consumers' activism against purchasing 'blood stained' ready-made garments made in Bangladesh. The Accord is a legally binding agreement between 200 companies from more than 20 mainly European countries (brands, importers and retailers) and 10 union bodies representing 2 Global Union Federations and their Bangladesh affiliates. Its principal purpose is to monitor and secure improvements in the health and safety and working conditions of RMG workers (https://bangladeshaccord.org/). This runs alongside the less ambitious Alliance for Bangladesh Worker Safety Accord formed by 29 North American brands and retailers.

According to the fifth and final report of Alliance (2018) and the Commerce Ministry of Bangladesh (https://www.textiletoday.com.bd/accord-alliance-leave-bangladesh-january-commerce-minister/), there were no reported cases of building collapse or fire hazards in the Bangladeshi RMG sector since 2013 and most of the 700 Alliance partners have been converted into 'green' factories (environment friendly and sustainable factories). Additionally most Accord and Alliance member companies plan to work through a locally based organisation to collectively monitor safety in their Bangladeshi outsourcing partners from 2019 onward (Cleanclothes.org, 2019). According to the Alliance (2018) report at least 1.6 million RMG employees have been trained in fire safety and a 24-hour confidential worker helpline reaches more than 1.5 million workers. Aside from fire and safety inspections and remediation programmes (buyers alliances, government and ILO have created a Remediation Coordination Cell (RCC) to sustain inspection and remediation activities) the major features of the Accord have been safety training, establishment of worker safety committees and providing workers with the right to refuse unsafe work (https://bangladeshaccord.org/). While the right to refuse unsafe work is sometimes workable in a developed nation context, it is unclear whether workers can effectively exercise this right in Bangladesh acting without appropriate support.

While workplace health and safety has gained major attention in the Western media leading to the revision of the *Bangladesh Labour Act, 2006*, the changes adopted in 2018 received qualified support from the ILO. The ILO criticised the requirement for unions formed at enterprise level to have a minimum membership of 30% of eligible workers in order to be legal. They also criticised restrictions on freedom of association and collective bargaining rights for workers in Export Processing Zones (UN News, 2013). Significantly in terms of the Decent Work agenda requirement for employee voice, the Accord required the formation of representative committees which have provided workers with a mechanism to discuss important workplace concerns with factory management. According to Khan and colleagues (2019) participants have acknowledged the effectiveness of Worker's Participation Committees (WPC) over the traditional labour unions in the RMG sector.

However, protests over the implementation of a new minimum wage structure in Ashulia on the outskirts of Dhaka in December 2018 cast doubt on Bangladesh's adherence to ILO conventions, particularly CO87 on freedom of association (UN News, 2013). The sight of striking workers being attacked, and their leaders being arrested raised concerns among international companies about workers' rights to freedom of association. Despite concerns by members of the US Congress and European Union member countries, there were further clashes between striking and protesting workers in Ashulia and Savar in 2019 with the police appearing to intervene at the behest of the factory owners (BDApparelNews, 2019). In addition it is reported that following industrial action in early 2019 approximately 12,000 RMG workers had their jobs terminated or were forced to resign by employers unwilling to pay higher wages and social security benefits (http://www.industriall-union.org/over-11600-bangladesh-garment-workers-lose-jobs-and-face-repression).

The Wicked Problem of Overseas Sweatshops

As explained above there are contrasting views on offshoring and the associated pay and working conditions of labour in developing countries. At the heart of this controversy is the argument that while the pay and working conditions of workers in underdeveloped nations producing for employers in developed nations are low by international standards, from the developing country perspective, this is part of an ongoing process of industrial development. In many cases the transition from grinding rural poverty to low wage industrial work with minimal rights represents a substantial improvement in their lives both economically and socially with the benefits of paid employment for large numbers outweighing the costs of poor working conditions and denial of basic human rights. Basic human rights as expressed in ILO Conventions and the Decent Work agenda cost employers more than otherwise, even if those costs are not high. We explore this dilemma using our Bangladesh RMG sector case and framing the discussion around the five core properties of a wicked problem (WP) as identified by Rittel and Webber (1973).

No Definitive Formulation of a Wicked Problem

In the case of a wicked problem, how it is framed has an impact on the identification of possible solutions. In the RMG sector, the 'sweatshop' framing raises the question of whether the problem results from the continuing demands of international buyers for cost reductions or whether it is rooted in the local work culture and broader socio-economic context. The Bangladesh Garment Exporters Association (BGMEA) points to the RMG sector minimum wage being higher than in other local factories; that is, that workers in the major export earning industry fare better than other workers. However, unions and labour associations argue that wage comparisons between industries must take into account workload pressure and other aspects of employment conditions in the industry. More generally in Bangladesh workers and labour associations' demands have traditionally been more focused on wage payments in terms of the level of wages, the extent of wage theft and the variable impact of minimum wage increases on the remuneration of different categories of workers (see Chapter 4).

However, in the past, wage rises have not led to significant improvements in living condition or higher purchasing power for garment workers because increases in rent and other living expenses intervened. Specifically, providers of goods and services in the residential areas close to the factories responded opportunistically by raising their prices in many cases (Ahmed & Nathan, 2016; Khan et al., 2019; Oxfam, 2019). Therefore, unlike 'tame' problems, cost of living pressures continue to fuel labour unrest despite tripartite collective bargaining success in improving the minimum wage (Ahmed & Nathan, 2016). Consequently, we view RMG sweatshop conditions as resulting either from the relentless pressures imposed by the overseas brands on their subcontracting partners or local socio-economic conditions that see prices of goods and rents rise in direct response to wage rises (Khan et al., 2019) Accordingly, we can either frame this problem as externally or internally driven.

Solutions to Wicked Problems Are Not True-or-False but Good-or-Bad

Experts have different solutions to the problem and each may be correct when viewed from a particular perspective so there is no consensus on whether an intervention is good or bad. For example, the Accord required improvements to building safety and consequently many factories could not operate profitably. Even in factories which are compliant with the relevant standards, safety monitoring and auditing expenses increased the employers' costs and some factories were reportedly selling their products at cost price (Ahmed & Nathan, 2016; Khan et al., 2019). While the Accord monitoring processes protect workers in Tier 1 organisations (operating in the Export Processing Zones), in other factories these processes effectively pushes other workers into unemployment and poverty (https://rmgbd.net/2019/04/apparel-pay-bgmea-rejects-tib-report/).

According to Transparency International Bangladesh (TIB, 2018) 400,000 Bangladeshi RMG workers lost their jobs as a result of Accord and Alliance mandated inspections and the surviving compliant factories have increased their production targets by 30%–36% to maintain their low-cost advantage in the international market; this puts increased production pressure on workers. According to the BGMEA increased production pressure is a response to the lower production efficiency of Bangladesh workers compared to competitors in the ready-made garments sector such as China, Vietnam and Turkey. The BGME further commented that : "To the best of our knowledge there was no correlation with the increase in the minimum wage and efficiency as considered by the Minimum Wage Board" (https://rmgbd.net/2019/04/apparel-pay-bgmea-rejects-tib-report/).

Coakley and Kates (2013) acknowledged that increasing the minimum wage standards has both good and bad consequences but they concluded that higher minimum wages, result is a net increase in workers' well-being. Others view sweatshop conditions as temporary and poverty as being preferable to unemployment. Therefore, any solution to a wicked problem may appear good or bad to different stakeholder groups or advocates of opposing views while none of these can be marked as true or false.

Every Solution to a Wicked Problem Is a "One-shot Operation"

Once an intervention is directed to a wicked problem, there is no erasing its impact, according to Rittel and Webber (1973). In response to the Accord and Alliance monitoring and compliance activities some RMG factory owners and managers opted for factory closures. Some owners reported that they could live off savings following a factory closure (Khan et al., 2019), whereas for others closure led to bankruptcy for the owners (TIB, 2018).

As we outlined above government and union interventions historically resulted in the payment of bribes, coercive subscription to union funds and settlement money paid to the politically appointed union leaders with negligible benefits for workers in terms of wages, working conditions or rights (Khan et al., 2019; Khanna, 2011). Transparency International Bangladesh (2018) reported that post Accord-Alliance some factories even lost their businesses due to some buyers' 'immoral' behaviours'. Such negative experiences associated with regulatory interventions ensured that representatives of overseas buyers and Accord-Alliance and government monitoring were unpopular not just with managers but also employee in the RMG sector (Khan et al., 2019). Once these interventions were in place, there was no going back or erasing the impact.

Every Wicked Problem is Essentially Unique

Due to the unique and complex socio-economic and political issues, worker exploitation and abuse in Bangladesh factories are particularly harsh even in comparison to factories in Vietnam (Oxfam, 2018). These factors are summarised as the weakness of formal institutions compared to the entrenched informal institutions which divert the various social actors into the pursuit of corrupt benefits and the pursuit of partisan political agendas. It was the manifest and continuing failure of national regulation and governance that made the transnational governance mechanisms of the Accord and Alliance possible. As the Bangladesh Commerce Minister observed, no other country would have allowed for the implementation of transnational governance mechanisms in the RMG sector (https://www.textiletoday.com.bd/accord-alliance-leave-bangladesh-january-commerce-minister/). While Bangladesh opposed the extension of these mechanisms beyond January 2019, the minister acknowledged that there had been no fire or other catastrophic accidents reported in the Bangladeshi RMG sector since the factory monitoring and rectification measures were implemented.

Wicked Problem Can be a Symptom of Another Problem

The 2013 labour law reforms were not generally opposed or criticised by relevant NGOs or human rights welfare advocates. However, the process of implementation was viewed as tainted by the local culture, the flawed judicial system and the questionable ethical standards of the law-enforcing agencies and government bodies (TIB, 2018). The general lack of respect for democratic solutions in the local political culture may also reflect on these RMG sweatshop issues.

Based on our assessment of the case of Bangladeshi RMG sector using Rittel and Webber's (1973) Wicked Problems framework we argue that the predicament of overseas sweatshops in an emerging economy is indeed wicked in nature and requires systems thinking in the sense of a holistic response to providing solutions. Therefore, each component of the problem and the relationships between them should be diagnosed systemically and collaboratively by involving all actors and stakeholders.

The Future of Global Outsourcing and Overseas Sweatshops

Globally we are in the midst of a much-vaunted transition from an industrial economy to a knowledge economy (sometimes tagged the Fourth Industrial Revolution) and at the same time the UN 2030 Sustainable Development Goals have gained unprecedented traction with many corporations and governments reporting their progress towards achieving these goals. Together these developments may warrant redefining the elements that constitute a sweatshop to better capture the emerging reality and a reshaping of the nature and process of outsourcing between regions.

The ILO's Decent Work agenda prescribes workers' right to a decent wage, basic health and safety conditions, social safety nets, employee voice and choice of work (Khan et al., 2019). These standards have extended the scope of employee welfare beyond the traditional sweatshop emphasis on basic rights such as a minimum wage and workplace health and safety. According to Khan et al. (2019), many subcontractors in emerging economies are struggling to remain financially viable while meeting the requirements of the Decent Work agenda, something which may be ultimately self-defeating. The view that a 'sweatshop stage' is necessary for economic development finds support in the examples of former sweatshop economies such as Hong Kong, Taiwan, Singapore and South Korea moving from a pre-industrial stage to achieve first-world living standards within a generation (Powell, 2014, 2018; Powell & Skarbek, 2006). In a similar vein it has been argued (e.g. Zwolinski, 2007) that sweatshops are exploitative but workers right to accept a job should not be restricted if there is no alternative employment available.

However, a recent report, *Made in Poverty – The True Price of Fashion* (Oxfam 2018), paints a grim picture of the lack of financial and personal well-being of female RMG workers in Bangladesh and Vietnam due to the low minimum wage paid by overseas subcontractors. The report essentially appeals to Western buyers and consumers to pay 1% more on the price of their apparel in order to ensure a decent work life for the minimum wage earners in these emerging economies. This solution appears to be feasible because at least 55% of total profits are received by offshore buying companies (Salam & McLean, 2014). The Federation of Bangladesh Chambers of Commerce and Industry has suggested that this figure could be as much as 70% (https://www.daily-sun.com/post/332660/2018/08/30/No-trade-unions-in-97.5-percent-RMG-factories:-CPD-survey). It is not clear what mechanisms would ensure that the small increase in price would be passed on to the workers.

Though the classic tension between the differing ethical perspectives on offshoring and overseas sweatshops remains unresolved and the question of superior moral responsibility to ensure a decent work life in the emerging economies is far from being answered, the positive response of some buyers such as K-Mart in Australia to Oxfam's (2019) call for a 1% increase in apparel prices seems to be a move in the right direction although it falls short of a comprehensive solution to the complex issues surrounding offshore sweatshops. If K-mart's response does not have a significant negative impact on profitability, other retailers are likely to follow in order to enhance their reputation for ethical trading. Consideration should also be given to Anderson's (2015) proposed research agenda which highlights the potential benefits of offshore outsourcing on international human resource development practices (Blodget, 2012), knowledge transfer, organisational culture, training and development. Over the longer term this can enable companies to increase the level of value added through improved operational efficiency while not infringing the core ILO conventions. While higher aggregate wages and improved working conditions are a concomitant of economic development, improved operational efficiencies may not come about without effective government intervention. In this regard Salter's theory of technical progress and in particular his view on the impact of higher wages in driving efficiency is apposite (Salter, 1960).

Our comments above also highlight the importance of consumers who increasingly present as stakeholders in the global production of goods and services. Many European consumers have expressed their willingness to pay more for retail products if they are convinced that their contribution will help solve a social problem such as sweatshop exploitation ("BBC New Report, June 30, 2013, retrieved on 28th February 2019 from   https://www.youtube.com/watch?v=XSn2gTLx8iU"). However, both foreign buyers and the consumers expressed concern about whether this increased price would benefit the minimum wage earners or help alleviate overseas sweatshops conditions. One way to exercise more control over the overseas suppliers is to provide conditional financial advantage to subcontractors. For example, Apple paying Foxconn more for their iPhone production may not necessarily improve wages and working conditions, but conditional profit sharing may enable companies to require offshoring partners to provide specified pay and conditions. A similar approach has brought some success in improving working conditions in the Bangladeshi RMG sector following the release of the Oxfam report (2019). However, as we argue the overseas sweatshop issue reflects most of the features of a wicked problem, imitating any solution without considerable contextual modification is unlikely to succeed.

Finally, the continuing use of the term sweatshops, particularly in relation to pay, working conditions and harsh management in factories, has been a durable feature of the industrialisation process, though increasingly, the worst abuses have shifted to developing nations. What distinguishes the present epoch however is that increased consumer and public awareness of these abuses and a growing consensus on the importance of labour standards as evidenced in the prominence of the SDGs is changing the discourse around sweatshops. While this is seeing some amelioration of the worst practices of industries such as clothing manufacture, there is insufficient evidence to conclude that sweatshops are in decline. On the contrary, the wickedness of the problem suggests that if anything it is taking new forms.

Notes

1 https://www.oxfam.org.au/what-we-do/workers-rights-2/are-your-clothes-made-in-sweatshops/
2 https://databank.worldbank.org/data/download/poverty/33EF03BB-9722-4AE2-ABC7-AA2972D68AFE/Global_POVEQ_BGD.pdf

References

Ahmed, N., & Nathan, D. (2016). Improving wages and working conditions in the Bangladesh garment sector. In D. Nathan, M. Tewari, & S. Sarkar (Eds.), *Labour conditions in Asian value chains* (p. 51). New Delhi: Cambridge University Press.

Alliance. (2018). *An industry transformed: Leaving a legacy of safety in Bangladesh's garment sector.* Retrieved from https://www.alliance.co.nz/media/1912/annualreport2018.pdf

Anner, M. (2015). Worker resistance in global supply chains: Wildcat strikes, international accords and transnational campaigns. *International Journal of Labour Research*, 7(1/2), 17–34.

Anderson, V. (2015). International HRD and offshore outsourcing: A conceptual review and research agenda. *Human Resource Development Review*, 14(3), 259–278.

Barrientos, S., Mayer, F., Pickles, J., & Posthuma, A. (2011). Decent work in global production networks: Framing the policy debate. *International Labour Review*, 150(3–4), 297–317.

BBC New Report June 30, 2013. Retrieved on 28th February 2019 from https://www.youtube.com/watch?v=XSn2gTLx8iU

BDApparelNews. (2019, January 18). Criminals will be punished, BGMEA says on labour unrest. *bdapparelnews.com*. Retrieved from https://www.bdapparelnews.com/Criminals-will-be-punished-BGMEA-says-on-labour-unrest/233/233

Blodget, H. (2012, January 22). Why Apple makes iPhones in China and why the US is screwed. *Business Insider Australia*. Retrieved from https://www.businessinsider.com.au/you-simply-must-read-this-article-that-explains-why-apple-makes-iphones-in-china-and-why-the-us-is-screwed-2012-1

Carlson, L. A., & Bitsch, V. (2018). Social sustainability in the ready-made garment sector in Bangladesh: An institutional approach to supply chains. *International Food and Agribusiness Management Review*, 21(2), 269–292.

Centre for Future Work, Australia Institute, Committee Hansard, 21 February 2018, p. 28. Retrieved from https://www.futurework.org.au/research

Chamberlain, G. (2011, May 1). Apple factories accused of exploiting Chinese workers. *The Guardian*. Retrieved from https://www.theguardian.com/technology/2011/apr/30/apple-chinese-factory-workers-suicides-humiliation

Chan, J., Pun, N., & Selden, M. (2016). Apple, Foxconn, and China's new working class. In R. P. Appelbaum, & N. Lichtenstein (Eds.), *Achieving Workers' Rights in the Global Economy* (pp. 173–189). Ithaca, NY: Cornell University Press.

Chowdhury, R. 2017. The Rana Plaza disaster and the complicit behavior of elite NGOs. *Organization*, 24(6): 938–949.

Chowdhury, S. D., & Mahmood, M. H. (2012). Societal institutions and HRM practices: An analysis of four European multinational subsidiaries in Bangladesh. *The International Journal of Human Resource Management*, 23(9), 1808–1831.

Cleanclothes.org. (2019). Retrieved from https://cleanclothes.org/safety/support-for-the-bangladesh-accord

Coakley, M., & Kates, M. (2013). The ethical and economic case for sweatshop regulation. *Journal of Business Ethics*, 117(3), 553–558.

Emran, S. N., Kyriacou, J., & Rogan, S. (2019). *Made in poverty the true price of fashion*. Retrieved from Oxfam Australia https://whatshemakes.oxfam.org.au/wp-content/uploads/2019/02/Made-in-Poverty-the-True-Price-of-Fashion.-Oxfam-Australia..pdf

Faraci, D. (2019). Wage exploitation and the nonworseness claim: Allowing the wrong, to do more good. *Business Ethics Quarterly, 29*(2), 169–188.

Flanigan, J. (2018). Sweatshop regulation and workers' choices. *Journal of Business Ethics, 153*(1), 79–94.

Guardian. (2019, January 14). Bangladesh strikes: Thousands of garment workers clash with police over poor pay. *The Guardian*. Retrieved from https://www.theguardian.com/world/2019/jan/14/bangladesh-strikes-thousands-of-garment-workers-clash-with-police-over-poor-pay

Horgos, D. (2011). International outsourcing and the sector bias: New empirical evidence. *Review of International Economics, 19*(2), 232–244.

Horlings, L. G., & Marsden, T. K. (2014). Exploring the 'new rural paradigm' in Europe: Eco-economic strategies as a counterforce to the global competitiveness agenda. *European Urban and Regional Studies, 21*(1), 4–20.

Hoskins, T. (2015, April 10). Rana Plaza: Are fashion brands responsible for those they don't directly employ? *The Guardian*. Retrieved from https://www.theguardian.com/sustainable-business/sustainable-fashion-blog/2015/apr/10/rana-plaza-are-fashion-brands-responsible-for-those-they-dont-directly-employ

https://books.google.com/ngrams/graph?content=sweatshops&direct_url=t1%3B%2Csweatshops%3B%2Cc0#t1%3B%2Csweatshops%3B%2Cc0. Retrieved on June 6, 2019.

https://bangladeshaccord.org/. Retrieved on June 6, 2019.

http://www.industriall-union.org/over-11600-bangladesh-garment-workers-lose-jobs-and-face-repression. Retrieved on February 13, 2019.

https://www.ilo.org/dhaka/Areasofwork/workers-and-employers-organizations/lang--en/index.htm. Retrieved on June 6, 2019.

https://www.textiletoday.com.bd/accord-alliance-leave-bangladesh-january-commerce-minister/. Retrieved on June 6, 2019.

Jabbour, L., & Zuniga, P. (2016). The outsourcing of research and development in global markets: Evidence from France. *The World Economy, 39*(3), 339–368.

Jinnah, S. I. M. (2013). *Land and Property Rights of Rural Women in Bangladesh*. Dinajpur, Bangladesh: Community Development Association.

Kedia, B. L., & Lahiri, S. (2007). International outsourcing of services: A partnership model. *Journal of International Management, 13*(1), 22–37.

Khan, S. I. (2013). High performance work systems in the context of the banking sector in Bangladesh. Retrieved from http://arrow.latrobe.edu.au/store/3/5/1/3/7/public/MasterVersion.pdf

Khan, S. I., Bartram, T., Cavanagh, J., Hossain, M. S., & Akter, S. (2019). "Decent work" in the ready-made garment sector in Bangladesh: The role for ethical human resource management, trade unions and situated moral agency. *Personnel Review, 48*(1), 40–55.

Khanna, P. (2011). Making labour voices heard during an industrial crisis: workers' struggles in the Bangladesh garment industry. *TRAVAIL, capital et société, 44*(2): 106–129.

Knight, J. (2010). Internationalization and the competitiveness agenda. In L. M. Portnoi, V. D. Rust, & S. S. Bagley (Eds.), *Higher education, policy, and the global competition phenomenon* (pp. 205–218). New York: Palgrave Macmillan.

Maitland, I., Beauchamp, T., & Bowie, N. (1997). The great non-debate over international sweatshops.

Marchant, B. (2017). Life and death in Apple's forbidden city. *The Guardian*. Retrieved from https://www.theguardian.com/technology/2017/jun/18/foxconn-life-death-forbidden-city-longhua-suicide-apple-iphone-brian-merchant-one-device-extract

Mol, M. J., Van Tulder, R. J., & Beije, P. R. (2005). Antecedents and performance consequences of international outsourcing. *International Business Review*, 14(5), 599–617.

Moore, S. M. (2011, July 21). Apple, HP and Dell among companies responsible for 'electronic sweatshops', claims report. *The Telegraph*. Retrieved from https://www.telegraph.co.uk/technology/apple/8652295/Apple-HP-and-Dell-among-companies-responsible-for-electronic-sweatshops-claims-report.html

New Age Business. (2018, August 30). No trade unions in 97.5pc Bangladesh RMG factories: CPD. *NewAge Business*. Retrieved from www.newagebd.net/article/49447/no-trade-unions-in-975pc-bangladesh-rmg-factories-cpd

Ok, S. T. (2011). International outsourcing: Empirical evidence from the Netherlands. *Journal of Business Economics and Management*, 12(1), 131–143.

Oshri, I., Kotlarsky, J., & Willcocks, L. P. (2015). *The handbook of global outsourcing and offshoring*. London: Palgrave Macmillan.

Oxfam (2019). Made in Poverty, The True Price of Fashion. Retrieved on February 13. 2019 from https://whatshemakes.oxfam.org.au/wp-content/uploads/2019/02/Made-in-Poverty-the-True-Price-of-Fashion.-Oxfam-Australia..pdf

Powell, B. (2014). *Out of poverty: Sweatshops in the global economy*. New York: Cambridge University Press.

Powell, B. (2018). Sweatshop regulation: Tradeoffs and welfare judgements. *Journal of Business Ethics*, 151(1), 29–36.

Powell, B., & Skarbek, D. (2006). Sweatshops and third world living standards: Are the jobs worth the sweat? *Journal of Labor Research*, 27(2), 263–274.

Preiss, J. (2014). Global labor justice and the limits of economic analysis. *Business Ethics Quarterly*, 24(1), 55–83.

Pun, N., Shen, Y., Guo, Y., Lu, H., Chan, J., & Selden, M. (2016). Apple, Foxconn, and Chinese workers' struggles from a global labor perspective. *Inter-Asia Cultural Studies*, 17(1), 166–185.

Rahman, M. T., Habibullah, M., & Abdullah-Al-Masum, M. (2017). Ready-made garment industry in Bangladesh: Growth, contribution and challenges. *Journal of Economics and Finance*, 8(3), 1–7.

Rittel, H. W., & Webber, M. M. (1973). Dilemmas in a general theory of planning. *Policy Sciences*, 4(2), 155–169.

Salam, M. A., & McLean, G. N. (2014). *Minimum wage in Bangladesh's ready-made garment sector: Impact of imbalanced rates on employee and organization development*. Paper presented at the HRD: Reflecting upon the past, shaping the future: Proceedings of AHRD European Conference. Edinburgh: UFHRD.

Sartor, M. A., & Beamish, P. W. (2014). Offshoring innovation to emerging markets: Organizational control and informal institutional distance. *Journal of International Business Studies*, 45(9), 1072–1095.

Salter, W.E.G. (1960). *Productivity and technical change*. Cambridge University Press, Cambridge.

Stiglitz, J. E. (2002). *Globalization and its discontents*. New Delhi: Penguin.

TIB. (2018). *Good governance in RMG sector: Progress and challenges*. Retrieved from Bangladesh https://www.ti-bangladesh.org/beta3/index.php/en/highlights/5584-good-governance-in-rmg-sector-progress-and-challenges-executive-summary-english

Tripathi, D. (1996). Colonialism and technology choices in India: A historical overview. *The Developing Economies*, 34(1), 80–97.

UN News. (2013). Revised Bangladesh labour law 'falls short' of international standards – UN agency. Retrieved from https://news.un.org/en/story/2013/07/445222-revised-bangladesh-labour-law-falls-short-international-standards-un-agency

Zwolinski, M. (2007). Sweatshops, choice, and exploitation. *Business Ethics Quarterly*, 17(4), 689–727.

11 About Not Predicting the Future ...

Chris Brewster and Peter Holland

As we set out at the start of this book, there are significant changes going on in the world of work. Many commentators described this as an age of acceleration (Colville, 2016; Friedman, 2016; Schwab, 2018). What we wanted to explore in this context was the changing dynamics and boundaries of work that has occurred in the 21st century as we come to the end of the second decade. Second, we wanted to look at the impact of the changing nature of work, much of which is underpinned by technological change during a period that Schwab (2017), founder of the World Economic Forum, argues is unlike anything we have experienced before. However, we argue at this juncture we can choose how this will play out. This book is published more than 70 years after the anniversary of George Orwell's '1984', and some have described these emerging issues in either dystopian or utopian terms. What we have sought to highlight is that these changes, however minor on the surface, have impacted and are profoundly impacting on the ways we work and the quality of work. But it was perhaps ever thus. For example, the statement 'adapt or perish' seems an appropriate line written for our changing time, when in fact it was made by H.G. Wells nearly 100 years ago in 1922. In the foregoing chapters our experts have shown us some fascinating (and in some cases unforeseen) developments that are being enabled by new patterns of work, often facilitated by new technologies. In some cases, these create or allow new and perhaps 'improved' versions of what has always happened in work; alternatively, they provide a pathway to new forms of work intensification and impoverishment.

The book starts with arguably the type of work that most defines the changing nature of the labour market in advanced economies in the 21st century – the platform economy. Kaine et al. (Chapter 2) identified that a key feature and impact of ICTs has been the creation of the 'gig' economy with its ability to 'disrupt' sectors or industries which in many cases were staid, traditional and almost monopolistic. From the taxi industry (Uber) through to the hotel section (Airbnb) new services streams have been developed. However, as Kaine et al. point out, there are both utopian and dystopian views of this work. Much is made of the new empowering work where people can become entrepreneurs by hiring their skills and services, all built around their lifestyle. This very much speaks to the future Toffler envisioned 40 years ago where people would work like traditional artisans, as and when they needed, from their 'electronic' cottages (Toffler, 1980). However, as Kaine et al. note, there are polarised views of how the 'gig' economy works or doesn't work for various groups. Whilst, those who are highly skilled or have products in demand can pick and choose their work, schedules and price. There are those (arguably the majority) who provide (low level) skills and services, effectively working as contractors but providing the capital (Uber drivers), and those who compete on platforms for work as a form of race to the bottom where the cheapest offer prepared to do the work gets the job. In all this, there is no safety net or minimum wage to protect the most vulnerable because there is effectively no employment contract. For many therefore a more dystopian rather than utopian future of work has emerged in the 'gig' economy.

Following this utopian theme of increased control and leisure as machines often linked to artificial intelligence (AI) take over more of the work we do, the assumption is we will work less and less hours. However, long hours have been a well-established feature of the economies of developed societies for many years. Holland and Liang (Chapter 3) note that as deregulation has swept the world since Toffler's time we have seen an increase in longer working hours despite research showing the dangers inherent for both workers and organisations. A major side effect of these extreme working hours is that it burns out workers – very few people over 50 years of age can sustain these hours – and it forces people to select out – a form of discrimination. In addition, the case studies highlight the rhetoric and reality of management in dealing with the impact of these working patterns. These issues can be extended beyond the examples cited to include the way that new technology has enabled the possibility of 24-hour connection to work for many people, especially in the service sector, so that people are now taking calls, logging in and working in the evening, at weekends and during their 'holidays'. The technology that has enabled 24/7 provision of services has also enabled 24/7 demands on workers. Most would see this as a dystopian view of work in the context of quality experience.

An increasing area of interest is the relationship of extreme danger and violence to worker in their workplace. Whilst these issues have been an aspect of many workplaces and there is no convincing evidence that this has got either worse or better in recent years compared to say 50 or 100 years ago, Meacham et al. (Chapter 7) note the problem is now much more visible. This perhaps leads to an increasing feeling that such behaviour is in some way acceptable – after all, 'I saw it on TV' or on social media or in the papers. However, for emergency services who are increasingly dealing with people affected by Class A drugs and the ageing populations of the advanced market economies seeing an increase in dementia patients, the erratic nature of these patients behaviour increases the perceived risks and dangers of those working in the emergency services. Technology has increased the visibility of such behaviour though various outlets such as television documentaries and social media posting. This has raised the attention of the authorities and employers to address these issues; the technology not only highlights the issue but may be part of methods for ameliorating the problem – it is now possible to show unequivocal evidence of perpetrators' misbehaviour, through body cameras and other devices.

An extension of these issues takes us to those working in dangerous locations. People have always lived and worked in places where there is political unrest, and nasty governments, war, famine, natural disaster. In most cases they have had little choice; and this is still the position for most people in such circumstances. However, recent developments have seen the arrival into such locations of foreigners, who have either come to help and improve the situation or are there because their employer has identified an opportunity. Richard Posthuma and his colleagues (Chapter 6) point us towards some of the occupations involved and discuss what can be done to help people in such cases. Technology may have made it easier for these foreigners to get into and out of dangerous locations, but it does not seem to have made much impact on the dangers they face. In fact, in some cases it has enhanced the risk, with social media platforms linked to the value of propaganda for terrorist cells uploading footage of hostages from smart devises posting threats and demands for their release, which get international coverage.

Another perspective on the use and advances in technology is that extreme work is only possible or enhanced by new technology. Working in dangerous conditions and doing long hours at a stretch in off-shore deep sea research, in the middle of jungles or deserts or, specifically in this case, in the Antarctic, would not have been feasible without the improvements in transport, storage, clothing and communication that have taken place in recent years. Norris et al. examined the personal, interpersonal and organisational aspects of such work. They suggest that working in extreme situations is likely to increase and that this will put added pressure on the individual and those who manage such workers and will require policies that support the experience in the face of the danger and isolation and living away from home for extended periods. What they also found was that whilst technology enables working in this harsh environment, it is also a potential destabilising factor with social media and other forms of ICTs contact with family thousands of miles away strictly managed. Creating what can be described as 'deadly combination' with other management practices and resources designed to enhance the ability to work and function in such isolated and extreme environments for up to a year. This is linked to the expectation people have, that social media and other e-platforms emerging in the 21st century are universal and available.

The increasing electronic monitoring and surveillance of workers that has emerged in the 21st century may be conceived as a continuation of former practices – indicated in words like 'supervisor' and 'overseer', with their connotations of a person physically looking down on the workers they controlled. These roles were once common in manufacturing and are far from unknown today. But this is an area where the technology has created a paradigm shift in possibilities, so that it might be considered that we are now in a new situation or what has been called 'Super Vision'. Holland and Tham (Chapter 9) have shown us how electronic monitoring and surveillance has spread into a very wide range of industries and occupations; and they note the developing power that it provides for managers take this monitoring and surveillance even further. Much of this is invisible: people may know that their use of their mobile phone or other smart devices, or their keyboard activities, can be monitored, but they are rarely aware of whether such data are collected or how they are used. There are already instances of employees in the USA and Sweden agreeing to have microchips inserted under their skin, so that their employer can monitor them (effectively at all times). An increasing reflection of the point noted earlier regarding the 70th anniversary of George Orwell's 1984, what was fiction then is very much fact now. Not least dystopian is how advancements in ICT and biometrics can help effectively monitor individuals across the globe.

Continuing this theme of changes technology has brought, is the sweatshops, which, have existed in one form or other for centuries. However, the new technologies have created the possibility of first, linking up sweatshops in many third-world countries with major multinational corporations and second, distancing the first-world organisation (despite signing up for code of conduct and regulations) from the poor and extreme working conditions – highlighted by major incidents such as Rana Plaza. As Teicher and Khan (Chapter 10) have shown, this model is now emerging in the high technology sector with sweatshops in China associated with major brands like Apple identified as having appalling working practices and conditions linked to high suicide rates. For these workers technology has provided an alternate avenue for poor and extreme working conditions. At the other end of the spectrum is what Teicher (Chapter 4) identifies as (first world) wage theft. In an era of hi-tech human resource information systems (HRIS), it is hard to see these high-profile cases as anything but systemic theft by global organisations such as Caltex, 7-Eleven, Pizza Hut and Domino's Pizza. Reflecting on the changing nature of work through the changing location(s) of work, Wheatley (Chapter 8) provides an historical and contemporary evolution of where we work. This can be as large as the corner office and as small as the smart device in your hand. Indeed, places like Starbucks coffee shops actively encourage people to see their shops as an extension of the workplace.

Future Trends

So, what are the experts telling us about the future trends in work? Perhaps unsurprisingly, much the same thing. Most of these experts are technology specialists and they make a variety of predictions. However, most debates appears to be around the amount of jobs technology and in particular AI will change and consume, ranging from 10% to over 60% of current jobs in the next generation (Arntz, Gregory, Zierahn, 2016; Frey & Osborne, 2017; McKinsey Global Institute, 2017; Nedelkoska & Quinitini, 2018). These significant claims come from the fact that the new technologies are having a substantial impact, in ways that many do not recognise as yet. As noted in the first chapter, AI has progressed from being about the collection and analysis of information ('big data' as it is sometimes called), and is now increasingly about replacing higher order human skills such as legal analysis, radiology, architecture many positions often considered to be too highly skilled to be threatened by technology or replaced by artificial intelligence-managed, robotised workers. Indeed, some futurologists argue that in the next step General Artificial Intelligence will be able to replace almost anything that humans can do.

One key mistake that many of these technologists make when they consider work, and what will happen to work, is to conceive work as a series of tasks. Work is, of course, much more than that. In *The Thought of Work* (2011) Budd noted that work is so much more than tasks – depending in part on one's class, power, gender and race it is an imposition, a source of freedom, a chance to serve – it is fundamental to how most people think of themselves. 'What do you do?' is a very common question and for most people the answer is that a significant part of their self-concept is concerned with the work that they do. Another mistake is to assume that whilst technology is increasingly likely to have a substantial effect on the nature of work, the march of technology is not inexorable. This is captured in what has become known in parts of the academic community in the UK as the 'car wash paradox'. For many years there were no such things as car washes: people washed their own car. As car ownership spread to the middle and lower groups it became a tradition amongst those who owned cars to wash their cars at the side of the road, mostly on Sundays, a tradition much mocked by comedians. Then, as technological solutions became applied to the problem of dirty vehicles, lorry and car fleet owners started installing automatic car washes on their premises. Gradually, as the long and variable hours culture that we have examined in the book spread, and as people came to have more disposable income (and less spare time), entrepreneurs installed publicly available car washes and most people stopped washing their own cars and used the public car washes. The technology developed and the car washes became smarter and better, able to offer washing, drying, polishing and even a degree of 'valeting'. But the accession to the European

Union of some of the ex-communist countries in Central and Eastern Europe opened up the UK labour market to people from these much less wealthy countries. Groups of such immigrants (in some cases, 'gangs', it has been alleged) offered an upmarket or personalised 'hand wash' option. People could take their cars to a car park or some other bit of waste land and six or ten migrants would descend on the car and give it a thorough clean, washing every single surface, inside and out, polishing and painting the wheels and even taking grit from the tyre treads. Significantly, they would do that at a price similar to, or below, that of the automatic car washes. As use of the automatic car washes declined, they became unprofitable, and then non-viable, and they closed. People went from having their cars washed in a highly technological, computer-controlled facility underpinned by IT, to having them washed in the most basic way possible. Technology could not compete with cheap labour and better service. So, one key question for the next few years will be to assess how these conflicting options play out in practice. As we noted the concept of work is very important to people and as the title of the chapter indicates it is the future that is difficult to predict.

Which Way Forward?

What conclusions can we draw from these changes emerging in the first two decades of the 21st century? We would argue that as we enter this fourth industrial age (Schwab, 2018), we have the opportunity to take a high road or utopian view of work or a low road dystopian view. What we mean by this is that these fundamental changes can create the opportunity for what can be described as meaningful work.

There is a growing stream of literature on the notion of 'meaningful' work (Chalofsky, 2010). This is one of those expressions that, like so many aspects of business and management scholarship (see, e.g. 'talent management', 'performance', 'corporate governance', 'sustainability', 'human resource management') where the terminology has become widely used, precisely because it is ill-defined (Abrahamson & Eisenman, 2008; Clark, 2004; Swan, 2004) and the literature has been critiqued on that basis (Both-Nwabuwe, Dijkstra, & Beersma, 2017; Lepisto & Pratt, 2017; Lysova, Allan, Dik, Duffy, & Steger, 2019; Rosso, Dekas, & Wrzesniewski, 2010). Understanding meaningful work involves addressing a number of paradoxes (Bailey et al., 2019). The same arguments could be made about the ILO notion of 'decent' work. Despite this, the concept of 'meaningful work' does direct us towards the importance of a positive, subjective, individual experience of work (Bailey, Madden, Alfes, Shantz, & Soane, 2018).

We note, of course, that meaningfulness in work has a 'dark side': it can lead to long working hours and poor employee well-being (Bunderson & Thompson, 2009; Michaelson, Pratt, Grant, & Dunn, 2014) and to stress on personal relationships (Oelberger, 2019). The positive side of meaningful work, which is now generating a significant literature (see the Special issue of the *Journal of Management Studies* of May 2019), is that the focus on what work means to individuals brings together research from a wide range of disciplines and with a wide range of consequences. How individuals view their work and how they evaluate it as meaningful have both an objective and a subjective element (Wolf, 2010); it is an individual and a social construct. The meaning of work will be different for co-workers and managers, although each does and will try to influence the meaning attributed to their work by any one individual. As has been shown in a much more entertaining and incisive way than the refereed journals are able to do (Graeber, 2018), most people have a fairly shrewd idea as to whether their jobs have any real purpose or not. Indeed, we see the concepts of 'bullshit' jobs (Graeber, 2018) and empty labour (Paulsen, 2014; Lyons, 2019) becoming main stream areas of discussion.

Much of the academic discussion on the meaning of work has focused on the outcomes of such meanings for organisations, in terms of issues such as attendance, motivation, commitment, performance and stress (Rosso, et al., 2010). However, much (meaningful) work – caring, nurturing, family-building, volunteering – has always been undertaken outside organisations; and this seems to be the trend of the future. Less and less work will be done in organisations; more and more will be done by individuals working, in some fashion, for themselves. We need to keep this in balance. In the near future, at least, substantial amounts of work will be done in organisations. However, a focus on work rather than employment will allow us to encompass all relevant activities.

A considerable amount of the research on 'meaningful work' has focused on workers who do not fit into the work usual patterns, such as volunteers (Alfes, 2018; Alfes, Shantz, & Bailey, 2016; Rodell, 2013; Yim & Fock, 2013), prison staff, people doing dirty work (Deery, Kolar, & Walsh, 2019) and, perhaps inevitably, university faculty (Knights & Clarke, 2014; Mingers & Willmott, 2013). In this whole area of work, the lack of construct clarity has meant that there are similar debates going on under different terminologies. There is a growing literature on 'good' and 'bad' jobs (Adamson & Roper, 2019): even if, again, the definitions are contested and there may be little coherence between objective and subjective measures (Kalleberg, 2011). The degradation of work, from good to bad jobs, has long been a concern (Braverman, 1974; Curley & Royle, 2013). New technologies, particularly AI, will change the nature of many jobs – will it be for the better or for worse? The situation at this point in time is that we have some choice.

For the future, the challenge is whether new technology will make work more likely to be good and meaningful or the opposite. As we have noted in this book, even small changes can create significant impact on the quality and nature of work. The answer is almost certainly that for some, in the games industry, in the arts and creative occupations, for example, work is likely to become ever more meaningful. But for a great many this seems unlikely: being a delivery driver (if we still have drivers) is not going to be seen by most people as meaningful work, and as the algorithms enforce increasingly exacting standards, it is likely to become even less meaningful. Even here, we need to remember that some people doing such work are happy doing it. The huge number of 'bullshit' jobs that Graeber (2018) describes are identified by the incumbents thinking of themselves as doing meaningless work. In this context, the 'economics of work doesn't work': that is, economists assume that if there is work (a job?) then it must show an economic benefit for the owner of the business, otherwise they would get rid of the job or the work. But this is demonstrably not true. Graeber's *Bullshit Jobs: A Theory* entertainingly points out that there are, he estimates, as many as 40% of jobs that have no real purpose – they exist because they make their manager seem more important, or to fix mistakes in other people's jobs, or to sell people things they do not need or to complete tasks required, or thought to be required, by some other agency. Graeber makes the point that such people know they are doing bullshit jobs. How does this fit with the notion that new technology is going to free up people to do more enjoyable, creative and artistic work? And, how does this fit with Fleming's critique that the growth of new technology has actually occurred at a time when developed societies have more or less full employment and are in many areas short of the skills that they need?

We think about these issues bearing in mind two (perhaps apocryphal) warnings. The first is from the late Danish physicist and Nobel Prize winner, Neils Bohr, who is supposed to have said that 'prediction is very difficult, especially about the future'. The second is 'Amara's law' (credited to the late Stanford scientist and futurologist Roy Amara) which states that the effects of technological change are almost always overestimated in the short run and underestimated in the long run. We need to be cautious about how the world of work may change under the impact of new technology over the next few years. But that major changes are developing is certain.

We believe that at the start of the fourth industrial revolution societies have options. We doubt whether there will be either utopian or dystopian futures as a result. In terms of work, at least, the result of the technology over the next few years is likely to reinforce existing patterns of ownership and benefits. In work, there is likely to be continuing duality, with good jobs getting better and bad jobs getting worse; old jobs disappearing and new ones created. There are options in terms of the trajectory of change. We fear that the impact of AI and robotisation increases the pressure for societies to expand the 'low road' approach to management.

The debates and the court cases about taxi services and food delivery workers have gone in different directions in the two countries we live in – at about the same time in a legal system that has many affinities with the British system, Australian workers in these sectors are losing cases to be considered employees. Where workers have had wins the company simply ceases trading. These cases may be seen as evidence of the problem of work without employment and workers without rights; or they may be seen as the last throw of the dice of older institutions and processes. It seems unlikely to us that the solution to the problems of work in the 21st century will be delivered by 20th-century legal structures, trade unions or indeed by 20th-century thinking. It is unlikely, for example, that someone working at home to supplement their state benefits by completing basic computer-generated tasks is likely to complain that the algorithm through which they are employed has not paid the full amount they were promised. The breaking of the work-employment assumption is best summed up by Valenduc and Vendramin (2019), who argue that it is not so much a world without work that should concern us but a world where employment relations have withered away. So the key question is – how do we maintain a quality working relationship in this 'new' era of work?

How Do We Get There?

Empirical results confirm that fair treatment has a more powerful effect in situations where people feel uncertain about their position and feel that they are not in control (van den Bos, 2001; van den Bos & Miedema, 2000; Diekmann, Barsness, & Sondak, 2004). Unfairness has been found to create doubt for people regarding their capacity to cope and subsequently to result in emotional exhaustion and organisational withdrawal (Cole, Bernerth, Walter, & Holt, 2010). These basic tenets of uncertainty management theory (see Lind & van den Bos, 2002) suggest that perceptions of un/fair treatment may be particularly important in the highly uncertain context of the new working environment. As such we see the framework of organisational justice as a useful way to structure this analysis, in terms of how people are treated in the context of the withering employment relationship.

Organisational justice has been identified as the glue that allows people to work together effectively (Cropanzano, Bowen, & Gilliland, 2007). Justice defines the very essence of individuals' relationships to their employer(s) (Rupp, Shapiro, Folger, Skarliki, & Shao, 2017), and, as such, has been identified as one of the dominant approaches within the human resource management (HRM) literature for examining how individuals come to view their situations as just and fair (terms that are used interchangeably in the literature). Discrete but integrated factors such as motives, processes and challenges impact individual's perceptions of organisational justice. A negative relationship, or injustice, is like a corrosive solvent and results in negative outcomes at the individual and organisational level (Jost & Banaji, 1994). Gonzalez-Mulé and Cockburn (2017) found in their study of the relationship between job demands, control, and death that for individuals in low control jobs, high job demands were associated with a 15.4% increase in the odds of death compared to low job demands. Fair treatment is therefore important because it can provide us sense of stability, predictability, safety and cohesion within and across groups (Tayler & Lind, 1992).

Of foundational importance to the study of organisational justice is Deutsch's (1975) principles pertaining to equity (e.g. whether perceived outcomes reflect the receivers' respective input), equality (e.g. whether received outcomes are equal across individuals within the same group), and need (e.g. whether received outcomes satisfy the receivers' relative needs). Individuals assess fairness by choosing one principle over the other to determine fairness. Four dimensions of organisational justice have been conceptualised and empirically confirmed, and measures have been psychometrically validated (Bies & Moag, 1986; Colquitt, 2001; Greenberg, 1993). These dimensions are: (1) *distributive justice*, the fairness of decision outcomes affecting employees such as pay, reward or performance ratings; (2) *procedural justice*, the fairness of the process and procedures used to determine allocation decisions including employee outcomes; (3) *informational justice*, the fairness of information provided to employees by decision makers regarding organisational issues that affect them in terms of specificity, completeness and timeliness; and (4) *interactional justice*, the fairness of interpersonal treatment of employees by decision makers with regard to politeness, respect, sensitivity and dignity (e.g. whether they explain decisions thoroughly).

Distributive justice assesses the perceived fairness of outcomes received in comparison to one's input, education and what others receive (Adams, 1965). Positive perceptions of distributive justice have been shown to impact positively on attitudes to work, work outcomes and supervisors (Moorman, 1991). In contrast, violations increase the desire to punish and impose harmful consequences on a putative wrongdoer (Skarlicki & Folger, 1997).

Procedural justice includes opportunities for control of the process and the outcomes, ability to genuinely express one's viewpoints (Folger & Cropanzano, 1998), consistency, lack of bias, availability of appeal mechanisms, use of accurate information, and following ethical and moral norms. Past studies show that procedural justice has a positive relationship with stress (Judge & Colquitt, 2004), organisational commitment (Cohen-Charash & Spector, 2001) motivation, performance and turnover intentions (Colquitte et al., 2001). One of the principal tenets of procedural justice is voice, meaning the opportunity for individuals to genuinely put forward their points of view during the process of making decisions that will affect them (Judge & Colquitt, 2004).

It has been established that people respond to uncertainty in their work lives by seeking information (Ashford & Cummings, 1985). Thus, information justice can be expected to be a key strategy for managing uncertainty and stress in the context of this new world of work, because a feeling of personal control can be a crucial coping resource during organisational transition, thereby reducing perceived stress (Ashford, 1988). Not being sufficiently informed about an upcoming change, especially if that change affects one directly, can cause perceptions of injustice (Bies et al., 2005) and is likely to foster poor adjustment, disengagement and turnover. Further, lack of information may inhibit coping and be related to emotional exhaustion (Stahl & Caligiuri, 2005).

Interactional justice, whether people are treated with disrespect in interactions, has been found to have a significant negative relationship with stress (Judge & Colquitt, 2004; Takeuchi, Lepak, Marinova, & Yun, 2007). Four different facets of interactional justice have been proposed (Bies et al., 2005). These are: (1) derogatory judgements when not true; (2) deception, such as feeling lied to, for example, in recruitment; (3) invasion of privacy and unwarranted disclosure of personal information and (4) disrespect, being ignored. It is clear that these perceptions have an impact on not only the individual, but also the organisation; therefore, it provides a cautionary tale to those who see the new unregulated world of work as an opportunity to exploit a vulnerable workforce.

The Grand Challenges

It is valuable, as we close our discussion of the future of work, to connect it to some of the bigger issues that lie behind the focus on work. Much of our scholarly work connects only very peripherally, if at all, to some of the Grand Challenges that the world faces (George, Howard-Greenville, Joshi, & Tihanyi, 2016), like those posed by poverty and hunger, climate change, rising income inequality and economic insecurity. These problems are accompanied by increased pressure for corporations to "contribute to the creation of economic and societal progress in a globally responsible and sustainable way" (GRLI, 2017, p. 3). The creation of the United Nations Sustainable Development Goals to end poverty, protect the planet and ensure prosperity for all is a reflection of these developments. But much of the business and management, and even the human resource management and industrial relations, scholarly work barely touches these concerns. We should perhaps be measuring work against these criteria too (Stahl, Brewster, Collings, & Hajro, 2020). As Teagarden (2019, p. 461) notes in this context, the question for HRM practitioners is, are they ready to embrace this new reality? For academics the question is how are we aiding organisational transformation in the fourth industrial revolution to build more valuable relations with their workforce and society?

Taking a sustainable HRM approach adds the social and environmental dimensions in which the organisation operates. As Kramer (2014, p. 1070) explains sustainable HRM literature can be seen as "an attempt to grapple with the relationship between HRM practices and outcomes beyond predominantly financial outcomes". Drawing on the Brundtland Commission's (1987) report, three pillars of sustainability; financial (or economic), social and ecological (or 'green') are identified. Adopting these three pillars, sustainable HRM can thus be seen as extending beyond strategic HRM definitions, which tend to focus on financial outcomes, to internal corporate social responsibility (CSR), with its focus on attaining social outcomes for a better society. As such the focus is on the expansion of HRM's focus to explicitly include social and ecological dimensions in addition to the traditional focus on economics. In developing these concepts, Kramer's (2014) definition of sustainable HRM also incorporates a temporal dimension, highlighting that a sustainable approach to HRM meets both current and future needs of employees, organisation and society. As Wagner (2013, p. 443) argues, a sustainable HRM approach should be designed to "meet the current needs of a firm and society at large without compromising their ability to meet future needs". A more sustainable approach to HRM acknowledges the importance of looking into the longer term, ensuring the approaches taken by HRM help support the availability of suitable labour into the future (e.g. through being an employer of choice, placing high value on employee health and well-being, training and developing meaningful work for employees in preparation for future positions), as well as supporting the overall business to long-term success (e.g. supporting staff to achieve business' economic, social and ecological goals, educating staff on environmental conservation efforts, creating policies to support staff contributing to social goals) (Ehnert, 2009; Ehnert et al., 2014). As we immerse ourselves in the fourth industrial revolution we don't think these positions are at odds with a workplace that people would want to work in.

References

Abrahamson, E., & Eisenman, M. 2008. Employee-management techniques: Transient fads or trending fashions? *Administrative Science Quarterly*, 53(4): 719–744.

Adams, J. 1965. Inequities in social exchange. In L. Berkowitz (Eds), *Advances in experimental social psychology* (pp. 267–299). Vol. 2. New York: Academic Press.

Adamson, M., & Roper, I. 2019. *'Good' jobs and 'bad' jobs: Contemplating job quality in different contexts*. London: SAGE Publications.

Alfes, K. 2018. People management in volunteer organizations and charities: Managing people in the not for profit sector. In C. Brewster, & J.-L. Cerdin (Eds.), *HRM in mission driven organizations* (pp. 47–77). London: Palgrave Macmillan.

Alfes, K., Shantz, A., & Bailey, C. 2016. Enhancing volunteer engagement to achieve desirable outcomes: What can non-profit employers do? *VOLUNTAS: International Journal of Voluntary and Nonprofit Organizations,* 27(2): 595–617.

Arntz, M., Gregory, T., & Zierahn, U. 2016. *The risk of automation for jobs in OECD countries: A comparative analysis.* Paris: OECD. Report 189.

Ashford, S. J., & Cummings, L. L. 1985. Proactive feedback seeking: The instrumental use of the information environment. *Journal of Occupational Psychology,* 58: 61–69.

Bies, R., & Moag, J., 1986. Interactional justice: communication criteria of fairness. In R. Lewecki, B. Sheppard, & M. Bazerman (Eds.), *Research on negotiation in organizations (pp. 43–55).* Vol. 1. Greenwich, CT: JAI Press.

Bies R. J., & Tripp T. M. 2005. The study of revenge in the workplace: Conceptual, ideological, empirical issues. In S. Fox, & P. Spector (Eds.), *Counterproductive workplace behavior: An integration of both actor and recipient perspectives on causes and consequences (pp. 65–82).* Washington, DC: American Psychological Association.

Bailey, C., Lips-Wiersma, M., Madden, A., Yeoman, R., Thompson, M., & Chalofsky, N. 2019. The five paradoxes of meaningful work: Introduction to the special issue 'meaningful work: Prospects for the 21st century'. *Journal of Management Studies,* 56(3): 481–499.

Bailey, C., Madden, A., Alfes, K., Shantz, A., & Soane, E. 2018. The mismanaged soul: Existential labour and the erosion of meaningful work. *Human Resources Management Review,* 27: 416–430.

Both-Nwabuwe, J., Dijkstra, M., & Beersma, B. 2017. How to define and measure meaningful work. *Frontiers in Psychology.* doi: 10.3389/fpsyg.2017.01658

Braverman, H. 1974. *Labor and monopoly capitalism: The degradation of work in the twentieth century.* New York: Monthly Review Press.

Brundtland Commission (The). 1987. *Report of the World Commission on environment and development: Our common future.* Retrieved from http://www.un-documents.net/our-common-future.pdf

Budd, J. W. 2011. *The thought of work.* Ithaca, NY: Cornell University Press.

Bunderson, J. S., & Thompson, J. 2009. The call of the wild: Zookeepers, callings and the double-edged sword of deeply meaningful work. *Administrative Science Quarterly,* 54: 32–57.

Chalofsky, N. 2010. *Meaningful work.* San Francisco, CA: Wiley.

Clark, T. 2004. The fashion of management fashion: A surge too far? *Organization,* 11(2): 297–306.

Cohen-Charash, Y., & Spector, P. E. 2001. The role of justice in organizations: A meta-analysis. *Organizational Behavior and Human Decision Processes,* 86: 278–321.

Cole, M., Bernerth, J., & Holt, F. 2010. Organizational justice and individuals' withdrawal: Unlocking the influence of emotional exhaustion. *Journal of Management Studies,* 47(3): 367–390. doi: 10.1111/j.1467-6486.2009.00864.x

Colquitt, J. 2001. On the dimensionality of organisational justice: a construct validation method. *Journal of Applied Psychology.* 86: 386–400.

Colquitt, J. A., Conlon, D. E., Wesson, M. J., Porter, C., & Ng, K. Y. 2001. Justice at the millennium: A meta-analytic review of 25 years of organizational justice research. *Journal of Applied Psychology,* 86, 425–445.

Colville, R. 2016. *The great acceleration*. London: Bloomsbury.

Cropanzano, R., Bowen, D., & Gilliland, S. 2007. The management of organizational justice. *Academy of Management Perspectives*, 21(4): 34–48.

Curley, C., & Royle, T. 2013. The degradation of work and the end of the skilled emotion worker at Aer Lingus: Is it all trolley dollies now? *Work, Employment and Society*, 27(1): 105–121.

Deery, S., Kolar, D., & Walsh, J. 2019. Can dirty work be satisfying? A mixed method study of workers doing dirty jobs. *Work, Employment and Society*. doi: 10.1177/0950017018817307

Diekmann, K.A., Barsness, Z.I., & Sondak, H. 2004. Uncertainty, fairness perceptions, and job satisfaction: A field study. *Social Justice Research*, 17: 237–245. doi: 10.1023/B:SORE.0000041292.38626.2f

Ehnert, I. 2009. *Sustainable human resource management: A conceptual and exploratory analysis from a paradox perspective*. Dordrecht, Germany: Physica-Verlag.

Ehnert, I., Harry, W, & Zink, K. 2014. The future of sustainable HRM. *Sustainability and Human Resource Management*, 35: 423–442.

Folger, R., & Cropanzano, R. 1998. *Organizational justice and human resource management*. Thousand Oaks: Sage.

Frey, C. B., & Osborne, M. A. 2017. *The future of employment: How susceptible are jobs to computerisation?* Paris: OECD. Report 202.

Friedman, T. L. 2016. *Thank you for being late: An optimist's guide to thriving in the age of accelerations*. New York: Allen & Unwin.

George, G., Howard-Grenville, J., Joshi, A., & Tihanyi, L. 2016. Understanding and tackling societal grand challenges through management research. *Academy of Management Journal*, 59(6): 1880–1895.

Globally Responsible Leadership Initiative. 2017. *Developing the next generation of globally responsible leaders: A call for action*. Retrieved from https://grli.org/about/global-responsibility/

Gonzalez-Mulé, E., & Cockburn, B. S. 2017. Worked to death: The relationships of job demands and job control factors with mortality. *Personnel Psychology*, 70: 73–112.

Graeber, D. 2018. *Bullshit jobs: A theory*. New York: Simon and Schuster.

Greenberg, J. 1993. The social side of fairness: Interpersonal and informational classes of organizational justice. In R. Cropanzano (Ed.), *Justice in the workplace: approaching fairness in human resource management* (pp. 79–103), Hillsdale: Lawrence Erlbaum Associates.

Judge, T., & Colquitt, J. 2004. Organizational justice and stress: the mediating role of work-family conflict. *Journal of Applied Psychology*, 89(3): 395–404.

Jost, J., & Banaji, M. 1994. The role of stereotyping in system-justification and the production of false consciousness. *British Journal of Social Psychology*, 33: 1–27.

Kalleberg, A. L. 2011. *Good jobs, bad jobs: The rise of polarized and precarious employment systems in the United States, 1970s to 2000s*. New York: Russell Sage Foundation.

Knights, D., & Clarke, C. A. 2014. It's a bittersweet symphony, this life: Fragile academic selves and insecure identities at work. *Organization Studies*, 35(3): 335–357.

Kramer, R. 2014. Creating more trusting and trustworthy organizations: Exploring the foundations and benefits of presumptive trust. *Public Trust in Business*, 7(3): 203–235.

Lind, E., & van den Bos, K. 2002. When fairness works: Toward a general theory of uncertainty management. *Research in Organizational Behaviour*, 24: 181–223.

Lepisto, D. A., & Pratt, M. G. 2017. Meaningful work as realization and justification: Toward a dual conceptualization. *Organizational Psychology Review*, 7(2): 99–121.

Lyons, D. 2019. *Lab rats: Why modern work makes people miserable*. London: Atlantic Books.

Lysova, E. I., Allan, B. A., Dik, B. J., Duffy, R. D., & Steger, M. F. 2019. Fostering meaningful work in organizations: A multi-level review and integration. *Journal of Vocational Behavior*, 110: 374–389.

Michaelson, C., Pratt, M. G., Grant, A. M., & Dunn, C. P. 2014. Meaningful work: Connecting business ethics and organization studies. *Journal of Business Ethics*, 121: 77–90.

McKinsey Global Institute. 2017. *Jobs lost, jobs gained. Workforce transitions in a time of automation*. New York: MGI.

Mingers, J., & Willmott, H. 2013. Taylorizing business school research: On the 'one best way' performative effects of journal ranking lists. *Human Relations*, 66(8): 1051–1073.

Moorman, R. H. 1991. Relationship between organizational justice and organizational citizenship behaviors: Do fairness perceptions influence employee citizenship? *Journal of Applied Psychology*, 76(6): 845–855. doi: 10.1037/0021-9010.76.6.845

Nedelkoska, L., & Quintini, G. 2018. *Automation, skills use and training, OECD social, employment and migration*. Working Papers, No. 202. Paris: OECD Publishing. doi: 10.1787/2e2f4eea-en

Oelberger, C. R. 2019. The dark side of deeply meaningful work: Work-relationship turmoil and the moderating role of occupational value homophily. *Journal of Management Studies*, 56(3): 558–588.

Orwell, G. 1949. *Nineteen eighty-four*. London: Pan Books.

Paulsen, R. 2014. *Empty labor: Idleness and workplace resistance*. Cambridge: University Printing House.

Rodell, J. B. 2013. Finding meaning through volunteering: Why do employees volunteer and what does it mean for their jobs? *Academy of Management Journal*, 56(5): 1274–1294.

Rosso, B. D., Dekas, K. H., & Wrzesniewski, A. 2010. On the meaning of work: A theoretical integration and review. *Research in organizational behavior*, 30: 91–127.

Rupp, D., Shapiro, D., Folger, R., Skarlicki, D. P., & Shao, R. 2017. A critical analysis of the conceptualization and measurement of 'organizational justice': Is it time for reassessment? *Academy of Management Annals*, 11(2): 919–959. doi: 10.5465/annals.2014.0051

Schwab, K. 2017. *The fourth industrial revolution*. UK: Penguin.

Schwab, K. 2018. *Shaping the future of the fourth industrial revolution*. Cologny: World Economic Forum.

Skarlicki, D. P., & Folger, R. 1997. Retaliation in the workplace: The roles of distributive, procedural, and interactional justice. *Journal of Applied Psychology, 82*(3): 434–443. doi: 10.1037/0021-9010.82.3.434

Stahl, G. K., Brewster, C., Collings, D, & Hajro, A. 2020. Enhancing the role of human resource management in corporate sustainability and social responsibility: A multidimensional, multi-stakeholder approach to HRM. *Human Resource Management Review.*

Stahl, G., & Caligiuri, P. 2005. The effectiveness of expatriate coping strategies: The moderating role of cultural distance, position level, and time on the international assignment. *Journal of Applied Psychology*, 90(4): 603–615.

Swan, J. 2004. Reply to Clark: The fashion of management fashion. *Organization*, 11(2): 307–313.

Takeuchi, R., Lepak, D., Sophia, M., & Seokhwa, Y. 2007. Nonlinear influences of stressors on general adjustment: The case of Japanese expatriates and their spouses. *Journal of International Business Studies*, 38: 928–943.

Teagarden, M. 2019. The future of work. *Thunderbird International Business Review*, 61: 461.

Tyler. T.R., & Lind, E.A., 1992. A relational model of authority in groups. In M. Zanna, Ed., *Advances in Experimental Social Psychology* (p. 192), Vol. 25, New York: Academic Press.

Valenduc, G., & Vendramin, P. 2019. *The mirage of the end of work*. Brussels: ETUI.

van den Bos, K. 2001. Reactions to perceived fairness: The impact of mortality salience and self-esteem on ratings of negative affect. *Social Justice Research*, 14: 1–23.

van den Bos, K., & Miedema, J. 2000. Toward understanding why fairness matters: The influence of mortality salience on reactions to procedural fairness. *Journal of Personality and Social Psychology*, 79(3): 355–366.

Wagner, M., 2013. 'Green' human resource benefits: Do they matter as determinants of environmental management system implementation? *Journal of Business Ethics*, 114: 443-456. doi: 10.1007/s10551-012-1356-9

Wells, H. G. 1922. *A short history of the world*. Harmondsworth: Penguin Books.

Wolf, S. 2010. *Meaning in life and why it Matters*. Princeton, NJ: Princeton University Press.

Yim, F., & Fock, H. 2013. Social responsibility climate as a double-edged sword: How employee-perceived social responsibility climate shapes the meaning of their voluntary work? *Journal of Business Ethics*, 114(4): 665–674.

Notes on Contributors

Editors

Dr. Chris Brewster is now a part-time Professor of International Human Resource Management at Vaasa University in Finland; Henley Business School, University of Reading in the UK, specialising in international and comparative HRM. He had substantial industrial experience and got his doctorate from the London School of Economics before becoming an academic. He been in involved as author or editor in the publication of more than 30 books, more than 100 chapters in other books and well over 200 articles.

Dr. Peter Holland is a Professor of Human Resource Management and Director of the Executive MBA at Swinburne University of Technology, Melbourne. Previously he was appointed at Monash University and was Director of the Faculty Research Centre – The Australian Consortium for Research on Employment and Work (ACREW) and Head of the Human Resource and Employee Relations Discipline in the Department of Management. Peter has worked in the Australian finance sector and consulted to the private and public sectors in a variety of areas related to human resource management and employee relations. His current research interests include employee voice, workplace electronic monitoring and surveillance and extreme work. He has authored/co-authored 12 books and over 100 journal articles, monographs and book chapters on a variety of human resource management and employee relation issues.

Contributors

Tom Barratt is a Lecturer at Edith Cowan University's School of Business and Law. He is a labour geographer who has published work related to Global Production Network theory, mining regions and the emerging gig economy. His work focusses on how spatial variability explains and generates variation in the terms and conditions of work between locations and over time.

Professor Timothy Bartram's expertise covers human resource management (HRM) and high-performance work systems, employment relations, nursing management, workers with disability, Men's Sheds and Indigenous communities. Much of Tim's research is multi-disciplinary and promotes the innovative use of HRM especially in the healthcare sector inclusive of hospitals and healthcare industry.

Dr. Jillian Cavanagh is a Senior Lecturer at Royal Melbourne Institute of Technology University. Jillian's commitment to research is predominantly in the area of human resource management, employer support and the employment of workers with disabilities, Men's groups and sheds, community development and engagement, Aboriginal and Torres Strait Islander men's health and participation in men's sheds.

Caleb Goods is a Lecturer of Management and Employment Relations at the University of Western Australia Business School. He is a co-investigator on a national Canadian research project entitled Adapting Canadian Work and Workplace to Climate Change. His research focusses on the concept of creating green jobs and the interlinking of greening work, the broader economy and contemporary society. His research also focusses on work and workers' lived experiences in the 'gig economy'.

Dr. Rob Hecker is an adjunct with the Tasmanian School of Business & Economics at the University of Tasmania. After long careers in business and academia, primarily teaching in organisational behaviour, his research interests continue in the areas of employee voice and extreme work.

A/Prof Sarah Kaine completed a PhD at the University of Sydney and is currently Research Director: Future of Work, Organising and Enterprise in the Centre for Business and Social Innovation (University of Technology Sydney Business School). Sarah is active on a number of boards. She is a founding Director of the McKell Institute and is a member of the advisory group for the Centre for Future Work and is a member of UTS Council. Sarah is interested in innovation in employment relations and regulation– beyond the bounds of traditional labour law, Corporate Social Responsibility and its link to industrial relations and the regulation of labour standards in domestic and international supply chains. Specifically, Sarah has explored possibilities for regulatory alternatives in a number of industrial contexts including publicly funded care service provision and in privately controlled road transport. Her current research explores multi-stakeholder regulation of domestic and international supply chains and work in, and regulation of, the digitally enabled economy. Sarah frequently appears in the media commenting on industrial relation issues, particularly emerging issues in the gig economy and is frequently requested to speak in a variety of forums on these issues (including government enquiries and industry association conferences). Sarah's research has appeared in journals such as *Human Relations, Journal of Business Ethics, Economic and Industrial Democracy, Human Resource Management Journal, Australian Journal of Labour Law* and the *Journal of Industrial Relations.* Prior to becoming an academic Sarah worked as an industrial relations practitioner and a consultant to not-for-profit organisations.

Dr. Sardana Islam Khan is a Lecturer at CQUniversity, Australia. She has earned a PhD in management from La Trobe University, Australia. She served as the Associate Professor and Deputy Executive Director of East West University Center for Research and Training from 2014 till 2016. During that time, she has successfully managed the World Bank-funded 'Higher Education Quality Enhancement Program (HEQEP)' sub-project on capacity building and knowledge sharing in East West University. She has published in international journals such as *Personnel Review, Journal of Developing Areas, International Journal of Economics and Management* and *International Business Research,* among others. She has edited two volumes of the 'East West Journal of Business and Social Studies' as the Assistant Editor. Her papers have earned several international awards such as GBMF UN OMAHA Best Paper Award 2008, Australasian Conference on Business and Social Sciences Best Paper Award 2015 and 'Best Innovative Paper' award in Sydney International Business Research Conference 2015. Her main research interests are the role of human resources in international business, high-performance work systems, decent work and organisational performance.

Dr. Xiaoyan Liang is an academic at the School of Business and Law of CQUniversity, Melbourne campus. Her research areas include volunteer management, human resource management, business ethics, leadership and qualitative research methods.

Dr. Hannah Meacham is a Lecturer in the Department of Management at Monash University. Hannah holds a PhD in the creation of meaningful and inclusive work for people with intellectual disabilities. Prior to her appointment, Hannah worked within the HR industry in both Australia and the UK specialising in strategic HR management and workplace relations.

Dr. Kimberley Norris is a Senior Lecturer in the Division of Psychology, School of Medicine within the College of Health and Medicine. Her overarching research and academic interests are focussed on maximising human health, well-being and performance in both normal and extreme environments.

Ms. Patricia Pariona Cabrera: Patricia is a current PhD student at RMIT University, currently researching in the Healthcare Industry.

Richard A. Posthuma is the Mike Loya Distinguished Professor and Director of the PhD Program at the College of Business Administration at the University of Texas at El Paso. He has published on many topics including employee staffing, conflict management, high-performance work practices, organisational justice, international and cross-cultural issues, and age stereotyping. He earned a PhD in Organizational Behavior and Human Resource Management from Purdue University; J.D., Cum Laude, from Thomas M. Cooley Law School; and Masters in Labor and Industrial Relations from Michigan State University. He is Editor of the *International Journal of Conflict Management*.

Jase R. Ramsey is an Associate Professor at Florida Gulf Coast University where he teaches the Strategy (undergraduate), Global Strategy (MBA), and Doing Business in Latin America (MBA) courses. He earned his PhD in Management with a focus on International Business from the University of South Carolina and a MBA focussed on Latin American Business from Thunderbird. Jase has lived, studied and worked in many places around the world which has inspired his research and teaching.

Jase's research is focussed on international organisational issues, primarily in the Latin American Business context. Specifically, his interests include innovation and creativity as well as global work in Multinational Enterprises. He has published in multiple peer-reviewed outlets and has written two books on doing business in Latin America.

Jeffrey Saunders is an Executive Advisor, Strategic Foresight and Futures Expert. He is the Workplace Evolutionaries Denmark HUB co-leader. Previously, he was Director and Head of the Strategy & Innovation team at the Copenhagen Institute for Futures Studies (CIFS), Chief Consultant at SIGNAL Architects and a national security consultant in the United States. Jeffrey specialises in applying future research methodologies, including the scenario development, and behavioural science to solve challenges for large organisations – public and private. He has extensive knowledge about the future of work and workplace strategy. Jeffrey is a sought-out public speaker who has presented at such conferences as the International Association of Outsourcing Professionals, Nordic Workplace Evolution Summit, IFMA World Workplace, IFMA World Work Place Europe. He has published many articles and reports on corporate real estate, facility management, outsourcing as well as reports on identity formation and organisational culture.

Eric D. Smith is an Associate Professor at the University of Texas at El Paso (UTEP). He works within the Industrial, Manufacturing and Systems Engineering (IMSE) Department, in particular with the Master of Science in Systems Engineering Program. He earned a BS in Physics in 1994, an MS in Systems Engineering in 2003 and a PhD in Systems and Industrial Engineering in 2006 from the University of Arizona in Tucson, AZ. He earned a JD in 2011 from the Northwestern California University. He performs research at the interface of systems engineering, cognitive science and multi-criteria decision-making.

Dr. Julian Teicher is Professor of Human Resources and Employment and Deputy Dean (Research) in the School of Business and Law at Central Queensland University. In the early part of his career he worked as an industrial relations officer for two unions, one in the maritime and power industries and the other in nursing. His research is in two related fields: workplace (industrial) relations and public policy and management. He has published widely on topics including: conflict management, employee participation, voice and industrial democracy, bargaining and dispute resolution and training and skill formation.

Dr. Tse Leng Tham is a Lecturer of Human Resource Management at the School of Management, RMIT University, with a PhD form Monash University, Australia. Her research interests include workplace well-being, workplace climate and voice. She has published in the *Human Resource Management, International Journal of Manpower* and *International Journal of Nursing Practice.*

Dr. Alex Veen is an employment relations scholar in the discipline of Work and Organisational Studies, where he is teaching in the employment relations and human resource management areas. He was awarded his PhD from the University of Western Australia, Perth. He is currently working on several projects focussing on work and employment practices in the platform-economy as well as employer militancy and assertiveness in enterprise bargaining.

Daniel Wheatley is a Senior Lecturer in the Department of Management at the University of Birmingham, UK. His research focusses on workplace well-being including the quality of work, work-life balance, flexible working arrangements, spatial dimensions of work including work-related travel, links with other aspects of time-use including leisure and the household division of labour.

Yang Zhang is a PhD student at the University of Texas at El Paso. Her research interest includes: firm innovation, high-performance work systems and teamwork. Prior to the doctoral programme, she got her master's degree in Business Administration at California State University, Los Angeles. She obtained her bachelor's degree in Accounting in China.

Index

Note: Page numbers *italics* and **bold** refers to figures and tables.

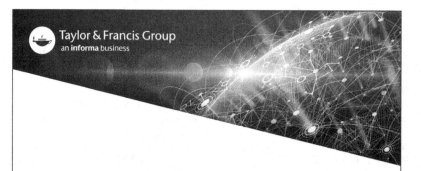

Printed in the United States
by Baker & Taylor Publisher Services